World Change-Maker

World Change-Maker

*Build Skills in International
Development and Social Work*

ANN McLAUGHLIN

*Foreword by
Cathryne L. Schmitz, PhD, MSW*

Toplight

Jefferson, North Carolina

Library of Congress Control Number 2022014740

British Library cataloguing data are available

ISBN (print) 978-1-4766-8711-7
ISBN (ebook) 978-1-4766-4474-5

Front cover image: two people with conical hats pushing
loads across a rickety bridge at sunset in Vietnam.
Photograph by Quang Nguyen Vinh/Pixabay

Printed in the United States of America

Toplight is an imprint of McFarland & Company, Inc., Publishers

Box 611, Jefferson, North Carolina 28640
www.toplightbooks.com

Table of Contents

Foreword
by Cathryne L. Schmitz

This book inspired a journey, one that kept me engrossed in the excitement of deep learning, from the personal to the global. Running through the book are narratives that guide the reader toward understanding poverty as it is lived by individuals, families, and communities. Ann McLaughlin threads our exploration carefully and skillfully, helping the reader move from critical self-reflection through theory, facts, skills, and change empowered at the local level. Stories highlight the complexity and ongoing nature of creating change. First, and as an interwoven thread, she asks us to learn what poverty feels like. Unless the reader struggles to understand the feeling and experience of poverty, they will not be able to understand the goal—joining as allies to support people as they strive to move out of poverty.

Those interested in helping are challenged to delve deeply into exploring their own context and stories. A part of those stories is learning what we can neither see nor feel. This means exploring culture, identity, privilege, and attitudes. As we come to know our own context and stories, we can begin to see the ways our words, attitude, and actions impact the relationships we want to build with others. As we come to know ourselves, the space opens to listen and join with communities. The process of learning, about self and others, is emphasized as a lifelong and intertwined process. As you learn about and experience others, ask yourself, "What did I learn from those interactions and experiences?"

Running parallel is the importance of learning about others, which is stressed as being local and contextualized. This comes to life as illustrations and examples humanize the complexity of social systems and structures. Lesson number one is to learn what you can before arriving in-country. Context is multi-layered, including history, country and region, culture, religion, geography, politics and power structures, income inequality, and living conditions. As emphasized, once there, learn by observing, asking questions, seeing what people have done, exploring what people want to know, and respecting the good work already occurring. Using what you have learned about yourself and the community, pace yourself in building relationships based on mutual respect and an equal partnership. Monitor your attitude, build empathy, check your sense of privilege, and become an ally rather than an expert.

The change systems proposed—international, community, and participatory development—address the complexity. These areas of practice are smoothly melded into an integrated response model. Introduced early, development models are delved into more deeply in each successive chapter. The application of development models is centered around local knowledge, expertise, and leadership. What is complicated becomes understandable, as stories again bring life to the evolving transitions. We are immersed in a multi-level process of relationship building and program development that respects people in context. In partnering with communities, it is possible to do assessments that recognize not only needs but also possibilities. By observing and listening to community stakeholders, local expertise, key players, resources and resourcefulness, power relationships, and gaps in services are identified. Organizing is an ongoing process that can create a base for the development of social movements.

As is underscored, the skills needed are grounded in the practical with programs often emerging out of necessity. Communities build capacity through experience and skill development. Provided are examples of how to develop from local needs and strengths using skills including problem solving, case skills, education, mentoring, and basic skills such as financial and economic literacy, grant writing, and critical thinking. The development is not done by an outside expert; it involves a collaborative learning-by-doing process, or what is referred to as mentoring while working.

For me, the chapter where McLaughlin's ability to bring clarity to complexity shines is the chapter on advocacy. Understanding the political, economic, and policy concerns is vital yet difficult to grasp.

Advocating for and educating the poor occurs at this intersection of economics, policy, politics, and activism. Change requires knowledge of laws, budgets, the International Monetary Fund (IMF), austerity measures, structural adjustments, and the World Bank. In one short chapter, she is able to explain debt, exploring the human cost of loans from systems designed to exacerbate inequality. I recommend this chapter for anyone who wants to understand the IMF, structural adjustments, austerity measures, and the historical role of the World Bank. These structures have crippled countries with loan programs designed to keep developing countries indebted to colonial powers. A debt crisis was created that has resulted in increasing inequality, the selling of land and forests, cheap exports and expensive imports, and environmental refugees. The global North sets the prices.

Further, she digs deeper to challenge us to reject paternalistic models and move beyond colonial and condescending attitudes. This takes the reader deeper into understanding the perpetuation of poverty through systems that create and enforce powerlessness. Moving beyond paternalism requires developing partnerships of equals. It is necessary to reject cultural imperialism and develop cultural humility.

This book is both grounded and hopeful in providing a guide for understanding what is and designing a different path forward. In one book, Ann McLaughlin has managed to pull together what would fill several academic textbooks and still lack a connection across theory and practice. Here several fields of analysis and engagement come together in a format that flows smoothly and is easy to grasp. Academically, this book offers a supplemental text that links across and expands disciplines and areas of study. It would enhance and expand courses in community organizing, international development, critical studies, peace and conflict studies, and environmental studies. It is an enriching book for social work courses including community organizing, policy, macro practice, diversity, social justice, and human rights. It is ideal for International Development and international social work practicum classes where the emphasis is on what you actually *do* in the field.

Equally well suited for the general public, this book is accessible for those who are curious about global issues and want to understand what is going on in the world. For people who are interested in international service or volunteering, who want to improve how they work in other countries, this book should be required reading. As people grapple to live in a world full of difficulties at both the local and global level, they are at a loss to find a manageable way to expand their knowledge about the complex relationships and dynamics that have led to growing inequality, environmental issues, and violent conflict. As we enter a post-pandemic world where so many are struggling, they are asking, what are the issues and how can I make a difference? This very practical book guides the way with its emphasis on self-growth, knowledge building, skill development, and exploration of how to create change.

Cathryne L. Schmitz (PhD, MSW) is a Professor Emerita in Social Work at the University of North Carolina Greensboro. She chaired Peace and Conflict Studies and was a Women and Gender Studies affiliate. She has coauthored numerous books focusing on diversity, vulnerability, empowering action, and social and environmental justice.

Introduction

Do you feel overwhelmed or paralyzed by hearing about the world's problems? Would you rather be empowered by learning what you can do to help change the world and how to build the skills to do it?

This book on international social work and international development will equip you to be a potent change agent. This book is meant to be a supplemental text in classes on international social work and international development classes. Though originally aimed at social workers, it is well suited for anyone who is interested in international development—ordinary citizens who hunger to help; those who volunteer abroad or do church or faith-based missions; and those from other disciplines, whether it is global or international studies or international relations. Or you may have a background in education, nursing, public health, medicine, public administration, entrepreneurship or business, engineering, environmental, political science or democracy building, agriculture or animal husbandry, or women or gender studies, or the trades, and are passionate about international development. What you studied in college may not be pertinent to where you end up in international work. This book has a much more practical emphasis. Out in the world, out in the field and on the ground in your work in other countries, what matters most are your skills and what you can *do*.

Have you searched for books that will help you enter international social work and found nothing? Did you find few books that describe what you will need to know and do after you unpack your bags in some far-flung place? This book aims to fill those gaps by walking you through the three most important factors in getting an international social work or international development job. In an age of wikiHow and YouTube videos on how to fix your lawn mower or make sourdough bread, learning *how* to do anything is empowering. If you passionately want to make a difference, but do not know *how*, this book is for you.

Over almost twenty years as director of NGOabroad: International Careers and Volunteering, I have observed where most peoples' gaps are. My twenty years as a psychotherapist and social worker plus my years working in international development inform the community trainings, grassroots consulting and international career counseling which I do. At NGOabroad, I help craft international placements for people so they can get much needed international experience. Thus, I have seen how people coming from the Global North or from privilege are often missing what is most essential.

There are three things that are critical to getting a job in international social work or development:

1. A grasp of poverty—how half the world's people live—which is the focus of international development.
2. The necessary and core skills.
3. Your attitude—how you "check your privilege at the border."

This book aims to illuminate and empower you in all three areas.

Mistaken About What Kind of Jobs There Will Be

Many new social work graduates come to me for international career counseling, and they would like to apply their counseling skills internationally. I have to admit I wanted to do the same thing, years ago!

It is important to understand that it is often not feasible, or perhaps not the most helpful use of resources, as counseling works with one person at a time, to provide direct emotional or mental health services. If there is a language barrier, agencies often can't provide—or may not even have—interpreters.

While there are many conflicts or situations in the world creating psychological trauma, there are few—though some—international social work jobs that provide trauma counseling. People in the developing world rarely request psychological help. More often, they ask for help with increasing the yield of their crops to feed their family; with generating enough income to pay their children's school fees; or for family planning to reduce how many mouths they must feed. Saying it another way, on Abraham Maslow's hierarchy of needs, survival needs come first.

Social work graduates coming to me for career counseling will say, "I want to work with child soldiers" or "I want to work with sex trafficking." In their studies, they gravitated to a particular issue and now want to pursue it after graduating. I explain to them: "You can count on one hand how many paid international jobs there are in sex trafficking ... or with child soldiers." It is not impossible, but simply very competitive, to get such "niche" jobs. But don't let this reality get in the way of your dreams! If there is not a job related to your passion, it may mean you must create your own social enterprise.

Some people think that international social work is transposing what social work is here in the developed world—working with the elderly, foster care, juvenile justice, substance abuse and mental health—to other continents. Few of these types of social work functions or services are found in many parts of Asia, Africa and Latin America. This relates back to Maslow's hierarchy of needs. The first step is helping people with survival issues. Once those needs are addressed, there will be the foundation to work with additional dimensions of life.

Interestingly, the types of social work that you see here in the so-called developed world that you would also find in other countries are hospice and palliative care. This is largely due to the AIDS crisis. In addition, disabilities or injuries are increasingly acknowledged as a factor in creating poverty. In most of the developing world, there are few social safety nets. Whether at a garment factory in Vietnam or Bangladesh or in a mine in South Africa or Bolivia, if the primary wage earner has been disabled on the job, it usually plunges their family into poverty. Thus, disability advocacy may be found in other parts of the world, as a way of addressing poverty.

Focus Is Helping People Move Out of Poverty

The lion's share of jobs in international social work is in international development. These jobs, in some shape or form, are empowering people to move out of poverty. Thus, this is the emphasis in this book.

Why do I not focus on migration, refugees and asylum seekers in this book? I cannot speak for other organizations guiding people in international careers, but from my perch at NGOabroad, I have seen a stampede of people who would like to work with refugees, especially Syrian refugees, because they believe this is the humanitarian crisis of our time. This is a horrific crisis, indeed. And addressing the issues that drive these refugee flows (war, tyranny, corrupt governments, and collapsed economies) is of vital importance.

However, this book aims to be practical, and because there are so many people who wish to help Syrian refugees, there is a glut of applicants for a handful of paid jobs. As a career strategy, I recommend people steer clear of such "feeding frenzies."

Additionally, refugee work is now complicated by the fact that some nations will not accept refugees or allow them to resettle in their countries. Al Jazeera reported: "Worldwide, 70 million people remain forcibly displaced, including asylum seekers, refugees, and those within their countries' borders. In 2019, of 1.4 million refugees estimated to be in urgent need of resettlement, less than 70,000 got the chance. ... In Barack Obama's last year in office, he set the refugee arrival ceiling for Fiscal Year 2017 at 110,000. In Fiscal Year 2018, Trump slashed that number to 30,000—the lowest ceiling set by any president since the US began its formal refugee resettlement program in 1980. In 2019, it was set at 18,000."[1]

With refugees stuck in transit countries—whether those are Greece or Turkey for the Syrians; Malaysia and Bangladesh for the Rohingya, or Kenya for Somali, South Sudanese and Congolese refugees—and not being able to resettle in final destination countries like Australia, the United States or countries in Europe, there are fewer international social work jobs with UNHCR (United Nations High Commissioner for Refugees). Your work helping those "stuck" refugees will more closely resemble international development work where you help with health, water and sanitation, education and "income generation."

There is an additional reason that I emphasize international development rather than work with refugees in this book: More than five million people fled Syria as barrel bombs devastated towns and cities. In contrast, three billion people—almost half the world's people—live on less than $2.50 a day.[2] People in other parts of the world have taught me that the slow grind of poverty is harder and more dispiriting and discouraging than war and conflict. For example, a Congolese refugee woman explained to me that fleeing conflict and even the rapes in those conflict zones in the eastern Congo were easier than hunger during the lean months or watching your child die from malaria because you could not afford a mosquito net or to get to the clinic.

Why do I not focus on human rights in this book? Some universities confer a master's degree in human rights, and some schools of social work study human rights in their international social work curriculum. I also believe that to be an educated world citizen requires learning about and safeguarding human rights.

However, the study of any topic—such as human rights—can be misleading. It implies that there are jobs in the human rights field. People come to me for international career counseling, saying that they would like to work in human rights. To which I answer, "Do you mean the detention part, the torture part, or the killing part?" What people aspiring to work in human rights often fail to realize is that human rights work is really, really dangerous. Authoritarian leaders or autocrats who perpetuate human rights abuses will not tolerate dissent and criticism. They jail the opposition to silence them.

It is not just authoritarian leaders which you must be wary of, but also corporations whose profit you may be interrupting. I read just yesterday that Mexicans who were trying to preserve the Butterfly Forest in the Sierra Madre mountains have been found dead.[3] "Global Witness annual figures show at least 207 land and environmental activists were killed in 2017 across 22 countries, almost four a week, making it the worst year on record."[4] So that is why there are so few job openings in human rights.

Additionally, I will not examine refugees and human rights in this book because I believe they are symptoms of authoritarian regimes.

While many books on international social work are academic or theoretical, this book is intentionally practical and skill-based because building the necessary skills is crucial to getting the job.

Social work is respected in international development because of our emphasis on practical skills; we are not just a theoretical social science. Yet there are no books that tell you in simple language what you do "out in the field." In my experience at NGOabroad, many people report feeling lost. Social work and international development courses need to better prepare people.

Additionally, too few people from North America, Australia or Europe truly understand or know poverty, so they don't get the job. International employers have told me that people who have grown up with a flush toilet whine about using a pit toilet; that Westerners may be totally off-target in the programs or interventions they design because they have no "lived experience" of poverty. Thus, one whole chapter of this book will try to paint a picture of life and daily realities for people on other continents so that you can gain this essential perspective and understanding.

I found as a clinical social worker that I could not have all the "lived experience" of my clients. I had not experienced sexual abuse; I did not have an eating disorder or a meth addiction. But I found I could partially compensate by voraciously reading life stories—trying to walk in others' shoes and get inside their heads—and on the inside of their experiences, gleaning insight from both ordinary people and experts. I propose that you do likewise regarding poverty in other corners of the earth. Whether through TED talks, videos (ideally not made by Westerners), music, social media or forums, learn as much as you can before you venture out of your culture and into the realities of people with whom you will work.

The third gap that this book aims to rectify is attitude. Attitude is everything. In the same way that people smile when you try to speak their language, even if you are mangling it, people will notice that you are trying to "get it." If you are trying to understand the travails and trials of their daily life; if you respect their fortitude, dreams and talents, this will be appreciated. You are not oblivious; you are an ally.

Unwittingly many people from the richer countries—myself included!—assume that we have the answers and may unconsciously impose those on others. Local citizens—and potentially the people with whom you work—will not tolerate such paternalistic, patronizing attitudes. In the chapter "Partner to the Poor and Participatory Development" and in the final chapter on attitudes and privilege, we will look at the ways you can work as an equal partner.

A Comment on Words and Wording, and Any Other Gaffes or Glitches

First, let me comment on my plain-spoken writing style. It took me *decades* to learn how to talk so that people understand me. I had to purposely jettison the polysyllabic words learned in my university years. In the blue-collar navy town that I worked in after graduate school, they would spit, "You and your $10 words!" Now, I don't want to use big words that make others feel small. Before, I talked in paragraphs; now I speak in short declarative sentences. (It is easier to translate when working in other countries.)

My communication has grown more direct and to-the-point to reduce misunderstandings between cultures. Over the years, I have learned how to speak more concretely, as it better bridges cultural divides. Likewise, I tell more stories so people "get the picture." Jesus spoke in parables, as did the griots (traditional storytellers of West Africa). Across cultures, stories seem to have more meaning than facts and numbing numbers. Stories, utilizing the functioning of the right brain, are often better remembered.

Second, I found it difficult to write about poverty without stumbling over words that imply superiority and inferiority, or powerful and powerless.

More importantly, I use the term "the poor" because this is the term used by the World Bank research team of development experts, such as India's Deepa Narayan. I sometimes refer to the "developed" and "developing" world, while some refer to the "majority world" or the "Global South." More nuanced terminology would be "least developed country"; "other low income countries"; "lower-middle income countries"; "upper-middle income countries." Often I say Asia, Africa and Latin America; and this is so broad it can be offensive.

In the chapter on poverty, I point out that Hans Rosling believed it misleading to refer to "the West and the rest." But in this book, I want to point out how the "have lots" may be oblivious to the lives of the "have nots." But yes, I agree with Hans Rosling and Deepa Narayam that poverty is mutable; that someone is not forever cast in this lot; that the overarching goal of international social work and international development is to help people move out of poverty. Joseph Heinrich, in *The WEIRDest People in the World: How the West*

Became Psychologically Peculiar and Particularly Prosperous, coined the term WEIRD (Western, educated, industrial, rich and democratic). So please forgive my stumbling words. Over time, I believe we will create less onerous and oppressive terms that reflect hope, courage and possibility.

Third, this book has more quotes from others than you will find in most books. This is deliberate. I want you to hear not only my ideas, but also the voices and experiences of people from all over the world, and from luminaries in the field of international development, ideally in their own words.

In summary, social work is one of the degrees that can help you get your foot in the door in international development. But there are definitely many paths up the mountain, so despair not if you have taken a different route. Please bear with the social work shop talk if you have a different background.

Working in international development is both fascinating and challenging. It requires lifelong learning.

Poverty is not just your level of income or whether you can afford or access an education or health services. It is not just whether you have shoes in which to walk for miles to fetch water or firewood. Most importantly, poverty is a predicament, often a state of powerlessness in which you are denied the ability to control decisions which impact your daily life. An economist hailing originally from India, Amartya Sen, calls these "unfreedoms" in his ground-breaking book *Development as Freedom*.[5]

The pinch, the punch and the pressure of poverty is the powerlessness, feeling helpless or hopeless. It is being disrespected. It is the deflated feeling when you are told to come back another day after you have spent the entire day trudging to that clinic or office, when you are told there is nothing that can be done. It is hard enough to not have food, or a home, clean water or medicine. What is salt in the wound are the doors slammed in your face when you try to improve your life and your family's.

Thus, in this book, we will discuss the skills that help people gain power and improve their own lives:

- **Needs Assessment to Program Design**: How you do a needs and strengths assessment and how this forms the foundation for program design and development.

- **Capacity Building**: How you build the strengths and skills of the local people so they can take over when you leave.
- **Partner to the Poor and Participatory Development**: How you work as equals and how the poor ultimately identify their needs, lead the discussion, design the programs and run an organization.
- **Community Organizing**: How you help people shape the decisions which impact their daily lives.
- **Advocacy**: What are the policies that dramatically impact poverty in Asia, Africa and Latin America? What have people tried to do about those policies?

The skills presented in this book build on each other; they are meant to be stacked like building blocks. The first skills discussed form the foundation for the more complex or nuanced skills later in the book.

This book is meant as a foundation to equip you to do international social work and international development. Because I am a dyed-in-the-wool social worker, I believe that a book is two-dimensional: that these skills come alive as you practice them in your internship or out in the field in other countries, as you tug at them in discussions with classmates or colleagues (see the "Discussion and Skills Development" section at the end of the book), or as you discuss these skills and apply them in international training and career consultations with me. There is no end point where you contentedly sigh and say to yourself, "Now I have learned everything I need to know." I would say: "Wrong, my friend." International development is fascinating because it requires a lifetime of learning. For those who love learning, burrow into the bibliography and wade through all the endnotes to see other books to read or videos to watch.

This book is meant as a launching pad.

I

Perspective

1

Why Social Work Is
So Valued in International
Development

Whether you are a social worker or you are approaching humanitarian or development work from another route, this chapter is designed to help you learn what skills are most useful in international development. Social work is one of the most valued credentials in international development work for several reasons:

1. Social work has a strong emphasis on poverty.
2. Social work dates back to Jane Addams and Hull House.
3. Social work training is practical rather than theoretical.
4. Social workers are trained to work with individuals, couples, families, groups, and communities.
5. Most social workers have strong people skills.
6. Students are trained in how to do needs and strengths assessments.
7. Social work also teaches how to design programs.
8. Social workers are trained in leadership, management, and how to run programs or an organization.
9. Social workers are taught program evaluation—what you are taught in your research classes.
10. Social work is one of the only disciplines which teaches community organizing and advocacy skills.
11. Social work emphasizes empowering disenfranchised or marginalized groups.
12. Social work emphasizes case work skills and knowing the resources.

13. Social workers hone their interviewing skills.
14. Social work emphasizes cultural competence and sensitivity.

At NGOabroad, I do an immense amount of international training and career counseling, helping people enter or advance into international development work. I train people in the necessary skills. In this role, I see what international employers want, per their job announcements. I have talked to some of their human resource departments and directors in other countries about their priorities. Also, I see what international job seekers bring to the table.

While social workers are sometimes stereotyped as being too soft or naïve, we also have earned a reputation for accomplishing a great deal in human services, both at home and abroad. While you may not have total command of all the skills or qualities listed here when you graduate, you will ideally have the initial foundation upon which you can build. This book aims to help to build that base.

Let's look at each of the points listed above, one by one.

Emphasis on Poverty

In a world where ⅘ of the people earn less than $10/day, poverty is really the core issue for most.

As said in the introduction, I get many aspiring international social workers who say, "I want to work with child soldiers" ... or trafficking ... or trauma ... or mental health. They pick an issue or something that has fascinated them in their studies or that they have seen on a very powerful special on television. But it is important to understand that it is often difficult to find an international job this way. It is too narrow. There are not many paid international jobs on the above issues and specializations.

It is also important to understand that specialties of social work in North America, Europe, Australia or New Zealand—geriatrics, prisons and criminal justice, or child abuse—do not necessarily have counterparts in the developing world. It took decades for all these services to gain traction in the West, and in many parts of the developing world, traditional social work services are in their infancy. But they are coming.

But really, where most of the world's people would say they want support is in getting out of poverty.

People who work 70 hours a week in a garment factory—aka sweatshop—in Cambodia or Bangladesh and earn $60 a month for all that toil, and who may support five to ten family members on that meager income, will tell you that getting out of poverty is their highest priority.

Young women in Thailand or other parts of Asia who work as prostitutes to support their entire family often find their way out of poverty by marrying a "sugar daddy"—a richer man from Taiwan or America.

A turning point for me in understanding priorities was when an Australian social worker who was counseling Congolese refugee women who had been raped emailed to me: "Ann, the women here say 'Send no more counselors. Send people who can help with income generation.' The women say that if they can bring money into the family, their husbands will not reject them for being defiled."

Prior to this moment, as a social worker with twenty years of experience as a psychotherapist, I had put more emphasis on psycho-social interventions. Interestingly, based on the research done by the World Bank team in the books *Voices of the Poor* and *Moving Out of Poverty*, I am just now beginning to get a glimmer that some of those counseling and mentoring skills can be very useful in helping people move out of poverty and get to their goals.

But suffice it to say, social work in North America is the primary discipline that has the courage to look poverty straight in the eye. We are the primary discipline that has such a long and proud legacy of tackling poverty. (In contrast, social work in the UK and Europe puts more emphasis on case work.)

I believe that international social work really needs to ramp up and take tackling poverty to the next level. In future chapters and books in this series, we will talk about how social work and social workers can help vanquish global poverty; can transform a world where ⅘ of the world lives on less than $10/day—the have nots—while ⅕ of the world are the have lots.

Practical vs. Theoretical

When I was considering what discipline to study in my undergraduate years, and considering how to become a counselor, I went to four different departments at the University of Washington: psychiatry; psychiatric nursing; psychology; and social work. (I did not know then that I could have also talked to the educational psychology department.) But I am forever grateful to the adviser in the psychology department, who took me outside the building and took me by the shoulders and literally pointed me across the campus lawn at the School of Social Work. I still remember his wise words: "We run rats through mazes over here. If you want to learn about counseling, go there—to the School of Social Work."

We are the least theoretical and the most practical discipline in the social sciences. While many schools now confer degrees in counseling, many do not help you learn how to do it. Often students must scrounge up their own field practicum, and these are often not supervised. In contrast, social work has for decades had a tradition of supervised practicums, and then classes to discuss and help integrate what you are learning out in the field.

Trained to Work with Individuals, Couples, Families, Groups and Communities

Social work is so valuable because it works with people and their context. While psychology's contribution is intra-psychic and focuses on research, such as in cognitive studies or neuropsychology, social work has always had an emphasis on inter-psychic.

If you want to do a stellar job in international social work then, if it is at all possible, try to take classes in or get training and practice in all of these "layers of the onion": individual, couples, family, and community. (And I would even say it is helpful to expand your orb one layer out to a national level also—but perhaps further into your career.) This emphasis on context will serve you well when you work internationally because you may need to work with most of these "layers of the onion." It helps to be very versatile in this way.

This emphasis on context is important because often it is the context which needs to change.

To explain this further: I had an interesting conversation with a woman who aimed to become a child psychiatrist. After decades of counseling youth and children, my comment was clearly from this contextual and social work perspective: "Rarely is what is going on psychiatrically with a child or youth a medical issue. It is often an issue of something going on in their family—such as alcohol abuse, physical abuse or sexual abuse. And with youth, it really helps to see them in the context of their peer group and family." Likewise with international social work: it really helps to see what is going on with people in light of what is going on in their family, community and nation; to see the power structures that constrain or empower them; the rules and the roles which shape what they can or cannot do.

Strong People Skills

People going into social work usually have strong people skills. That is fairly obvious. What is crucial is how those people skills get stretched and strengthened over time.

Regarding people skills, my goal has always been to be equally comfortable talking to a beggar or to the queen. Albert Einstein famously said, "I speak to everyone in the same way, whether he is the garbage man or the president of the university." People skills are essential as you sit down with a village chief in Cameroon or any-where in Africa, or as you liaise with the minister of health; or as you scramble to find resources and build a network in Tajikistan or Timbuktu.

I found my people skills were challenged while working in Yugo-slavia when the director of their orphanage would get up at meetings and get red in the face as he'd rant, rant and rant in Serbo-Croatian. The proposed changes to the way orphanages were run were disrupt-ing everything he knew about running his institution. He was furi-ous that these changes in the social services structure would put all the orphanage workers out of work. I kept telling him they would just be working in outpatient rather than inpatient settings … to no avail, because it was foreign and new to him. Your ability to be poised under fire, to be able to de-escalate hot-headed people or heated exchanges, will be critical. I guarantee it.

I think that "people skills" are both innate and learned. Many people drawn to social work have been told throughout their life that they are good listeners, naturals with people. Working in social work, either in your home country or internationally, expands those people skills which are often forged by fire. Social workers are often thrust into the center of the crisis. I have had many new social workers tell me how they have learned to deal with a person wielding a weapon, or to gain the trust of someone in the midst of a suicidal crisis—someone about to cut themselves or jump off a bridge.

Since we are dealing with people—and as one person said, "People are funny creatures"—social workers invariably have to be emotionally and interpersonally savvy. They have to have strong emotional intelligence. This is especially true when you are working internationally, because you must also understand people of other cultures who may have dramatically different beliefs or suppositions. A Canadian social worker told me the story of when she was working in Papua New Guinea. She was part of a group huddled, waiting for a helicopter ride to another island. The helicopter finally arrived, and out got the pilot with a gun and pointed it at the group. The social worker—with that Canadian graciousness—talked him down and eased their way out of danger.

This is a very important qualification written between the lines on job announcements, especially in the conflict zones. You have to be able to sometimes handle gnarly challenges where your life and others' lives are on the line. International development workers, like river kayakers or mountain climbers, and like the Canadian social worker in Papua New Guinea above, have their "war stories"—how they defied death or danger.

Both domestically and internationally, important parts of "people skills" are thinking on your feet and creating a human bond that forms a lifeline or bridge. For example, a social work friend of mine tells the amazing story of when she was called out by 911 on an emergency to a hostage situation. (This was when the mental-health team worked with the sheriff responding to calls in the community … an idea that is again being advocated.) It was midnight and the SWAT team had surrounded the house. Inside the dining room my social work friend could see the tense stand-off: a man with his shotgun held to a woman. The police, the SWAT team and my friend the social worker stood shivering for hours surrounding the house. After hours and hours of patient waiting out in the cold, at about 5 a.m., the police and SWAT team gave the nod to my friend the social worker, and with their eyes implored, "What can we do? We do not want to escalate this." My friend slowly walked forward to the dining room window, and gently knocked on it. The guy with the gun looked up at her. They made eye contact. The social worker said: "I'm cold. Can I come in for some coffee?" She ever so gently built a bond; made a bridge to the solution. Thus she made the first step in and defused the entire situation.

Throughout this book and in the trainings and consulting I do at NGOabroad, I say to people: "I tell stories on purpose. Stories are stored on the right side of the brain and often are what is remembered while the facts on the left side of the brain fall away. The stories stick and stay."

Many social work students already have some "war stories" as social work is replete with crises. Social workers are not the only ones who have tales about getting out of a scrape, but most of the social workers who work at child protective services, in emergency rooms, in mental health, in schools, in prisons and in drug treatment centers get adept at pulling themselves or others out of peril.

I call your attention to this getting-out-of-a-pinch skill because it is often useful not just in international work but in international travel as well. On the NGOabroad questionnaire, I ask about resourcefulness and self-sufficiency because it helps me assess the "level of challenge" someone is ready for in international volunteering or international work. You learn "travel smarts" over time and through accumulated experiences.

So-called people skills—knowing how to make a human bridge or lifeline to another person or a group or a community—are crucial. In social work, we take this "emotional intelligence" for granted, but international employers do not. I often visualize this bridge as a delicate gossamer thread connecting me to person or community. Over time that bond or bridge grows stronger and more serviceable. It is a key, core skill, this bridge-building—you know how to put people at ease; you know how to connect, laugh and schmooze; you know how to leverage that connection to get projects and tasks done; you are both a team player and a leader; you can gracefully duck into a palm frond hut in the tropics, or enter a family or a community context. These sorts of skills will shine both in interviews and on the job.

Knowing How to Do Needs and Strengths Assessments

Social work is one of the only disciplines which train students how to do a Needs and Strengths Assessment. This is a very important skill in international development. For me personally, it shapes how I see and make sense of world events and is the foundation for my schema. Whether the Needs Assessment is done in an informal or organic way or more formally, quantifying and calculating the needs with scientific precision, it is often done early on in international development projects. However, I have met graduating MSWs who have not been trained to do or practiced doing a Needs and Strength Assessment. In my humble opinion, this is more important than knowing the English Poor Laws, so why is every school of social work not required to teach it? To ensure that you have not missed this key skill in problem solving, there is an entire chapter devoted to Needs and Strengths Assessments and how it lays the foundation for Program Design and Development.

Knowing How to Design or Build Programs

Usually in the first years after you get your MSW, you will be more of a "foot soldier," whether you work in your home country or internationally. That is, it is more comfortable to step into a pre-existing role and established job.

But often in international development, as a project or program manager, you must make things happen. There is not a program to step into; you have to help *make* that program. In the chapter on participatory development, we will look at how you include the community in the Needs Assessment and Program Design.

As one seasoned social worker who was getting additional experience so she could enter paid international social work wrote me from our NGOabroad program in northern Uganda, "Ann thank you so much for the expression 'Makin' somethin' outa nothin'." "When did I say that?!" "It is all over your website. It has really helped me navigate here. There are few resources; few materials or equipment. So I now understand what I am encountering is normal and just how it is. I must make somethin' outa nothin'!"

Right: international social work requires a great deal of improvising. You make most things from scratch.

This ability to improvise and make somethin' outa nothin' may not be something taught at the school of social work; it is more likely something you will learn out in the world or in other aspects of your life. The most helpful life experience I had as a foundation for international social work was rebuilding a house: you start with the foundation; then you lay the joists, upon which you put the plywood platform which is the floor; then you build up the walls—the 2x4 framework, then the sheathing or plywood on the walls, then the rafters and then the roof and the roofing. Every day in construction, you encounter wild obstacles and confounding puzzles, and every day you figure out a way to solve them. (Little did I know how intellectually challenging construction and carpentry are.) It was in this way that I truly learned how to build things from the ground up. It is certainly this building experience that imbues my writing with a very practical bent.

Though you may not have the opportunity or even the desire to build or rebuild a house first, by necessity you will learn how to build programs. Likewise, you *build* your skills; they aren't just handed to you. I have deliberately sequenced how I present the necessary skills so you can stack them like building blocks. I believe this analogy from construction is helpful: you start at the foundation. If you read Si Kahn's books about community organizing, he has this same common-sense way of building a community's strengths and responses to a challenge.

The joy of social work itself, and of building programs, is that it draws on so many parts of yourself or kinds of expertise—professional, vocational and avocational; child development; education and literacy; mentoring and building others' confidence and skills (more on this in the chapter "Capacity Building"). This last is often at the core of youth and women's programs. Additionally, gardening, farming, or agriculture, and crafts, vocational or trade skills sit at the heart of "income generation" programs. This list just scratches the surface. To do this discussion justice, we would have to start with the needs of the community and what challenges or obstacles they are encountering—we would have to custom fit the intervention or program design. Organizations and practitioners come to me at NGOabroad, and I act as a consultant on how to build or strengthen programs. Again, social work does a good job of preparing people to be such organizational development consultants; but that is usually after years of being out in the field.

But watch how over the years, as your skills and experiences—professional, personal and avocational—grow, you design better and richer programs. Watch how as you become a parent, you have a deeper affinity for that mother or father who has walked for miles to the clinic with their child in their arms, whether in Malawi, Nepal or Peru. Watch how your parenting classes become less pedantic and filled with more laughter, whether here or internationally. One of the most rewarding things about social work is that it provides the foundation to grow laterally in so many directions.

Often Trained in Leadership, Management and How to Run an Organization

When I was getting my MSW, there were two tracks in the School of Social Work: administration and clinical. There was no such thing as international social work, so I charted my own path. Though I chose the clinical track and never took any administrative classes, I osmosed the administrative track. And though you may be in the international track, I likewise encourage you to learn as many of the organizational skills as you can.

Throughout much of the world, many of the organizations which NGOabroad is partnered with are directed by social workers. This is because all over the world, the discipline that teaches you how to build and direct the organizations that respond to human needs is … you guessed it … social work.

Program Evaluation—What You Learn in Your Research Classes

When I was in graduate school, we had to do social work research. In the clinical track I had to quantitatively prove that my clinical intervention with this physically abused woman was making a difference. When I was in school, this was very new; now evidence-based research is integrated into social work education and clinical or organizational practice.

It is to social work's and international development's credit that there is this push to both monitor progress and also to evaluate at the end. Prior to this being a priority, international social work and international development were just hope, hope, hoping that they were making a difference. Now international organizations must account to their donors: did the program that the donor funded achieve the goals that it claimed it would?

After reading *Moving Out of Poverty: Success from the Bottom Up*, I realized that this program evaluation is not enough. Yes, a program may have met its goals. But we need to evaluate, really, how many people this program lifted out of poverty. Did the program reach those most in need? Deepa Narayan, Lant Pritchett, and Soumya Kapoor in *Moving Out of Poverty* found that only a minuscule number of the 60,000 poor who they interviewed attributed their move out of poverty to an NGO, either local or international, or social service. The new emphasis is impact.

Community Organizing Skills

Social work is the only discipline that I know of that teaches community organizing. There are some great institutes which also train people in community organizing—that is, you don't have to be a social worker to get training and work in this field! But I believe social work is the only academic discipline which puts an emphasis on community organizing, thanks again to Jane Addams. Later in this book, an entire chapter is devoted to how you rattle cages and pull the levers of power.

And though your school of social work may not offer community organizing or you may not have the time to take a community organizing class, I believe that this is something which you can gain through reading and experience. I gained insight into community organizing by reading every single copy of *Mountain Life and Work*, a journal out of Berea, Kentucky, which focused on the lives of coal miners. My school of social work library had *Mountain Life and Work* in its periodical section—not stuck in stuffy archives. Reading about black lung or other struggles of the mining communities,

I began to understand that Kentucky was a colony within the United States, where we sucked out the resources and wealth and gave little in return.

So even if you may not have time or opportunity to take a community organizing class, the books and magazines are likely in your school of social work library. There is an entire chapter on community organizing later so you can learn more about it and build the skills if the need arises.

Case Work Skills—Knowing the Resources

Whether doing discharge planning at a hospital or a congregate care facility, or working in the emergency room in your home country, part of social work is connecting people with resources.

Such case work and connecting-people-to-resources is another branch of international social work. I did international career counseling with a woman who really, really wanted a paid job with Syrian refugees. She had many graduate degrees, but alas, not an MSW. An MSW would have been her ticket to all the case work jobs that she was trying to get. Even if she had not done her practicum doing case work, it is very likely that an MSW would have helped open the career door for her.

The thing about social work is, it opens so many fascinating doors!

An interesting case work job was one that I interviewed for decades ago. This was with a mom-and-pop organization located north of Seattle. Originally it was just mom and pop, literally. They had created a website to try to connect to other parents whose children had died of the same kind of leukemia of which their son had died. Being the only resource online related to this rare form of cancer, it was their organization that got the email from a drug company which said, "We are willing to give this drug away free to anyone who has this disease. Can you help us find all the people in the world who have this kind of leukemia?"

Wow, what a challenge! How to find the people with this disease? How to get someone in remote Laos who has no bus money to get into Vientiane and to find the right doctor and give the doctor instructions on how this drug works? The challenge was a combination of needle-in-a-haystack and kid-in-a-candy-store combined.

Thus, while it was still just mom and dad running this organization, they were looking for medical social workers (which I am not) who could help with this daunting international case work. We discussed how to strategize tackling the challenge. Especially before Google Translate, one of the challenges was language. So I asked them, "Where are the most people with this kind of cancer?" It was a rhetorical question because I could accurately guess the answer: India and China. That was a no-brainer because they are simply the most populous countries. I recommended that they hire a medical social worker who could speak Mandarin and ideally Cantonese; and hire another who could speak Hindi. "Mom" spoke fluent Spanish and she was from South America, so she could take care of a hemisphere herself.

So at the very outset they were just a mom-and-pop operation. This is what I mean by "makin' somethin' outa nothin'." Checking their current website, I see that they have grown exponentially and that they are now a flourishing international health organization.

To succeed at case work, you have to know the resources. To do the above job, we had to figure out how to know the resources for almost every country on earth! I believe that "knowing the resources" is something else you osmose at the school of social work. It is not necessarily something taught or tested on, but something that most social workers are expected to know—so it is a skill you cultivate.

For the woman who wanted to work with Syrian refugees in Turkey, it would be crucial to know the resources in Istanbul and in southeast Turkey.

I am doing some career counseling and cover letter and résumé help with a man who has been in international development for ten years. He feels that his greatest asset—and I agree—is being thrown in somewhere, like Kurdistan for him, and building a network, learning from that network about other resources—what he accurately calls "snowballing"—and how to make things happen within that culture. Though not a social worker, he has learned how crucial networking is and how to make things happen. Networking in-country is not usually done on LinkedIn; it is more like at a teahouse or where the community congregates. This man talks about tugging on any thread of the social fabric and seeing where it leads him and then building from there—what he accurately calls leveraging.

His process is essentially what I said about building a foundation and then building up from there.

When I began my international quest, before there was such a thing as international social work, I would just scribble resources on Post-It notes or little pieces of paper or notecards. If you were to come to my office, you would see that one whole wall is covered with a pegboard of resources—each topic with cards about 50 cards deep. (Because I am so "hands-on," I do not like things on my computer or phone as much ... though I am keeping track more of resources on my computer now.)

Once you have done enough research on the resources, you can see "how things are wired." You can see programmatic priorities, gaps in services, key players and power relationships. Knowing how things are wired is what a discharge planner, community organizer or international social worker all need to know. E.g., if you want to get any funding, you go to the Rotary Club meeting that meets for breakfast every third Tuesday. E.g., in Morocco, if you want to make anything happen or get any question answered, you must go directly to the place and people and have a cup of tea and make a personal connection—a phone call or email is not the way things are done.

Interviewing Skills

There are doubtless some social work jobs in your home country which depend on your ability to interview people, such as working for child protective services or for crime victim assistance in court systems. Here the bulk of your job is meticulously getting an account of what happened—whether it was physical or sexual abuse or some other crime.

There are also international social work jobs that hinge on your ability to accurately grasp what occurred. Working at UNHCR—the United Nations High Commissioner for Refugees—is mostly about getting the story from refugees about why they fled to determine if they will qualify for resettlement. This can be fascinating work. A social worker in Kenya who has worked for UNHCR all over the world says that now the gay and lesbian people who have fled Uganda actually have highest priority as refugees because their lives are often truly at risk. Thus, your people skills and social work interviewing skills—your ability to form a connection, to probe and to listen—are at the heart of these jobs.

Cultural Competency and Sensitivity

Cultural competence and sensitivity may sound like an easy or "fluff" skill, but it is actually one of the most strenuous. It is likely where you will learn and grow the most over your career and lifetime.

At its foundation, cultural competence requires learning about people who are different from yourself, cultures that are different than your own. It is why, I believe, that Muslims are more likely to be picked for the jobs with Syrian refugees: they understand what "inshallah"—if Allah wills it—means and how it shapes a whole worldview.

Cultural competence and sensitivity is also where you are most likely to stumble and unwittingly make mistakes simply because you do not know that something is done very differently somewhere else. For example, a woman who has worked in international development for twenty-five years came to me when I first started NGOabroad and said, "Ann, it is brilliant that you have these cultural consultants on your team."

"Why do you say?"

"Because in all my years in international development, when we would hit the seemingly most tangled and insurmountable obstacles, that is when I would need to consult with many, many people from the culture or country so that we could actually find our way out of the maze and quit hitting our head against the same walls."

When you enter a culture that is not your own, this is where you can make the most gaffes. The one that I struggle with all over the world is to know how to behave as a woman. In the West, women have fought long and hard to make certain strides. I walk with a confidence and speak with an assertiveness that fits in this culture, or at least some parts of it. But in some other cultures, it may really offend people if I behave this way as a woman.

I do know that I inadvertently made a cultural error when I went to shake someone's hand when I was in Lebanon or Jordan. I knew intellectually that men and women do not touch in the Muslim world, but it had not sunk in enough. Shaking hands was just too automatic for me.

I think that I likewise blew it when I was trying to find an organization in Israel on a Friday. Same problem, I intellectually knew that Friday is the Sabbath (Shabbat), but I did not know that the elevator would not be working properly! None of the buttons would open the doors! I have since learned that Orthodox Jews do not use electrical devices on Shabbat. But when I was stuck in the elevator and none of the buttons opened the door, or made the elevator go up or down, you bet I pressed the little red button that rang the alarm. The doorman was furious, but I was relieved that I did not spend the night locked in the elevator. But what a culturally offensive blunder!

Cultural competence and sensitivity rests on our attitudes. It is why at the end of the book, we will look at our attitudes about our position of privilege in the world, and how people in other countries see us. Saying it another way, I am not so concerned with shaking hands with the wrong hand or wagging my head the wrong way; I am more concerned that I offend people by my privilege.

We will explore this further in the chapter on attitude. As a social work colleague said to me the other day about this question of privilege, "We acknowledge that we are going to make mistakes often, though almost always unintended. The key is an attitude of learning; a willingness to hear and heed when someone tells you that you have offended them; and even a willingness to ask."

Really, the best learning comes from trying, making mistakes and revising your course or behavior. Sometimes it can be a very steep learning curve—almost vertical. But it is this connection to other cultures and countries that draws people to international social work in the first place.

In conclusion, there is a reason that social work is so valued in international development work: we are trained and steeped in the many necessary skills and experience.

It is a rare MSW graduate who has all the skills and experience needed for many international development jobs when they first graduate. Many of the skills which I have listed above must be built over time. Employers want solid skills and experience. This is why I do international training and career counseling to help people plot the steps to get there; why we have placements that give you experience in addition to your practicums. As I say on the NGOabroad website, "It is usually not a leap but a climb."

So do not be discouraged if you do not get an international job offer right after you graduate. Build your skills, be realistic and be determined and you will get to your goal.

2

Know Poverty? How Does Half the World Live?

The primary focus of most international development work is on improving the lives of the 4 billion of the world's people who live on less than $8/day.[1] The priority is helping the three billion who live on less than $2.50/day move out of poverty.[2] It is these sheer numbers along with the huge effect poverty has on each of these people's lives that make defeating poverty the number one priority in international development.

Humanity Is Succeeding in the Fight Against Poverty

Hans Rosling and his son Ola and daughter-in-law Anna, in their work at the Gapminder Foundation, have shattered our notions about global trends and numbers. Hans Rosling was a medical doctor in Mozambique; he pioneered the research on konzo, a paralytic disease, in the Congo; he taught and chaired the international health department at Karolinska Institute in Sweden; and finally—and most important to him—he launched the Gapminder Foundation to debunk many of the myths we have about what is going on in the world.

The Roslings assert that the proportion of people in the world living in extreme poverty has halved in the last twenty years.[3] As Hans said, this is revolutionary; it is the most important change that has happened in his lifetime.

It is largely China that drove the huge change in the world's rate of poverty. For the Millennium Development Goals, China decreased the proportion of people living in poverty from 2 out of 4 in 1981 (634 million) to 1 in 10 (129 million) in 2004.[4]

In their TED talks, the Roslings expose how ignorant almost every audience is about the many improvements occurring all over the globe. Chimpanzees, the Roslings laugh, are more likely to accurately answer the questions (by clicking on buttons) about what is going on in the world today.

With their very vivid graphs, bubble diagrams and analytics, the Rosling team shows that in 1800, 85 percent of the world lived in extreme poverty; 50 percent in 1966; and 9 percent in 2017.[5] Hans Rosling describes what poverty was like in 1800: all over the world, people simply did not have enough to eat. Children had to work to eat; and in the UK, children started work at age 10. One fifth of the Swedish population fled to the United States to escape starvation.

Thus, the Roslings see poverty on a historical trajectory. For example, Vietnam by some measures is advancing to where the United States was in 1975. They comment:

> It's also interesting to look at a country like Vietnam, which has developed tremendously in the past 25 years. Today life expectancy there, for example, is the same as the United States was in 1975, the year that John McCain came home from Vietnam after being a prisoner of war there. But the GDP per capita in Vietnam is today only what it was in the United States in 1900. So we have a big gap between human resources and skills on the one hand and the salary level on the other.
>
> When you look at the people in Vietnam, they are pretty much the same as everybody in the world. The parents want a good life for their kids, they want shoes for them, a good school, perhaps a guitar and maybe a vacation at the seaside. So they have this standard of health, long life expectancy, which is at the 1975 US level and you can be sure that GDP is going to move up very fast from the 1900 level. They are very hardworking and motivated people.[6]

The World Bank research group that wrote *Voices of the Poor* and *Moving Out of Poverty* found that Vietnam stands out starkly as a very positive exception among the 23 countries studied. Focus groups at all sites in Vietnam said economic opportunities have increased, and poverty has declined substantially in the last ten years, thanks to changes in the government economic and social policy. The implementation of the Renovation and Open Door policies in the 1980s led to markets, land allocations to households and freedom to travel—changes that people perceived

Vietnam has a standard of health and long life expectancy equivalent to that of the U.S. in 1975.

as laying the foundation for increased opportunities. An emphasis on building assets and development of secondary sources of income such as raising livestock, gardening, tree cultivation and trading as well as an extensive network of credit provision has helped people generate income.[7]

Hans Rosling had (I say it in the past tense because Hans died in 2017) some very important insights about global poverty: "The world used to be divided in two but isn't any longer. Today most people are in the middle. There is no gap between the West and the rest, between developed and developing, between rich and poor. … Today, most people, 75 percent, live in middle income countries. Not poor, not rich, but somewhere in the middle and starting to live a reasonable life. Nine percent live in low income countries."[8]

When speaking at conferences, the Roslings point out that all over the world, people think things are getting worse, when in fact by many measures, they are improving around the world[9]:

- HIV: There were 549 million new cases of HIV in 1996, dropping to 241 million in 2016.
- Child mortality: 44 percent of children were dying before their 5th birthday in 1800, 4 percent in 2016.

- Hunger: 28 percent of the world population were undernourished in 1970, 11 percent in 2015.
- Literacy: Percent of adults (15+ years) who can read and write: 10 percent in 1800, 86 percent in 2016.
- Girl child education: Percentage of primary age girls enrolled in school: 65 percent in 1970, 90 percent in 2015.
- Clean water: Percentage with access to protected or potable water: 58 percent in 1980, 88 percent in 2015.
- Immunizations: Percentage of one-year-olds who received at least one vaccination: 22 percent in 1980, 88 percent in 2016.

But Much More Work Needs to Be Done to Eliminate Poverty

The advances above are all great news, but there is still much work to be done!

- For ten days, the world was focused on the Nepal earthquake in which 9,000 people were killed; in that same ten days, 9,000 children died from fecally contaminated water across the world.[10]
- In 2017, there were an estimated 219 million cases of malaria in 87 countries.
- In 2007, every minute, two children died of malaria.[11]
- Over 1.5 million children die annually from diseases that can be prevented by vaccination.[12]
- UNICEF reported in 2019 that 663 million people do not have access to clean water; 2.4 billion people don't have access to improved sanitation and 946 million people defecate in the open. Seven out of ten people are without access to improved sanitation, and nine out of ten people who have to relieve themselves in the open live in rural areas.
- At this time, one billion people in the world live in slums. By 2040 that number is estimated to double.[13]
- Though HIV infection rates have slowed, AIDS still ravages Africa.
- 36.9 million people in the world were living with HIV in 2017.[14]

The founder and headmistress of a high school in Uganda that is primarily devoted to AIDS orphans said to me: "I grew up in a family with seven siblings. Only two are still alive. All the others have died of AIDS." This woman had been a bank teller, her husband a respected entrepreneur. That is, AIDS impacts all strata of life on the African continent.

"Knowledge of suffering cannot be conveyed in pure facts and figures, reports that objectify the suffering of countless persons," observed Dr. Rebecca Chopp, former president of Swarthmore and Colgate and the first female chancellor of the University of Denver, who has a background in divinity.[15]

Numbers can be numbing. Often stories do a better job of helping you get the picture.

How Does Half the World Live?

In this chapter, the aim is to give you snapshots of how half of the world lives. Some will be the glimpses that helped illuminate my path in international social work and development, the experiences that helped me understand; and I admit I have a long way to go.

Glimpse: China, 1987 (much different than China today!): We were out by the Stone Forest near Kunming. It is a bit like Bryce National Park. I remember watching a girl in the village dip her toothbrush into a mud puddle and brush her teeth.

Luke was my first "ah-ha" awakening.

Luke, a very bright young man out in the village of Lamarck, several hours outside of Yaounde, the capital of Cameroon, taught me the most about poverty and "unfreedom," as Amartya Sen calls it.

Luke and I were engrossed in a fascinating discussion at the midday break from our Needs Assessment meeting in his village. Luke then sighed and lamented, "I don't know what to do. My wife is so very sick."

"What is she sick with, Luke?"

"Malaria." And then his wife came shuffling out of the side room past our meeting in the main room. She could hardly drag her feet.

"Luke, surely there is something you can do!"

"Yeah, Ann: I could put the two of us on a motorcycle taxi and get to the nearest town with a clinic."

"Luke, there is your answer!"

"Yeah, Ann ... but I do not have $5 for the motorcycle taxi man. And I do not have $5 for medicine at the clinic."

"Luke, surely there is someone in this room that has 10 bucks."

The others in the room heard that comment and lifted their heads and turned toward me. "Uh, I see, Luke. I am the only person in this room that has $10. Here's $10, please take your wife to the clinic."

When I was getting ready to leave Lamarck with the Cameroonian social work director—both of us and our packs on the back of a motorcycle taxi in the pouring rain—Luke came running out. He gave me a necklace made of seeds with a carved piece of wood the shape of Africa. I have the necklace taped to a door jamb that I often walk through. I want to remember Luke every day and all that he taught me.

It is one thing to go to Nepal, Brazil, Peru, Honduras, Ghana, or some other part of the developing world, and another to bring home those lessons learned. What you learn in other parts of the world, let that shape your life and over years, hold those people in your heart and help them. Do not forget them.

Luke's dilemma is what Amartya Sen describes as an "unfreedom." Amartya Sen is an economist from India who has moved the needle and changed the focus, so he deserves important credit. For decades, if not centuries, economists were concerned with numbers and crunching economic data. Sen has said we also need to look at quality of life and how the economy impacts living, breathing people.

Sen, who got the Nobel Prize in Economics in 1998 for his thesis that famines do not occur in democracies, gave a very important series of lectures to the World Bank. Those lectures were written up into the book called *Development as Freedom*, published in 1999, and they created a shift in thinking to look at quality of life, not just income and GDP. Sen writes, "Poverty is a deprivation of basic capabilities rather than merely as lowness of income... 'unfreedoms' are reflected in premature mortality, significant undernourishment (especially in children), persistent morbidity, widespread illiteracy and other failures."[16]

All over the world, people who are poor say that the hardest part is not having a voice in decisions which impact their daily lives, especially these unfreedoms—situations where you have no choice or freedom. Thus, the crux of poverty is this powerlessness, the despair and desperation that I heard as Luke told me his predicament. He felt there was nothing he could do. Though Luke is very bright, upbeat and energetic, a person who has much going for him, he felt cornered, afraid and hopeless.

The antidote to this powerlessness is helping people have a voice in the decisions that affect their lives. In the coming chapters, we will examine how empowerment—via capacity building, participatory development, community organizing, and advocacy—undergirds the work that you do in international development and social work; how much of what you do increases voice and power ... and thus, hope.

This conversation with Luke was an awakening for me. Though like all people on earth, everyone faces some kind of hard times, I never had been in Luke's shoes. Though well meaning, my can-do American attitude was a sharp contrast to the reality Luke and his wife faced. I was almost obnoxiously chirpy. This attitude or point of view that came from my position of relative privilege is often how foreigners may totally miss the mark. This is what we will explore in the chapter on attitude.

Like a domino effect, if we can solve poverty, many other problems will diminish.

In Africa, Asia and Latin America, poverty impacts your health, your housing, and whether you can get an education. The organization Oxford Poverty and Human Development Initiative deeply grasps how poverty impacts many aspects of someone's life. Their aim is "to build a multidimensional economic framework for reducing poverty grounded in people's experiences and values." They are doing cutting edge research that lays the foundation for important policy decisions.[17]

* * *

Another example of an unfreedom—an example of how extreme poverty affected health in the family—comes from the Canadian development journalist for the *Globe and Mail*, John Stackhouse. In his book *Out of Poverty*, Stackhouse was exploring the "chars"—which are here-today-gone-tomorrow sediment islands in the Ganges River delta of Bangladesh. Only the very poor live on these ephemeral islands, which are subject to the vicissitudes of the river flooding and typhoons.

Stackhouse described a woman named Hajera and her family, who lived on one of these islands:

Many of the poorest people in Bangladesh live on unwanted land by the sea or on sediment islands, and so they are vulnerable to flooding and typhoons. In the foreground is a simple latrine (Gonoshasthaya Kendra Archive).

"Her husband Shahor ... suffered from what a visiting doctor called Parkinson's disease. ... He sat quietly in the corner trembling. All the neighbors believed that Shahor was possessed by a spirit ... and Hajera could not afford the medicines to prove them wrong. The drugs alone cost 100 taka every 10 days or about $2 and were supposed to be supplemented with a high protein diet and lots of vitamin B foods like milk, spinach, eggs and liver—items Hajera could not afford. She could not even afford to buy basic medications for one of her sisters-in-law who had come down with malaria. The family's health had hardly been worse, now that several of the children were showing signs of measles, for which none had been vaccinated."[18]

The Price of a Latte Here Equals What Many Earn in a Day

For people who can afford a latte every day, it may be hard to grasp what it is like to live and perhaps support seven to fifteen family members on the same sum as the cost of that latte.

There are approximately 2 million garment workers in Bangladesh who work 7 days a week, often 15 hours per day, and sleep on the factory floor. If they put in 100 hours of overtime plus 63 hours a week of regular work they get a bonus which brings their total monthly earnings to $60/month. Garment workers make twice as much as those in agricultural work and laborers at construction sites in Bangladesh. So doing the math, a factory worker earns about $2/day; an agricultural or construction worker earns $1/day.[19]

Extreme poverty is earning less than $1 a day, on which it is difficult to even feed yourself properly. $2/day or more is the minimum to provide enough for food, shelter and clothing.[20]

Equally important, most people in Asia, Africa and Latin America support many dependents. In the example above, Hajera is supporting a disabled husband, children and her sister-in-law. Many people in the developing world make their living in the informal sector. They do not have a paying job, but they scrape by being a street vendor or busking or washing windows or windshields.

Scratching out a living in the informal sector is a way people scrape by.

In Peru and Bolivia, you get mobbed by shoe shiners when you get off the airplane. The shoeshine kids are making the money to support their family because mom and dad, after fleeing the cold and hunger of the altiplano (the high plain at 10,000 feet elevation), have not found work in the city.

In Reyna Grande's memoir *The Distance Between Us*, she describes the despair, disappointment and desperation if her mother was not able to sell any candies or small packaged food in front of the resort in her home town of Iguala de la Independencia, Guerrero, Mexico.

This is what I mean by "getting it"—understanding poverty and the disparities: The smart phone that you have paid $365 for is the equivalent of how much someone making $1/day earns in a year. This is why someone may want to "relieve" you of that burden of your smart phone. As Katherine Boo explains in *Behind the Beautiful Forevers: Life, Death, and Hope in a Mumbai Undercity*, or as they illuminated in the movie *Slum Dog Millionaire*, people make a living by theft if there are few or no other choices.

Duncan Green is an important writer and practitioner in international development, currently holding the position of Professor in Practice at the London School of Economics and senior strategic adviser at Oxfam GB, and previously senior policy adviser on trade and development at DFID (Department for International Development). In *From Poverty to Power: How Active Citizens and Effective States Can Change the World*, he writes: "'In La Paz, everyone works but no one has a job' jokes one Bolivian government official."[21]

According to the International Labor Organization (ILO), formal employment varies from 45 percent of the working population to a mere 30 percent in Sub-Saharan Africa. For example, in Malawi, only one in every 250 people has a formal job in the private sector.[22]

Duncan Green asserts, "In part, the informal economy flourishes because of the 'barriers to entry' for formal business. In Angola, starting a new business requires 13 different procedures and 124 days, and costs about 500 per cent of the average yearly income. By contrast, in the United States the same process requires just five procedures, five days and 0.7 per cent of average income of the American."[23]

This is why one of the most important findings of the World Bank research team that wrote *Voices of the Poor* and *Moving Out of Poverty* is this: One of the most effective ways that you can help people move out of poverty is remove the obstacles or barriers.

*   *   *

What's for dinner illuminates how people live.

I have traveled to many places in the world to consult and set up NGOabroad's international volunteer programs. In my travels I rarely stay at hotels but live as the people of that country do. It has opened my eyes.

- As I walked around a village in China years ago, where a girl was brushing her teeth in the puddle, I remember seeing a cat and I thought, "Will that cat be dinner sometime?"
- In Bolivia, the tilapia fishpond was definitely something to show off. It is hard to eke out a living in the high Andes. It is hard to grow food at or above 10,000 feet elevation. People eat guinea pig.
- In China, they eat anything and everything: anteater, snake, the webbed feet of Beijing duck, the tongue. It is fascinating to walk through a market.

On the coast of Ghana, many make their living fishing, so they sell the fish for income rather than eat it themselves. Usually fufu (cassava) is for dinner.

At one dinner in China I asked our national guide, "Mr. Ju, what is this?"

"Hmmm.... I can't say it in English." Then he triumphantly found the word: "Hedge!"

Indeed, that was my question. It looked like fried laurel hedge, and it was! Oh, I get it: the Chinese learned to eat anything and everything in the Great Famine from 1959 to 1961, when 30 million people died.[24] Or it may not be the famine that puts food that seems unusual to us on the dinner table in China. With an entirely different medical paradigm, traditional Chinese medicine, different foods are revered or appreciated for their medicinal value ... value that we are perhaps blind to because we think in an entirely different way.

Out in the remote, rural villages of Cameroon, I asked what they were cooking for dinner that night in the pot over the fire. I just about fainted when they told me: "Bush meat." In the lean months that are furthest from the harvest, you must forage and hunt in the forest and eat anything you can. My Cameroonian social work colleague saw my astonishment and said, "It's ok, Ann, we brought spaghetti noodles for you." She was savvy enough to know there is no extra food in the villages, so we schlepped heavy bags of all our food out to the villages.

In Mongolia, I ducked into the yurt where everyone was gathered. A wok was bubbling on the wood stove at the center of the yurt. I peered into the wok to see what they were cooking: all the guts of the sheep. This was about as appealing as bush meat in Cameroon. No thanks from this gastronomic wimp!

The next day in Mongolia, we ventured out across the wide-open steppes to visit herders—Mongolians who herd sheep and live in their yurts far, far, far from anyone else, surviving frigid winters just south of Lake Baikal in Siberia. Mongolians, like their famed ancestor Genghis Khan, are exquisite horse riders. (See the film *Eagle Huntress*, about the Mongolian girl who won the eagle hunting competition, so you can see the wide-open, stunning scenery that I savored.) We visited a female herder—a real rarity. She walked me over to where her horses were. She deftly took a mare and urged a young colt to suckle. Then she yanked the colt away and captured the squirting milk. Hmm, I thought, clever way to get some milk when there is no other source of milk.

Have you ever known hunger?

On the NGOabroad questionnaire that people fill out if they want international career counseling or to apply to our international volunteer programs, there is a very revealing question: "What makes you grumpy?" Many people from North America or Europe say, "Lack of sleep." Some people from Africa say: "An empty belly" or "hunger."

A man from Zambia opened my eyes: "Ten years ago lack of food was not such an issue. We had enough fertilizer to do what we wanted with. Now we are depending on things like mushrooms and caterpillars."[25] Depicting Africans as eating grubs can be a demeaning stereotype, but I mention this because people who have always had food on the table may never have known such hunger.

Binyavanga Wainaina was offended by this kind of portrayal of Africa. In attempting to paint a picture of poverty all over the world, I run the risk of perpetuating stereotypes. Binyavanga Wainaina, Kenyan writer and former director of the Chinua Achebe Center for African Literature and Languages at Bard College, wrote a scathing satirical essay, "How to Write About Africa."

"Make sure you show how Africans ... eat things no other humans eat. Do not mention rice and beef and wheat; monkey-brain is an African's cuisine of choice, along with goat, snake, worms and grubs and game meat."[26] Throughout this book, I have attempted to let the people of each country speak for themselves, to diminish these stereotypes.

For ease for the reader, I refer to Africa, Asia and Latin America. Where possible, I am more specific about a country. Wainaina was irked that people refer to Africa as a country when in fact it is a *continent* of fifty-four countries with 900 million people. He mocks generalizations about the continent, such as, "It is hot and dusty with rolling grasslands and huge herds of animals and tall, thin people who are starving."[27]

So to give a more accurate picture of what people eat that does not emphasize deprivation: in many West African countries they revere cassava; fufu is a favorite in Ghana, while baton de manoc (fermented cassava or manioc shaped into a bat) is savored in Cameroon. In Uganda, they treasure ugali, corn mush. I watched one colleague open her pot of ugali—it was like her birthday cake. In South Africa, they also eat corn mush or mealie meal. In southern India, they make scrumptious coconut pancakes. In Nepal, you are likely to eat lots of dal or lentils. In the Peruvian Amazon, laced with rivers, they served me fish for breakfast. (If the vines that grew like kudzu abundantly everywhere in the Amazon there were edible, then they would know no hunger.) What I do find is that often people will sell their eggs and the vegetables and fruit that they grow as a way to gain some income, rather than feeding themselves. So, indeed, people all over the world have been brilliant at figuring out how to eat and survive.

* * *

If you are going to work in international development, you must be honest with yourself: would you be content in a remote, remote, remote location?

In Bolivia, I remember driving straight up rocky slopes in a 4-wheel drive, with the Potosi director at the wheel. There was no road. I thought we were going to fall off the mountain! I asked to get out of the truck so I could walk—which was faster anyway and felt much safer. In Bolivia, it might take school children three hours to

Would you be willing to work in a remote location like this on the *altiplano* (high plain) of Peru with no movie theaters or latte stands?

walk to school and three hours to get home, in places that are incredibly remote.

In Uganda, we were driving from Gulu to Lira. On the map, which I had looked at back home before going, there were little symbols indicating it was a swamp. Having never lived near such a vast swamp, I didn't really believe there would be a swamp there. (I basically thought that the map makers did not know what they were talking about!) But it was definitely a swamp. I was definitely wrong. We had to drive just the right speed: fast enough to make any forward progress through the water, but carefully enough so that water did not come in the tailpipe. "Why don't you have a decent road and a bus between these two major towns?" I shouted from the back seat. Turning around, my colleague answered my question about the lack of a good road: "Just one word, Ann: corruption."

I asked a Kenyan friend, "Why is it that Kenya produces so many world class marathon runners?" He answered: "Well, I would have to do my chores before school. School was six miles away. I could not be late to school or I would be beat. Often times I would be running late after finishing my chores so I had to run like the wind to get there on time so I would not be beat."

So, "remote" is not really determined just by distance. Just like poverty is not just a matter of income, remote is not really measured by how far the crow flies. It is measured by how far you have to walk. Remoteness is a function of: is there a road? And are there buses or mini-buses to transport people and produce from the rural areas to the towns?

* * *

Where people live and their homes are just as revealing as what they eat.

I like small, cozy spaces—I prefer a harbor to wide open ocean or plains—so I enjoyed the coziness of a yurt, whether out in the countryside (wow, were the steppes wide, open with a dazzling canopy of stars!) or on the outskirts of Ulaanbaatar, Mongolia's capital. Six hundred thousand people out of Ulaanbaatar's one million live in the "gers," the yurt slums at the edge of the capital.

But "slum" is a misleading word. Of the many homes in the "gers" that I visited with the Mongolian director, most homes were more permanent than a yurt. Most had gardens on the side to feed the family unlike the nomads in the countryside who move their yurts along with their grazing sheep. I was impressed with how the frame of the yurt folds up accordion style to really compress when the herder and family move once again.

It is important to understand slums because approximately one billion people in this world live in slums.

The slum population is expected to double in the next 30 years.[28] Often, when people are struggling to survive in the rural areas, of almost any country—it could be Bangladesh, Pakistan, Peru, Ecuador, Bolivia, Nigeria, you name it—they move to the city, hoping to find work. Usually they do not find work but scrape by in the informal sector.

* * *

I stayed in Colombo, Sri Lanka, in an upgraded slum. The organization that NGOabroad works with does amazing work to improve the housing, livelihoods and health of the people who live in the slums.

Slums in many parts of the world are along railroad tracks,

because that is land they can squat on that no one else wants. I mean, how many people want the train coming through as you try to sleep?

(Interestingly, a friend recently told me that when he took the train from Seattle to Los Angeles, there were tents of the homeless along the railroad right-of-way down the entire coast. Thus, squatting on railroad right-of-ways is also what the poor in America do, for the very same reasons.)

Where I stayed in the upgraded area of Colombo was downright middle class. But as they showed me around the neighborhood the next morning, there were the railroad tracks. They also took me to the areas that had not been upgraded yet. Not so shabby. They would have community meetings to discuss which improvements were the highest priorities for the community: clean water, toilets, or a cobblestone path rather than a dirt path?

This community participation and prioritizing is the heart and soul of participatory development, which we will discuss in a later chapter. Participatory development does not just target tangible changes like the water, toilets and housing, but does it in such a way that people have input into the matters which impact their daily lives.

Each home that I walked past, though simple and fairly small, was clean and had personal touches like flowers outside the front door. They had swept the walk with palm fronds. Clothes were hanging to dry.

African colleagues of mine sometimes say that the image that is projected of them emphasizes the worst side of their reality. One of our African directors resented that the American volunteer wanted to share photos of kids in rags and the director insisted that instead they show the clean, crisp school uniforms the kids wear every day.

As director of NGOabroad, I have prepared many people to go to Asia, Africa or Latin America. Most people, I think, expect to find abject poverty. People think there will be squalor and rats. To be honest, I have seen more squalor in the United States; more rats too. In all my travels, I have only seen one rat. Rats are smart; they go where there is food. The rat that I saw was fat with pudgy cheeks—it had found the place where the villagers were drying the ground nuts (peanuts) with no wire mesh or anything to protect the peanuts from varmints. There are no leftovers in many parts of the world, so fewer rats.

In most parts of the world, they sweep the front stoop every morning. The women scrub the floors often. They draw the water from the well in India and wash the Ambassador cars almost daily. They take great care of what they have, and it shows.

In preparing to work abroad, I wasn't quite sure what to wear in-country. One of my mentors pointed out to me that people dress more smartly all over the world. The women in India put the coals of burning coconut shells and dried palm fronds in the iron to press their saris. My Congolese colleague would rise every morning early enough to press his shirt. It is only in America that hoodies and tee shirts would pass at work. It is primarily in America that there is a grunge look.

But getting back to abject poverty: I have to confess, I have not been to the slums in all corners of the world. But what I do know is that what matters to people who live there might surprise you.

In the townships of Cape Town, South Africa, I talked to a young woman who was getting water at the spigot. Here I was in Langa, where the apartheid government insisted that blacks and mixed race people live at the edge of the city. This Xhosa woman was absolutely thrilled to live in Langa. Why? Because where she had lived previously, in the Transkei—the Xhosa rural homeland where the apartheid government corralled the Bantu/ blacks—she had to walk miles and miles and miles to get water. She was overjoyed to live somewhere where there was a spigot and out the water came.

Continuum from Poverty to Prosperity

Hans Rosling did not talk about rich and poor, developed or developing, or have lots and have nots. He did not believe in defining a world view of the "West and the rest" or "us vs. them" and creating an adversarial dichotomy. He found it to be more accurate and to perpetuate fewer myths and less misinformation to talk about levels. The two levels that you will likely be working with in international social work and development are these:

Level One:

Your five children have to spend hours walking barefoot, back and forth, to fetch water from a dirty mud-hole an hour's walk away. On their way home, they gather firewood, and prepare the same grey porridge that you have

People, especially women, in the Global South spend hours each day fetching water.

been eating every meal, every day, for your whole life—except during the months when the meagre soil yielded no crops and you went to bed hungry. One day your daughter develops a nasty cough. Smoke from the indoor fire is weakening her lungs. You can't afford antibiotics, and one month later she is dead. This is extreme poverty. Yet you keep struggling on. If you are lucky and the yields are good, you can maybe sell some surplus crops, and manage to earn more than $2 a day, which would move you to the next level. (Roughly one billion live like this today.)[29]

Level Two:

You've made it. In fact, you have quadrupled your income and now earn $4 a day. Three extra dollars every day. What are you going to do with all this extra money? Now you can buy food that you didn't grow yourself, and you can afford chickens, which mean eggs. You save some money and buy sandals for your children, and buy a bike, and more plastic buckets. You buy a gas stove so your children can attend school instead of gathering wood. When there is power, they do their homework under a bulb. But the electricity is too unstable for a freezer. You save up for mattresses so that you do not have to sleep on the mud floor. Life is much better now, but still very uncertain. A single illness and you would have to sell most of your possessions to buy medicine. That would throw you back to Level One again. Another three dollars a day would be good, but to really experience drastic improvement you need to quadruple again. If you can land a job in the local

A step up in the world is having a bike to haul things or to travel more easily from your remote village to town.

garment industry you will be the first person in your family to bring home a salary. (Roughly 3 billion people live like this today.)[30]

People want a piece of the pie.

People all over the world want to improve their lives and are doing everything in their power to do so. They want to make those moves from Level 1 to Level 2 and even better. Your job in international development or international social work is to help people improve their lives and have a say about what matters most to them.

"At the heart of her bad nature, like many bad natures, was probably envy. And at the heart of envy was possibly hope—that the good fortune of others might one day be hers," Katherine Boo observed in *Behind the Beautiful Forevers: Life, Death, and Hope in a Mumbai Undercity*, which won the National Book Award in 2012.

Grasping the reality of how half of the world lives will affect whether you get the job.

Those who have a strong grasp of the realities of half the world's people—what it is to be hungry, to have to fetch water, to clear land with a machete, to get paid a pittance for back-breaking work—are more likely to get the job in international development or international social work. Why? Because you are more able to form strong bonds with the people you serve, and together design powerful programs that really make a difference in the lives of the people.

Thus, people from Afghanistan, Yemen, Sudan, Somalia, Liberia or the Congo, who know what the euphemism "insecurity" means firsthand; people from Delhi, Jakarta, Lagos, Nairobi or Mexico City, who are more likely to know what mega-city and "peri-urban slum" mean; these people have a strong advantage: they are more likely to "get it." Employers need people who grasp the realities of people's lives.

Employers want to know that you can handle a remote posting, whether it is western Nepal or the scrub land of Sudan. A good example of this: a Kenyan woman asked for my career help—though she was doing a phenomenal job forging forward under her own steam. She was posted in Sudan at the time. I ask for a form to be scanned back and the hard copy mailed by postal mail. She kindly asked, as is the way in East Africa, "I can scan it easily. Is it really necessary to send it by post? It is a two day walk to a post office."

Thus, I kiddingly say but am totally serious: Being from Yellowknife in Canada is a good prerequisite for work in Bolivia or Mongolia. Being from a small town, where you have learned how to make your own entertainment, helps. A social work friend who worked at a clinic in Madagascar loved how much they played cards. Can you handle it if there is no movie theater (and no Netflix) and no latte stand? Conversely, if you are from a huge, teeming city, you may feel at home in a megacity like Delhi or Lagos.

It also helps if you have not come from a privileged background in North America, Europe or Australia. People who have worked their way through school and perhaps worked in a factory here are more likely to understand the sweatshops in Bangladesh and Vietnam, or the maquiladoras in Honduras, Mexico or Dominican Republic. They are more likely to understand what it is to be dog-ass tired at the end of the day and discouraged by the pittance you are paid. This instinctive empathy undergirds the kind of community organizing that Si Kahn, one of the most important community organizers in the United States, does and that you may be a natural to do also.

Years ago in private practice, I had a client who joined the navy so he could have a job and a future. He told me, "We didn't have a refrigerator. We kept everything cool in the creek. We even built a little roof over this section of the creek so it would be shady and cooler. ... I had never had a pizza until I joined the navy." His family was ingenious and clearly knew how to "make somethin' outa' nothin'," thus he is likely more practically prepared than most for the rigors in other countries. Likewise, just the other day, I did a career consultation with a young man from a working-class background in an industrial town in the UK. He had never had the opportunity or income to go to college but deeply wanted to go into international development. He was pleasantly surprised to hear me say that coming from a working-class background and knowing how to scrape by can be an advantage in international development. Knowing poverty as a "lived experience" and overcoming adversity may enrich the contribution you make in international development.

In the same way that schools of social work value life experience, knowing that hardships forge and galvanize true leaders and create movers and shakers, international employers know this too. Thus, your cover letter and résumé should not just reflect book learning and have pat job experience. Of all the résumés that I see at NGOabroad, those that stand out in my memory are those which say, "I go to my grandparents' village every summer [in Greece, China, Palestine, Albania, Moldavia or Mexico]. They have no electricity or running water."

In summary, to do well in international development and international social work, you must understand poverty. Social work is so valued in international development because we have a long and proud history, dating back to Jane Addams, of addressing poverty.

Some of the best job candidates whom I have met are those who understand that poverty can be very close to home. They are the kind of people who plunge into the action where the needs are. Do you help at a soup kitchen or with the homeless? Do you teach English to new immigrants and refugees or literacy in prisons or help with the opioid crisis? Do you teach job skills to marginalized or at-risk youth? This is especially important, because one out of seven youth in the world have no job. At a global level, the youth unemployment rate is two to three times higher than it is for adults.[31]

You do not have to be rich and travel all over the world to work in international development. Those who have experienced poverty or hardship in their home country may be at an advantage, whether they are the Vermonters I met who hunt moose to put food on the table, or those who have lost their job or their home. What irks people, both at home and internationally, is being condescended to and patronized. Thus, more important than expertise and book learning, it is your attitude which will get you hired. You do not need to be rich and have traveled all over the world, though international experience is definitely valued, as is work and life experience. You simply have to have your eyes open and be willing to learn and help.

As an international career counselor, consultant and trainer at NGOabroad, time and time again I see that one of the biggest impediments to someone's getting an international job is that their background is too Western and too privileged. I advise the person: "Go wade out into the world and see how half the world lives; go get your hands dirty."

II

Skills

3

Needs and Strengths Assessment to Program Development

At NGOabroad, I help people enter or advance in international development work.

Several years ago, a newly graduated MSW came to me. She wasn't getting any interviews in response to all the applications she had sent out, so she was getting discouraged. She asked for my help. We started with a career counseling session and some basic training about international development.

At the end, as we discussed steps and strategies, I recommended that she get more international experience because most employers ask for three to five years of international experience. I recommended that she do our internship in Rwanda, followed by our internship in Sierra Leone. I said, "The Rwanda organization that you will work with is much like international development organizations all over the world. It has many departments and ways you can get experience. The director is bright and wonderful but harried. He runs himself ragged each day, which is true for most international development directors, so try to lift the load off of his shoulders."

I continued to explain why I recommended this sequence of experience: "After Rwanda, I recommend that you work in Sierra Leone with Ebola orphans. Though the organization is not as big as Rwanda's, the needs are greater. It will be a great place to get experience with needs assessment and program design."

I assumed that every school of social work in North America, if not the entire world, teaches how to do a needs assessment. I was wrong; she had not learned this. So I want to dedicate this chapter to this MSW who alerted me to the fact that there is a need to learn how to do a needs assessment.

Being able to do a needs and strengths assessment is at the heart of all social work and, as explained in an earlier chapter, is one of the reasons why social workers are so valued in international development work. Note: it is not just the needs or problems which you assess. It is equally important to gauge the strengths of the person, the community, and the country with which you are working. What are the talents, interests, attitudes and beliefs that you can access and build upon to form solutions?

So how would you do a needs and strengths assessment in Sierra Leone?

First, do your homework. Before you even leave your home country and arrive in Sierra Leone, it is smart to do this. Read everything that you can about Sierra Leone and talk to anyone you can from Sierra Leone so that you get the broad, basic brush strokes.

Just a cursory online search reveals The Borgen Project's blog by Carolina Sherwood Bigelow:

- Approximately 60 percent of Sierra Leoneans live below the national poverty line.
- Around 70 percent of youth are unemployed or underemployed.
- Sierra Leone holds only a 41 percent adult literacy rate.
- Sierra Leone has one of the world's highest maternal mortality rates, at an estimated 1,165 deaths per 100,000.[1]

Let's compare that to Rwanda[2]:

- Rwanda's global income ranking has improved from the seventh poorest in 2000 to the twentieth in 2015. This is due to the government's commitment to strong governance and to the principles of market economy and openness.
- At least one million Rwandans have been lifted out of poverty in the last five years.
- Although more than 60 percent still live in extreme poverty, Rwanda has reduced the percentage of people living below the national poverty line from 57 percent in 2005 to 45 percent in 2010.
- During the years 2006 to 2011, Rwanda posted an average

annual growth of real GDP of 8.4 percent. This was driven mainly by higher productivity in the agricultural and industrial sectors.

- The decline in poverty can be attributed to three main changes: an increase in farm productivity, an increase in non-farm employment, and an "increase in the number of livelihood activities in which an individual engages, such as running small businesses," according to United Nations Assistance Mission for Rwanda (UNAMIR).
- The country's Vision 2020 plan is a strategy that aims to "transform the country from a low-income, agriculture-based economy to a knowledge-based, service-oriented economy with middle-income country status by 2020," the World Bank reports.
- Since 2005, the mortality rate of children under 5 has been halved from 152 to 76 deaths per thousand.
- Participation in secondary schooling has doubled since 2006, and primary education has far exceeded the set target.

So when I summarized the difference between the two countries for this MSW, I said, "Sierra Leone is poorer and less educated." How is that difference reflected in the organizations that she would work with? As I said to her, the Rwandan director and organization are more sophisticated. The Sierra Leonean director, though one of the best in the country, does not have the same resources and organizational infrastructure as in Rwanda. I explained, "So there will be more room in Sierra Leone to apply your international social work skills; there is a great deal of latitude in how you add, improve or bolster what they are doing. Much of paid international social work jobs are not stepping into a prescribed role or pre-existing program. Often you have to make programs from scratch. Because the Sierra Leone program has lots of needs and less structure than Rwanda, you can get more practice at needs assessment and program design."

Second, learn history, so you grasp context and why people believe and behave as they do.

Ideally, you do even more research to grasp the history of the country into which you are stepping. Possible ways to do this: read Human Rights Watch Backgrounder reports and glean from Wikipedia:

- The Sierra Leone Civil War (1991–2002) began on March 23, 1991, when the Revolutionary United Front (RUF), with support from the special forces of Charles Taylor's National Patriotic Front of Liberia (NPFL), intervened in Sierra Leone in an attempt to overthrow the Joseph Momoh government. The resulting civil war lasted 11 years, enveloped the country, and left over 50,000 dead. During the first year of the war, the RUF took control of large swathes of territory in eastern and southern Sierra Leone, which were rich in alluvial diamonds.
- In 2014 an Ebola virus epidemic occurred in Sierra Leone, along with the neighboring countries of Guinea and Liberia. On March 18, 2014, Guinean health officials announced the outbreak of a mysterious hemorrhagic fever "which strikes like lightning." It was identified as Ebola virus disease and spread to Sierra Leone by May 2014. The disease was thought to have originated when a child in a bat-hunting family contracted the disease in Guinea in December 2013. Consumption of African bush meat, including rats, bats, and monkeys, is commonplace in Sierra Leone and West Africa in general.
- The CDC (Centers for Disease Control and Prevention) reports that 3,956 people died of Ebola in Sierra Leone from 2014 to 2016.[3]
- Lisa O'Carroll reported in the *Guardian* on March 4, 2015, "More than 12,000 children have been orphaned by the disease in Sierra Leone ... some children, rejected by their friends because of the stigma of Ebola, have tried to take their own lives, while girls are being forced into commercial sex work to earn money for food their parents would have previously provided. ... Apart from day-to-day survival, one of the biggest challenges ahead for orphans is education. Schools are scheduled to reopen on 30 March and although many are desperate to get an education, some will be unable to afford to do so in their new roles as heads of their households."[4]

In researching the background regarding the Ebola orphans in Sierra Leone, you begin to learn about some of the needs: the Ebola orphans are vulnerable and unprotected—some of the teenage girls who are now head of household after parents have died have been raped; as very young heads of households they need help with viable ways to earn income ("income generation"); and often the Ebola orphans do not have a way to pay school fees, so they are being left out of an education.

These will be the things for the MSW to watch for once she gets to Sierra Leone and can do a more thorough, on-the-ground organic or informal needs and strengths assessment.

Your first impressions as you enter the country form a foundation.

Imagine being that MSW as you fly in over the indigo ocean on the coast of Sierra Leone and the plane banks so that you catch a first glimpse of Freetown, the capital. You think, "Hmm, not such a big place—looks more like a town than a city from the air. Where are all the people—the 802,000—people that give life to this place?" Ah ha—then you realize there are more people in each house—maybe a family of eight or ten. There are no green lawns surrounding each house to make a suburban sprawl.

You finally land and deboard and see that the airport is quite small and unadorned but clean as you walk in from the tarmac, enjoying the tropical heat and sun. Without much hassle, you come through immigration and then see the throng of taxi drivers and touts hounding you for your business. You slowly walk down the long line of mostly men holding placards of hotels or NGOs. You are relieved to finally find the placard with your name on it and the simple words "for Ebola orphanage." You are grateful for the driver sent by the orphanage. "Hi, let me take your bag." He slings your small backpack—just the right size to fit in carry-on space—over his shoulder and leads you to the car. The first thing you notice as you get in is the cracked windshield. You point to it as if to ask. Your driver explains, "Many cars in Sierra Leone have cracked windshields. Our government paid the French contractor millions to build the roads between cities. They brought the gravel and graded it, but never tarred over the top. The French contractors made off with millions of dollars and never finished building the roads! Now the gravel on the road flies up and cracks the windshield!" he says indignantly.

But the little Toyota sedan feels like a limo after being on a crowded, packed-like-sardines-with-no-leg-room airplane. You must board a small ferry that takes you across the estuary between the airport and Freetown. As you wait for the ferry and chat, the driver tells you that he has a degree in mechanical engineering and another in computer science, but he can't find a job in these fields in Sierra Leone, so he works as a driver for local and international non-government organizations (INGOs). The driver takes you to a small guesthouse that is clean and simple, only a block from the beach and only $10/night. He says, "I will be back in an hour or so and we can go get some dinner."

You jump in the shower just to wash away all the grime and weariness of travel. You were up at an ungodly hour to hurry-up-and-wait at the airport in Rwanda and then begin the journey here. You are grateful for some time to yourself. The driver comes back so that you can walk to a restaurant together. It is pitch black as you walk. Hmm, no streetlights. The night is a velvet black that feels remarkably safe. People—total strangers—greet each other on the street. You tuck into a hole-in-the-wall restaurant that has four tables covered in red and white checkered plastic tablecloths. A restaurant staff person bustles out of the kitchen and deposits the menu in front of you. You gaze at the choices: rice, greens and Fanta. Your choices are first, second, third, none of the above, or all of the above. (Actually, you can get complicated and consider all the permutations: rice with Fanta; rice with greens; greens and Fanta…) So as not to tax your brain or the waiter's, you look up at the cook, busser and wait staff all rolled in one: "I'd like all of them."

Walk Around Town to Get to Know and "Get a Feel"

The next day in Freetown, you are awakened before dawn by the rooster crowing. You pull the pillow over your head hoping to go back to sleep, cursing the cacophony that seems to start before dawn in most developing countries. Finally you resign yourself to the fact that the day has begun and drag yourself out of bed.

You have wisely asked the Ebola orphanage staff to have the first day to nose around Freetown and get oriented and get to know the place. You learned that this kind of nosing around is essential in social work. Your social work supervisor at Eastside Mental Health back home at your first practicum encouraged you to get to know each town and city that the Eastside team worked in: you popped into the only grocery store in the town of Carnation and asked when Carnation Dairy went out of business and how Carnation is surviving now; you wandered the main street of Issaquah and could see that it is clearly becoming a suburb and bedroom community of Seattle and Bellevue; you wandered through the cemetery next to the church that the Eastside Mental Health team operated out of and could see the headstones of miners who had come a century ago to mine coal. Wandering through the heart of Bellevue was a stark contrast: much wealthier … especially after Microsoft and all the dot coms set up shop on the east side of Lake Washington. Your social work supervisor had taught you that this kind of settling in and getting to know a place is part of a needs assessment or prelude to doing counseling or social work or community organizing in any locale.

So once again, you are grateful for your chum the driver, who shows up to escort you around town. The downtown core is thick with people milling in the streets—none of the fast-paced bustle and mow-you-down that you would find in New York, Chicago or Toronto. A man comes up with a board of Styrofoam with sunglasses poked into it. He shakes the board in front of you, gesturing and eyes imploring, "Want to buy?" You smile and shake your head "No." A young girl, about ten years old, approaches you with a plate of hard candies and gum, and likewise asks if you want to buy. "No thanks, I don't chew." As you walk down the street, you almost crash into the woman with a mountain of fruit on her head. "Wow," you marvel, "what neck muscles she must have!" (Or maybe it is just a very sore neck at the end of each day!) You point to her foot-high delicately balanced mountain of fruit, and ask, "Can I have a banana?" It is just what you will need for breakfast tomorrow.

As you make your way down the river of people, you realize that commerce is done differently here. Back home, people would sell their wares out of a shop. Here, they cannot afford the rent on a shop, so they must be portable units. They sell something that they can carry.

Then the big realization hits: Hmm, this is how people make a living. And that guy selling sunglasses is probably lucky if he sells a pair or two of sunglasses a day. You realize few people jostling their way down the crammed street have the money to buy such a frivolity as sunglasses. It slowly dawns on you: this is how people make less than a dollar or two a day.

There are not lots of fancy art galleries in Freetown. Just like the street vendors, the history and culture are dished up in a different way. On one cement wall along the sidewalk, artists have hung their paintings and carved masks. There are simple bead makers. Like at a street fair, they sit in front, eager to sell. There are not fancy museums to tell you the history of the country or the city, either. But you notice bullet dents on some of the walls. The driver nods that, yes, those are from the war in 1991–2002. You both go down to the beach lined with lavish hotels. In the sand in front of the hotels is a group of young men playing volleyball, hooting and diving into the sand to make saves.

Then your pal the driver has a great idea: "Want to go to the garbage dump?" (The only other place that you know a garbage dump to be a major attraction is Alaska or Prince Rupert, British Columbia, where you can watch the grizzly bears forage for food.)

"Ah … yeah … sure, whatever. But why would we want to go to the garbage dump?"

"So that you can see how they live at the garbage dump."

Well, now that you mention it, that's exactly why I go to other countries; more than museums, I want to see how people live. Just

The market is much like the farmers' market back home, because it is exactly that: where local farmers and fishers bring their produce, fish or wares to sell.

like in Thailand, which has an NGO devoted to those living at and off the dump, you see moms and kids, clothed in rags, pawing through the garbage.

Hmmm, you muse to yourself: Even in America people live off of what others have discarded: the homeless on our streets "dumpster dive," and people salvage copper or other treasures they find in what others have thrown out. At the side of the mound of garbage are very simple, cobbled-together shacks made of scrap wood and metal.

You are grateful to be escorted back to your guesthouse and have the evening to yourself. Enough stimuli! After several days of being sleep deprived, you crash early ... and wake early to the Muslim call to prayer from the mosque nearby. You feast on some peanut butter you have brought from Rwanda and the banana that you bought from the fruit lady the day before.

What needs do you see or hear at the Ebola orphanage itself?

The wonderful driver comes to fetch you and take you to the Ebola orphanage. When you walk in, you see the many, many kids in their one big, unpainted cement block room. "Not too much for the kids to do," you think to yourself, "and not many adults or caregivers amongst 100+ kids, either."

The grey-haired, in-charge female director of the orphanage comes scurrying out of her room and herds you into her office. Launching right in, she says that they have approximately 100+ kids. At any given moment, there are more kids coming in, but also kids being assigned to new foster or adoptive families.

"Great," you mentally note, "they are on it." The director goes into a side room and summons their social worker to come in and join the discussion. In walks a very young woman, with an armload of files. "Yes, we have been working almost night and day to find local homes for all the kids orphaned by the Ebola crisis. But it is not an easy task. Most families in Sierra Leone struggle to feed their own kids, so are not in a position to take in one more mouth to feed and pay for school fees."

"How do you find willing adoptive families in Sierra Leone?" you wonder out loud.

"Like I said, it is not easy," laments the social worker. "But we have found that if we approach people through their religious organizations, it appeals more to their good will."

"As you may know, there are many Muslims in Sierra Leone—77

percent of the population. Arab traders came down the coast of West Africa centuries ago. Twenty-one percent are Christian. So we have approached the chief imam of the Freetown Central Mosque, Sheikh Ahmad Tejan Sillah. He is also the spiritual leader of the Sierra Leone United Council of Imams, which has meant that we can connect with even more imans and mosques."

"Good strategy!" you comment. "So you do not really need help in placing kids in homes, then?" you ask.

"We'd love another hand," answers the Sierra Leonean social worker, "but where we really need help is here at this center, before the kids are placed in a foster or adoptive home in the local community."

You are now nose-to-nose with the challenge: how do you assess the needs of the kids at the center?

How Would You Figure Out What the Children and Youth Need?

- Ask the orphanage director and the social worker their ideas. That's a good place to start.
- Observe and talk to the kids and youth. Ask their stories, struggles and experiences.
- Recall some of what you learned in your pre-arrival research.
- Apply everything that you have learned in child development and social work.

You see that the orphanage director and social worker are already scrambling to just find families for these kids, so they have had no time to design any program of activities. So you plunge in. It is a great opportunity for you to jump in over your head—stumble, stammer and finally gain some traction and succeed.

In your mind, you are sketching out some ideas of what you want to do with the kids:

- Help with grief and loss
- Help the teens who have been thrust into head-of-household responsibilities
- Bolster education, as the Ebola crisis has meant years of schooling derailed and lost

You recall from your child development class that children or youth who have experienced trauma may act aggressively or regressively as they wrestle with the loss or trauma. You don't initially see signs of this with the Sierra Leonean kids, but you keep an eye out for how the Ebola crisis has impacted them. You also recall from your child development class that when things have happened to a child—things out of their control—it is ideal to give them some sense of control. Likewise, when a child's life events have been unpredictable, you want to balance that with predictability, as it is essential to a child's emotional, social and intellectual development.[5]

Gently, at the periphery, you start interacting and launching activities.

You have the savvy to know that you want to gently enter these kids' world, ever so gently. Rather than forcing your way into their world, you sit in the doorway or at the periphery. You just sit doodling or writing in your notebook. Out of the corner of your eye, you see several kids watching you. You look up at them and smile and make eye contact, then go back to your doodling. Two of the kids, a boy about age seven and a girl, probably nine years old, come closer

When children have lost parents or have been through trauma, you approach gently, starting unobtrusively at the periphery.

to you to see what you are doing. You show them your doodle and offer them each a pen and paper, with a smile.

See? You have let the children be in control, you don't force yourself on them. You watch over their shoulders as they draw. "Hmm," you mentally note, "I wish that I had some background as an art therapist!" But you don't need extensive background to be able to get the message. Both are probably drawing the family members they have lost. But you don't assume too much; you ask: "Please tell me who is in the picture and what are they doing?"

"This is a picture of my mom when we lived in Kenema. Then we came here with my dad after my mommy died. Then my dad died too. Then we came here to this center with all the kids."

Other kids are gathering round to see what you and the two kids are doing. You wish that you had brought crayons, because they do not have any supplies at the orphanage. So you lead the gathered kids outside. You find a stick and begin to draw in the hard dirt. Other kids find sticks and begin to draw. You wander amongst young artists asking them about their drawings.

This is how informal and gentle therapy with kids who have lost so much should be.

Good "program design" is often not theoretical or done from the top down programmatically, but instead uses your clinical skills to see what interests the kids or local people.

The next day the cock crows and you do not cover you head with the pillow. You stretch and get ready to walk to the orphanage and see what the kids are doing. When you unobtrusively enter the room and sit down on the periphery, they are preparing to eat. The cook sets a pot of rice among twenty or so kids; five circles of kids scramble to scoop some rice from the pot with their fingers. "Hmm," you muse, "they need to wash their hands. But they may not have soap. I will ask the women if they know how to make soap for an income generation project."

After the children and youth have finished breakfast, you start humming and quietly drumming on your thigh. Again, a few children watch you quizzically. A few gather round you once again. You want to use music to help with the healing of grief and loss. You know music can help release the sad and melancholy feelings and also the pent-up mad or energetic feelings, but you are stumbling because you do not know any local Sierra Leonean tunes or songs that everyone sings here.

So you nod to the fourteen-year-old girl who you had talked to last night, who became a head of household when her parents died of Ebola. You beckon her to come join you. "Hey, Amina, I do not know the songs that you sing here. Will you help me?" Perfect move: facilitate the kids' being in control. She is happy to become the center of attention—she gets everyone clapping and then she breaks into song, and the kids join her. You can't even understand the language, the Krio, but you get the message. After hours of singing, the teenagers start everyone dancing. You have stepped out of the spotlight, and they are clearly carrying the show.

This is how needs and strengths assessments are intertwined. When you first talked to Amina, you were amazed by her resilience, determination, intelligence and maturity. You noticed what a natural leader she is; how unintimidated she was in shouldering the responsibility of becoming head of household; how resourceful and scrappy she was in figuring out how to simply find food to eat.

With each of the children and youths, as you begin to interact with them, you look for their strengths. What are their interests and talents? What are their goals and what motivates them? These strengths form the foundation upon which you will build.

You assess the needs of the older kids who are heads of households and have missed school.

When there is a quiet moment, you beckon to Amina and some of the older kids. You gather them and ask about what they have experienced and thus explore what they need. Some of the youths have harrowing tales of how their parents and relatives died of Ebola—how this seemingly mysterious disease felled their family. They talk almost matter-of-factly about how they scratched and scraped to get by and take care of their younger siblings.

You ask what would be helpful to them now. They tell you:

"We'd like to learn some ways to make some money, some skills so that we do not have to be so poor again."

"All sorts of guys were preying on me once my protectors died. I'd really like to learn about how to prevent getting pregnant."

"I had to leave school to raise my brothers and sisters. I was a star student before and now I am afraid that I will never get back to school."

"Once you are in a foster or adoptive family, some of your needs will hopefully be addressed," you explain. "These are all really important ideas. Let me talk to the director and see if we can begin to talk about sexual health; and I can tutor you in the afternoons so that you can catch back up in school. Income generation skills may require more time and training. Let me find out if there are resources in the community that can help with this, but we can begin some of that here." Note: "Income generation" is a term I would hear often, all over the continent.

Observing the children's and youth's needs helps shape the program and therapeutic activities which you do. In this way a needs and strengths assessment and a program design are intertwined. This process does not need to be formal and rigid. With children and youth this spontaneous, organic and informal approach has more vitality and is often more effective.

In this way if you are a program manager or project manager you would do a needs and strengths assessment at a programmatic level. If you are the country director, you would do a needs and strengths assessment at an organizational and national level.

As Country Director: From Needs Assessment to Program Design

Let us say that after you have worked in program manager and project manager positions in Bolivia, India, Nepal, Yemen and Sudan, Save the Children recognizes the wealth of experience that you have had, especially in war-torn Yemen and Sudan, and hires you as country director in Uganda.

Save the Children has never had a branch in Uganda, so it is your job to lay the cornerstone. You fly into Entebbe and meet the driver who you have pre-arranged, who works closely with the simple guest house or Airbnb where you will stay. Where to begin in assessing the needs?

As with Sierra Leone, it behooves you to do your homework because that will help determine where you start your "Listening Tour." You learn that Uganda is one of the most generous countries to refugees from neighboring countries: Uganda gives a plot of land so refugees can grow crops and sustain themselves. From your work in Sudan, you know that one million South Sudanese refugees have poured into Uganda—making it the second biggest refugee crisis after the Syrian refugee crisis. You know that in 2018, over 3,400 Congolese refugees arrived in Uganda each day. You begin to map out the situation:

When you are country director, your needs assessments ultimately result in program development. If you are really a phenomenal country director, you include the community in all of these discussions and program development, rather than dreaming it up by yourself in an echo chamber. We will talk about this approach further in the chapter on participatory development.

The above framework of problems and needs, and solutions and strategies, gives the country director a starting point. It is a hypothesis. The next step is to talk to a great many people all over the community and country—community leaders, clergy, chiefs (something more pertinent in other parts of Africa), CBOs (community-based organizations)—to see what is already being done and what they believe the problems and solutions are. After all, you do not want to recreate the wheel. Additionally, this networking may reveal CBOs that you want to ally or align with in rolling out interventions.

What you may find is that the stakeholders are different in Uganda than in Los Angeles or Montreal. The stakeholders you will want to talk to in Uganda may be more like who you would talk to in Kansas or Saskatchewan. That is, the movers and shakers are not

Problem or need	Solution	Strategy
Refugees both Sudanese & Congolese	Assess what the needs are of refugee children	1. Talk to UNHCR & UNICEF 2. Go to refguee camps
Education Girls are now included in education but teachers do not come to school because they are not paid	1. Kerala, India is model of quality education and quality of life on low budget. 2. Engage parents & teach them so invested in their kids education -> + early childhood education	1. Coordinate with "citizens" schools that fill the gap. 2. Borrow model from Bangladesh how paraprofessionals do outreach to bolster education.
Poverty Uganda director said President Museveni has no interest in developing a jobs program so youth scrape by in the informal sector	1. Teach entrepreneurhship skills 2. Create network of mentors to help entrepreneurs flourish	Coordinate with CBOs that do income generation to discuss successes & future steps about economic empowerment
Health Foul water & sanitation are main health issues in refugee camps + malaria (and throughout country)	1. Develop WASH programs - Water, sanitation & hygiene. 2. + malaria prevention. Will address other health concerns after tackle these first.	1. Coordinate with Kenya org about portable, composting toilet to use in refugee camps. 2. Create Training of Trainers to disseminate WASH program 3. Coordinate w/ UNICEF & UNHCR re mosquito prevention

Needs Assessment of country director in Uganda (author photograph).

as multi-layered as in a big city, but they are the people with whom it is wise to consult. Don't think that you should only be talking to leaders. It is equally helpful to talk to taxi drivers, farmers, laborers, prostitutes, shopkeepers, teachers, and parents to get your "pulse of the planet."

In addition to trying to wrap your head around what the needs are in Uganda, you are simultaneously noting strengths as you talk to community leaders and ordinary citizens, as you listen to the music and what popular culture tells you about the country. You notice that there is a strong thread throughout the country of people grumbling about the president and the corruption. You see in the news that Bobby Wine, the rapper and a member of the parliament, was jailed for his criticism of the president.[6]

You see the movie *Queen of Katwe*, about the young woman chess whiz from the slums of Kampala. You see the video done by Patrick Ssenyonjo, the eight-year-old rapper, who raps about the realities of poverty and its impact.[7] You talk to many Ugandan organization directors who had scholarships to Makerere University, Uganda's best, who after graduating want to give back to their community. Still new to the country, you do not draw conclusions, but you know that you will build on the strengths that you find all over Uganda: intelligent, resourceful, creative, committed, sometimes cheeky people.

From your needs and strengths assessment, you then design the programs. Together with the community, you decide that the greatest unmet need is in the Sudanese and Congolese refugee camps, so you will seek funding to pilot some of the programs there.

1. WASH (water and sanitation, hygiene)—you get Stewardship Foundation (because they emphasize clean water and youth) monies to
   - employ refugee youth to dig new latrines that are not near a water source;
   - employ brigades of women, men and youths to train about how to purify water (sanitation is often the first issue that needs to be addressed with refugees or after an earthquake such as in Haiti).
2. Education—you get UNICEF monies for an empowerment campaign; you meet with refugees to discuss if they want

a school for themselves and their kids. If they do, then you have a small budget to help in the building of the school.

But it will be the refugee women, youths and some men (many of the men have been killed) who will press the bricks and actually make the school—thus learning an important trade, but more importantly learning that they can take care of their own needs and make anything they set their minds to.

- You invite anyone who is interested to come learn how to read and write. You also teach math. Then this core group of people, in turn, are the mentors and instructors for the next cohort that wants to learn to read and write. Once you have a strong group of people committed to reading and writing, then they can teach the kids.

You have obtained funding to roll out these two programs over two years. Later, you can develop other programs associated with the needs identified in your needs assessment. You are committed to doing this with the active involvement of local communities, thus doing participatory development. You can now hire your program managers to help implement these programs. You understand that these are innovative approaches, that you may encounter strong headwinds, and that you are new to this role as country director, so you want to start with only two programs and build your success from there.

It has been a long, winding, rewarding journey as a social worker: years of work with children, youth and families in your community back home so that you could refine your skills and build your launching pad. Then you knew that you had a lot to offer, so you branched out and waded into deeper water when you entered international social work as a program manager in several places around the world.

After years of incrementally gaining experience and years of studying various models of how different countries have addressed their needs, you finally are ready to take the reins as country director.

There are only a few concerns or cautions to add to the above framework or method of operation.

1. More and more presidents and prime ministers resent INGOs (international non-government organizations)

coming in to do development work. More leaders have their own grand plan how to improve life in their country. Or sometimes they have no idea of how to improve lives of their citizens and perhaps just resent outsiders showing them up. So more and more, it is wise to do your homework before you even enter the country to assess the political climate. Assess if it would be wise to consult the president, prime minister and pertinent ministers, for example of welfare or education or health. Weigh whether it is smart to include these stakeholders in your needs assessment and program design.

2. Sometimes the above framework is just too tidy; it may not be how things are done in real life. Usually it is more complex. "In a situation that needs changing we can gather enough data about a community and its problems, analyze it and discover an underlying set of related problems and their cause, decide which problems are the most important, devise a set of solutions and purposes or outcomes, plan a series of logically connected activities for addressing the needs and achieving the desired future results, as defined up front, cost the activities into a convincing budget, raise the funding then implement the activities, monitor progress as we aim to keep them on track, hopefully achieve the planned results and at the end evaluate the program for accountability, impact and even something for learning."[8]

3. Has your project or program not only accomplished its goals, but also improved the quality of life for the people? That is, have you impacted at the macro, not just the micro level? Often the real litmus test is this: how many people has your program helped lift out of poverty?

A Model of Needs and Strength Assessment as Melinda Gates Would Do It

Melinda Gates, co-founder of the Gates Foundation, one of the world's biggest philanthropies, essentially does needs assessments all over the world to determine what the most pressing needs are to which the Gates Foundation will devote its money and programs. Meanwhile, Bill Gates, founder of Microsoft, dreams up and tackles interventions much as he would dream up innovations for Microsoft; Melinda is "yin" to Bill's "yang." For example, it was Bill's idea to develop a malaria vaccine.

In contrast, Melinda does many more "listening tours." In her book *The Moment of Lift: How Empowering Women Changes the World,* Melinda writes about how she will talk to women at clinics and community centers, and sitting on their floor eating chapatis. One mother in India beseeched and begged Melinda to take her two Indian children and for Melinda to raise them, because this Indian mother could not feed, clothe or provide for her children. From these many conversations, and listening to many heartbreaking stories, and because so many women have asked Melinda how they can have fewer children, Melinda believes that priority should be placed on family planning. Read *Moment of Lift* as a fascinating way to learn about how to do a needs and strengths assessment.

And notice how Melinda humbly says that all the data-driven research the Gates Foundation does to shape its policies, practices and decisions is dwarfed by her conversations with those she calls the "experts." Melinda humbly acknowledges that she has learned the most by talking to the poor themselves and by going to remote and impoverished places to listen.

In summary, the needs and strengths assessment, and how it shapes program design and development, together are the foundation upon which much of international development work is built. I have attempted to outline how to incrementally learn this important skill so that you are more likely to be hired and be more effective in serving on the job.

4

Capacity Building:
Creating Collaborators,
Not Passive Recipients

In international social work and international development, you not only incrementally build your own skills; you also help build the strengths and skills of the local people. This is what capacity building is.

In international development, you are, more often than not, a facilitator or mentor. Expatriates commonly picture themselves as being the primary change agent. But often you are not the central actor, and more emphasis is put on being a facilitator, animator or mentor. There is more emphasis on helping build individuals' and communities' strengths and skills. In international development, we call this *capacity building*.

Development professionals have written about and debated the merits of capacity building for decades. Deborah Eade wrote a very practical book, *Capacity-Building: An Approach to People-Centred Development*.[1] Eade explained, "Strengthening people's capacity to determine their own values and priorities, and to organize themselves to act on these, is the basis of development."[2]

The Food and Agricultural Organization of the United Nations defines capacity building like this: "Human resource development (HRD) is an essential part of development. ... Education and training lie at the heart of development efforts ... helping participants ... to increase their knowledge, skills and understandings and to develop the attitudes needed to bring about the desired developmental change."[3]

And in Africa especially, "capacity building" is an expression which you will hear often. Sometimes, it simply means "We would

75

Dr. Zafrullah Chowdhury, of Gonoshasthaya Kendra in Bangladesh, believes that to provide health care to the many Bangladeshi who need it, you must build capacity and empower villagers to engage with their health (Gonoshasthaya Kendra Archive).

like training" on something like strategic planning or grant proposal writing.

Capacity building is often built into how your work teams are arranged.

For decades, international development work was failing because foreign aid workers would come in and run the program and/or organization and then depart, leaving the locals empty handed. Now international staff and locals are often paired and work side by side as equals. The local staff knows the local realities, beliefs, language, culture and communities. International staff may bring models that have worked elsewhere, new techniques or technologies. The goal of capacity building is that the local staff acquires the skills they will need to have to run the program and organization.

But the important point here is this: Yes, there will be job openings for country directors and program and project managers, but there will also be jobs where you mentor local talent so that they can be the country director or program manager.

This is true across all professions, not just in social work. So likewise, many nurses think that they will do nursing in hospitals and clinics all over the world just like they do back home. But often international nurses are needed to mentor and build the strengths and skills of the local nurses.

For example, consider the following job opening for a nurse mentor in Malawi with Partners in Health, one of the most esteemed health organizations in the world. Many people have heard of Paul Farmer and his work in Haiti, where Partners in Health was launched. (See more about Paul Farmer in the later chapter "Partner to the Poor and Participatory Development.")

> The NCD (Non-Communicable Disease) Nurse Mentor will be based ... at the two hospital-based advanced NCD clinics and will help oversee nurses on a clinical team. This team will also be responsible for providing broad NCD mentorship in Neno. The NCD Nurse Mentor will work closely with the NCD Physician Lead ... and the other clinical and community programs in order to provide holistic care to the patients in the district. ... He/she will also be a key collaborator with the MOH [Minister of Health] in Malawi, both locally in Neno and in Lilongwe. The candidate for this position must be self-motivated, have superb interpersonal skills, be passionate about nursing care and social justice, and show creativity in tackling clinical and organizational problems as they arise.

A Nutritionist's Résumé

Another example of capacity building is reflected in this nutritionist's résumé. Her capacity building was as important as her direct nutrition work. Notice that she not only figured out the nutritional formula which would help malnourished infants gain weight and survive, but that in every place where she worked, she was training health teams or local people how to take over when she leaves.

Bamako, Mali

Medical Nutrition Coordinator, February 2008–December 2008

- Coordinated [organization]'s nutrition, health promotion and HIV/AIDS prevention programs in Mali, including strengthening local partnerships via joint community mobilization events that combined different types of media and social channels.

- Successfully mobilized resources for the implementation of four projects (targeting 600,000 beneficiaries, total budget 3.2 million euros).
- Provided technical assistance to Minister of Health (MoH) in strengthening Essential Nutrition Actions (ENA) programming and in developing standardized monitoring tools
- Promoted best practices for integrated CMAM (Community-based Management of Acute Malnutrition), including mainstreaming nutritional surveillance and emergency response in training modules to strengthen local capacity in these specific areas.
- Participated in the evaluation of new food technologies to support local food fortification initiatives and multiple micronutrient supplementation.
- Managed HR and financial aspects of projects, including staff evaluations, proposals and budget administration.

Juba, South Sudan

Medical Nutrition Coordinator, April 2007–January 2008

- Coordinated [organization]'s nutrition surveillance and treatment programs in South Sudan, including local capacity building in integrated CMAM, setting up early warning systems in vulnerable zones and reinforcing emergency preparedness and response.
- Successfully mobilized resources for the implementation of 3 projects (targeting 450,000 beneficiaries, total budget 2.1 million USD)
- Coordinated nationwide nutrition surveys; formulated advocacy plans based on results in collaboration with government counterparts and partners.
- Led the first NGO pilot project in South Sudan on sentinel site nutritional surveillance as an early warning tool to monitor child nutrition and food security trends at the household level.

Democratic Republic of Congo

Nutrition Program Manager, August 2006–March 2007

- Supported 36 health centers and two district hospitals in integrating nutrition promotion and therapeutic services into routine health service delivery.
- Worked alongside local authorities and community-based organizations to promote eight key family practices in health and nutrition, including IYCF (Infant and Young Child Feeding). Participated in the development of standardized promotion strategies and tools.
- Facilitated trainings for health authorities and a network of 200 community health workers on CMAM and IMCI guidelines to reinforce community-based detection and referral of malnutrition.
- Conducted joint field assessments and interventions with partner agencies in response to cholera and measles outbreaks.

Pakistan

Nutrition Program Manager, January 2006–June 2006

- Set up and managed eight emergency nutrition feeding and breastfeeding support centers targeting 10,000 IDPs after the earthquake.
- Monitored health and nutrition trends through ongoing assessments and data analysis in order to identify evolving program needs and opportunities.
- Actively participated in weekly [organization]-led nutrition cluster meetings to ensure coordination of humanitarian interventions and common priority actions.
- Designed and led a capacity building project for traditional birth attendants and Lady Health Workers (LHWs) in maternal health and hygiene promotion and the detection-referral of acute malnutrition.
- Monitored and evaluated impact and performance of the emergency program.

Niger

Nutrition Program Manager, June 2005–December 2005

- Launched 30 mobile emergency nutrition feeding centers (CMAM approach) reaching over 25,000 beneficiaries in response to the food crisis.
- Organized and conducted ongoing assessments and rapid evaluations to determine gaps in coverage, which led to the establishment of four additional feeding centers.
- Produced situation analysis reports and proposals for emergency funding; secured additional funding for post-emergency phase of program.
- Introduced new community mobilization approach by directly involving mothers of program beneficiaries in nutritional screening, door-to-door sensitization and follow-up of malnourished cases. This strengthened detection-referral systems between the community and health centers.

The nutritionist's résumé also reflects the other responsibilities which are required in international development. Often in the job announcement they ask for strong skills in "liaising." To liaise is to establish a working relationship, typically in order to cooperate on a matter of mutual concern.

As a program manager, which the nutritionist was in all the above jobs, she often liaised with the minister of health, public health workers, and hospital and clinic staff. Often you coordinate and work with all the main "stakeholders"—another term that is often used in international development.

Mediating

A corollary skill that is needed is mediating. In international social work or international development, you often must juggle various, potentially conflicting, interests or parties. One woman commented on her work in refugee camps. To paraphrase her:

We had refugees pouring in from many countries, twenty-seven to be exact. There were seventeen languages spoken in the camp. There was squabbling among the refugees about the little bit of space that we could offer them to sleep and live and call their own home. Then there were the NGOs (non-government organizations) and the national government. Everyone had different needs and different opinions about what should be done. The most important skill, really, was mediating.

When they ask for strong interpersonal skills in the job description, those skills will likely be put to the test. The ability to be graceful and gracious under pressure and at the same time be assertive is essential.

How do you actually do capacity building? Lest you think of capacity building as outside your reach, it is really an extension of social work or people skills which you likely have been polishing in your home community: communication skills with couples, parenting skills, empowerment, encouraging expression, and assertiveness and leadership skills for disenfranchised groups such as youth and women.

Capacity Building Is Like Coaching

How exactly do you build people's skills and confidence? It is much like coaching, whether you are a soccer coach or a ballet teacher. You notice what the soccer player or ballet student is doing correctly, and you applaud it. Why? Applying the tenets of behavior therapy, positive reinforcement is more powerful than negative reinforcement. Praise what is done well and the person who you are lauding will shine and the behavior you are applauding will flourish. This forms your foundation and bolsters your bond. They then are more likely to have the courage to take one more step or stretch further.

Once they feel confident in what they are doing well or correctly, then you can comment on what they could do differently. The basketball coach will say, "When you are coming in for your lay-up, you are dragging your left foot. You will get more lift off if you aren't dragging that foot."

Coaching is nudging people to make small changes that will make a big difference.

Capacity Building Is the Foundation for Empowerment

As people gain more confidence, they are more likely to speak up in the groups or community discussions. If you are facilitating a group, include the people on the periphery; make their voices or opinions welcome in the group, thus also building the foundation for leadership skills. Through capacity building, you build the foundation and fabric of participatory development, which will be discussed in a future chapter.

Starting small is wise, because even that is likely a formidable challenge. Urge people to have an impact in smaller orbs of influence: e.g., help with how a woman can have more voice in her family, which in many countries is a huge step. In most parts of the world, women are still considered the property of their husband, with no rights of their own. In some parts of the Muslim world, women must be accompanied by their husband or a male relative whenever they leave their home. Malala Yousafzai, the youngest Nobel Peace Prize laureate, was shot in Pakistan for advocating that girls get an education—a major step in Pakistan. It is wise to start with small steps, because often you cannot anticipate the results or repercussions. Change comes one step at a time. These small but assertive steps are the root of empowerment.

Role models are important in capacity building. One of the simplest ways to learn almost any skill is to imitate someone who does that skill well. Rather than describing how to hit a baseball or cricket ball with a bat, you just show the person, and they imitate. Rather than describing salsa or tango or ice skating, have people learn by doing.

It is crucial to have role models, heroines and heroes who beckon and light the way.

It is helpful to be well-versed in the heroines and heroes of the culture or country into which you are stepping. For example, going to work with young women in Kenya? Get to know the life story of Tegla Chepkite Loroupe, Kenya's famous long-distance runner and marathon champion. Know the irreverent environmentalist and activist Wangari Maathai? You increase your credibility if you know who the local people look up to and who they emulate and admire. Every country in the world has remarkable people who create music and art, pioneer innovations, or become leaders in their society. Get to know these role models and you will have deeper insight and more success working in that country.

Your attitude may be more important than your expertise. Capacity building and empowerment are very nuanced and influenced by the attitudes that you bring, which undergird your work and interactions.

Thankfully, attitudes are being scrutinized. In *Mistaking Africa: Curiosities and Inventions of the American Mind*, Curtis Keim explores the often unconscious stereotypes which we have about Africa: Troubled Africa; Helpless Africa; Unchanging Africa; Exotic Africa; Sexualized Africa.[4] When asked to list words they associate with Africa, Westerners will say: impoverished, conflicts or safaris. Wangari Maathai—the Kenyan Nobel-Peace-Prize winner for the environmental work she did in launching the Greenbelt Movement—sardonically said (paraphrased): "There are more than lions and elephants here; there are people here too."

Check out, on YouTube, Trevor Noah's "Great Britain Is Not So Great." Trevor Noah, a comedian and social commentator from South Africa, had his British audience chortling at how condescending colonial attitudes are.[5] While you are nosing around Trevor Noah videos, find his sketch of the Malibu surfer's questions about Africa. Like Curtis Keim has pointed out, too many people, like the Malibu surfer, think Africans live in the trees like Tarzan.

Keim also writes about the attitude that Africa needs help and that we North Americans and Europeans are the saviors who can provide that help. I know many African directors who are bewildered by how many Americans who have read Keim do not want to work or volunteer in Africa now. The African directors feel abandoned. Rejecting the "savior" role and learning how to work as equals is the key.

Robert Chambers, eminent professor emeritus at University of Sussex and a development pioneer (whom you will meet again in the chapter on participatory development), says there is a simple but profound way around this dilemma: "put the first last." Reverse roles; discard the dominant-subordinate power relationship of "one-up/one-down." Build interactions based on mutual respect, a partnership as equals.[6]

How do you establish that relationship of equality? In the later chapter on partnering with the poor and the chapter on attitudes, we will look at the privilege and power you may bring to the work you do in international development and what to do about it. Leading thinkers of the white privilege movement would say, first, be cognizant of how you are thinking, before you even get off the plane. Second, you have to get in step with the community and country into which you are entering. When you first arrive, wander the local area, getting to know its people, its pulse and its rhythm as the MSW did when she first arrived in Sierra Leone.

Do you know what "pacing and leading" is and how to do it?

Learn Their Pace and Spirit So You Can Get in Stride with Them

One of the first steps is making bonds: you start with some casual bonds in your walk-about; and then further, you begin to make bonds with new in-country colleagues, with important stakeholders and decision-makers.

In family therapy, this bond building is sometimes called "joining," as you must be accepted into the family. An executive director who does youth programs all over the world astutely calls this "relationship building." This bond-building may sound obvious, but without strong bonds, all further steps founder and fail.

Through your walk-about and the first bonds you build with people, you get in stride with the organizations and community with which you will work. Do tangible things together: wake at dawn and go gather water or firewood. In this way you will learn their realities, and how and why they do things the way they do. Peel potatoes or squish the fermented cassava into "baton de manioc" with Cameroonians. Thus, they will be the experts guiding you how to do it, and you will all be laughing together. Go see if you can fix the water pump or cut trees with a machete. You must be in stride before you can propose or introduce any new directions or interventions.

Richard Bandler and John Grinder, who developed neurolinguistic programming (NLP), call this "pacing and leading."[7] Neurolinguistic programming emerged from studying how Milton Erickson's powerful hypnotic techniques were so effective in creating therapeutic change. More pertinent to international social work and international development, you can apply this concept from NLP to capacity building. Pacing and leading is really at the heart of good capacity building.

For example, I just did a debriefing with a woman who did some environmental work in Vietnam. She was baffled by why the Vietnamese environmental team did not want her to make some solar energy calculations. (She is an engineer.) My comment: "They may not have known what you were talking about: they are a more educational program and less technical." She lamented, "The Vietnamese team took me to see the places where they had installed solar, rather than learning more about solar."

We talked about how pacing and leading pertained to this dilemma which she encountered in the field. She and I had talked about pacing and leading in capacity building before she left. I told her:

> Yes, go see the work they have done which they proudly want to show you. Applaud it. Use that field visit as an opportunity to glean what their skill and understanding level is. The Vietnamese team is doing amazing environmental education work promoting the idea of people painting their roofs white so it reflects the heat, and even encouraging the Vietnamese to make green gardens on their roofs to capture carbon. These are huge advances in Vietnam. But do they have the skills of a photovoltaic electrician to actually install and wire solar? They are not a solar company; they are an environmental educational organization. Praise them for the many presentations they have put on all over the country; this is the way you get in stride with them; that you "pace" them. Either on that field visit or back at the office, ask them what they want to add to what they are doing; what they want to learn about in environmental work. These are the new directions that they have identified, that you might lead. This is how pacing and leading could have helped with the capacity building you were doing.

Another example: I did a consultation with a Canadian woman who called from Peru to ask why her entrepreneurial efforts were not succeeding. She said, "I think that the Peruvians could start a small enterprise in essential oils, but they are not interested."

"Hmmm," I mused, "who thought up this idea of essential oils? It sounds like a foreign idea. Essential oils are more a luxury item among Peruvian people who would like shoes for their kids and food to eat in the high Andes. More familiar to the Peruvians might be alpaca or llama weaving."

"Huh, I never thought of it that way, but I saw essential oils for sale at the market in Lima," she commented.

"Then invite some of the women you are working with to come with you to Lima next time that you go. Let them see if essential oils are something that they are interested in producing. Help close that gap."

We discussed how she might rectify the situation: build stronger bonds in the community to gain credibility and get in stride with them, thus putting her in a better position to propose a new idea or direction.

As my best clinical social work professor would say, "Start with where the client is." Much of what is taught in the clinical track of social work applies to international work. A clinical social worker assesses the situation, challenges and strengths of a psychotherapy client; you essentially do the same initial assessment or intake to determine the starting point for your work with a community or person in another country.

Here is a shining example of how to do it right.

I had a young Canadian nurse come to me and ask if I could help her get international experience. I said, "Sure, NGOabroad has an ever-changing and ever-growing range of international placement opportunities in many fields—social work, education, nursing/medical, public health, business/entrepreneurship, environmental, engineering, and political science, democracy-building, and human rights. So yes, we have some great places to get international experience in nursing. I recommend Sri Lanka—doing nursing in the clinic in the slums and then later working in the clinic and village outreach in remote northern Uganda."

Wow, did she do a phenomenal job! Actually, I knew she would: she had such an attitude of equality and she makes such strong bonds—she is clearly a bridge builder.

How did she do it? She really got in stride. She helped with the chores at the home stay (in international volunteering, the home stay is where one lives with a local family in order to become more intimate with the culture) in the slums in Colombo, Sri Lanka. She laughed at herself as she learned Sinhala from the clinic staff. In exchange, she taught them English. In this way she was laying the foundation for how they would work together as equals. She did this not because she was following a "recipe" or was taught this, but because without guile, she simply loves people and embodies this belief in equality. Then as their bonds and relationships were built, she noticed where there were gaps in their nursing skills or knowledge. (She was informally assessing the needs.) She taught her Sri Lankan nursing colleagues some things from Western medicine, and they taught her about Ayervedic medicine.

She then did a repeat extraordinary job in northern Uganda. In the same way, she let the local staff be her teachers as she stumbled to learn Acholi. Like in Sri Lanka, she watched what they were doing for a long time. She observed their strengths and skills, and where she could contribute something. She noted that they were skilled in diagnosing and treating malaria, a disease they work with frequently. The health clinic director had told me that none of their nurses were trained in anatomy and physiology, so the Canadian nurse had brought books and showed them and discussed them. She learned a tremendous amount from her Ugandan colleagues, and they also learned from her.

In this way, it is a reciprocal relationship. As they say in education, it is not a teacher-student hierarchy; we are all learners. There is not a one-up, one-down relationship, but a profound equality.

This is why I say attitude is more important than expertise. Expatriates who think of themselves as experts may have unwittingly lost this attitude of equality and respect.

As mentioned earlier, a further way that you can remove yourself from the role of expert is through what Robert Chambers calls a reversal of power. Chambers, in his important book *Whose Reality Counts? Putting the First Last,* has some very concrete ways in which you can avoid dominating, in which you encourage participation: don't stand at the blackboard or poster paper with marking pen in hand, calling on people to speak, because then you control too much—who speaks and how it is represented. Chambers much prefers drawing things in the dirt. (His methodology is called participatory rural appraisal, often involving work with farmers.) Farmers or villagers are gathered around; there is no podium; people are more likely to interject or amend the diagram being made.

Don't Expect to Always Be Greeted with Open Arms

In various countries, presidents and governments are declining offers of aid, some saying that international aid impairs building the capacity of their own people and country.

Though most major international development or humanitarian

organizations responded to the 2004 Boxer Day earthquake in Banda Aceh, Indonesia, and the tsunami that hit in India, Thailand, and Sri Lanka, and to the earthquake in Haiti in 2010, there are occasions where nations decline assistance. After one of strongest earthquakes in the world, the 8.8 quake that hit Chile on February 27, 2010, President Michelle Bachelet initially declined offers of foreign aid. But as the death toll mounted and after seeing the devastation of the quake and tsunami, she reversed her position and accepted help, reported Sara Miller Llana of the *Christian Science Monitor.*[8] After the earthquake in Nepal on April 25, 2015, that killed 9,000 people, Nepal asked for everything from blankets to helicopters to reach rural villages devastated by the quake that were now impossible to get to because of landslides on the mountain roads. Several nations sent helicopters, but the *Guardian* reported: "RAF Chinooks were recalled from Nepal quake effort without flying a mission."[9]

But to be honest, after Hurricane Katrina devastated New Orleans and the Gulf Coast in August 2005, the United States declined 54 of 77 aid offers from three of its staunchest allies: Canada, Britain, and Israel.[10]

Additionally, in an international context, authoritarian governments or leaders may not welcome foreign NGOs, also called INGO (international non-governmental organizations). Deborah Doane reported in the *Guardian* about the situation in India:

NGOs, including Greenpeace, Amnesty and Cordaid, were accused of "serving as tools for foreign policy interests of western governments by sponsoring campaigns to protect the environment or support human rights." ... Accusing development NGOs of being anti-development is somewhat of a paradox—but it's a growing global trend. Reported Civicus, the global civil society alliance, "Particularly for those activists who dare to challenge economic and political elites, the environment in which civil society operates has continued to deteriorate."[11]

It is wise to be aware of this trend and sentiment in some countries, as it may impact how and where you get a visa, and how and where your international development organization is welcome to operate. Some presidents and governments see international development organizations as a threat because they interfere with their agenda or interfere in building the capacity of their own nation and people.

Thus, doing capacity building well—working with an attitude of equality and respect—impacts the future of international development. There is a shift to capacity building from within.

Yesterday, I was very moved by a director in The Gambia who said, "I have started this school so that the next generation does not dream of leaving the country but of building it." Capacity building, at its best, is not something that comes from outsiders or foreigners but is built from within the country, by the people of that country.

This is important to know about in international development, because not always will a country want outside help. For example, Rwanda's president Paul Kagame has made it a core policy for Rwandans to develop their own solutions and self-sufficiency, to build their own capacity.

More than many countries, Rwanda is very aware of capacity building. Rwanda is rightfully very proud of their University of Health Equity, which is devoted to advancing global health delivery by training a new generation of global health leaders who are equipped not just for building, but also for sustaining, effective and equitable health systems. They are proud that they have achieved the Millennium Development Goals in Health and equally proud of their universal healthcare coverage. Agnes Binagwaho, MD, former minister of health in Rwanda, explained that Rwanda's community-based health insurance program (Mutuelle de Santé) was transformed to a system of tiered premiums to make it more affordable to all Rwandans. Their goal—health coverage for as many Rwandans as possible—has been achieved and serves as a model for many other nations. By 2010, more than 90 percent of Rwandans had health insurance under Mutuelle de Santé.[12] Because of this, Rwanda has accepted few international health organizations to work within their country, though they do work closely with Partners in Health.

Nations, including the United States, make national plans and policies. For example, Lyndon Baines Johnson's War on Poverty and the launching of the Head Start preschool program were important nationwide initiatives. Nations want to see if their programs will work, so sometimes they do not welcome international aid organizations that will confuse or complicate their efforts. That is why the core tenet of capacity building—working side by side as equal partners—is so important. You might say that capacity building at a national level is equally important.

But let us detour to examine why Rwanda and Partners in

Health have such a strong relationship, given Rwanda's very selective policy about which organizations they will allow to work in the country, and what this tells us about capacity building and trends in international development.

As the Partners in Health website says of their own work and philosophy: "We go. We make house calls. We build health systems. We stay. ... We work in close partnership with local government officials and the world's leading medical and academic institutions to build capacity and strengthen health systems. And we stay, committed to accompanying the people and communities we serve for the long term."

Partners in Health strives to achieve two overarching goals: to bring the benefits of modern medical science to those most in need of them and to serve as an antidote to despair. "At its root, our mission is both medical and moral. It is based on solidarity, rather than charity alone."

The name of the organization, Partners in Health, emphasizes the very important precept that you work together as equal partners. The organization was founded by Ophelia Dahl, Jim Yong Kim and Paul Farmer, but it is Paul Farmer who is best known. Central to Paul Farmer's work as physician and medical anthropologist is the connection between poverty and disease, the maldistribution of medical technologies in the world, and "immodest claims of causality" that scholars and health bureaucrats have of these phenomena.[13]

Partners in Health, after years of collaboration with Rwanda's minister of health, Agnes Binagwaho, MD, helped launch the University of Global Health Equity. Dr. Paul Farmer's vision for Partners in Health was harmonious with the Rwandan vision of pulling people up by building a "knowledge" economy while delivering care.[14] In short, Paul Farmer's and Partners in Health's philosophy fits Rwanda's: both believe in building the capacity of Rwanda. PIH has, since its inception, had an attitude of humility, of equality, of service, and of solidarity with the poor. As we shall see in the chapter on attitude, a very new ethos is sweeping out and into international development. The partnership between Rwanda and Partners in Health is, I believe, a harbinger of the future of international development.

5

Capacity Building:
Other Steps to Empowerment

It is possible to take capacity building further. Don't just think of capacity building as confined to the activities of your job role, take it one more step: really work with local staff to build their strengths and skills. As you do lots of coaching, mentoring and confidence building, it can strengthen the bonds. The following skills are ones that organizations around the world have asked our help with, so check if the local team that you are working with would also find some of these additional skills helpful.

Invite local staff to work with you so they learn the skill. Whatever your job is, don't work until midnight writing a grant proposal by yourself. Invite some of the local staff to first look over your shoulder to see how it is done, and then delegate pieces of the grant proposal to them. Yes, it is more work to train people in grant writing, but that is an example of what capacity building really is.

In the beginning, you do most of the work. As you grow more adept at certain skills such as management, proposal writing, and budgets, then you also become better at capacity building: you are better at including others in the work so that their skills, strengths and capacity grow.

How Do You Build Financial Literacy Skills?

Within the context of your work, you may also find the opportunity to teach local staff how to do the math to take care of the budget. At its most basic level, teach how to keep track of income and expenses. Like grant writing, it is easier to work until midnight yourself poring over the budget. It takes longer to train others how Excel or QuickBooks works and how the budget should balance.

In Jacqueline Novogratz's book *The Blue Sweater: Bridging the Gap Between Rich and Poor in an Interconnected World*, she does the accounting herself and finds that one of the directors was embezzling money from their microfinance organization in Rwanda.[1] Later in Novogratz's career, when she became founder and director of Acumen Fund, she not only worked side-by-side with local staff but also put much more emphasis on capitalizing on local ideas, initiatives and talent, for example in Pakistan. She is a brilliant example of someone using capacity building across cultures to ensure financial literacy and market-driven, successful local development.

Financial Literacy Is Essential in Fighting Corruption

Corruption plagues many countries. For example, my Sierra Leonean colleagues told me that they had arranged to get a container load of bicycles from the UK. They did not have to pay for the bikes; or so the UK group intended. But when that container came into the Freetown port, the port authorities would not release the container of bikes. The port authorities made up bogus excuses for why my colleagues could not claim the bikes. And for every day the container sat at the port, the port charged my colleagues $100. The port authorities played this game for a month, until the bill owed to the port added up to $3,000! This is a huge sum to people who do not have a penny in their pockets. But they scraped the money together so that the efforts and the generosity of the UK bike organization would not be in vain. That is what you call corruption.

It was in Uganda, though, that I witnessed how being financially literate is a way of preventing corruption. I went out to lunch with the hospital administrator of a government hospital. Later she was going to show me around the hospital, and we could discuss how volunteer nurses, nurse practitioners and doctors from NGOabroad could help.

When we got back to the hospital, there was great uproar and chaos. Water was spewing in the air on the front hospital lawn. The television news crews were arriving to film the bedlam as this administrator quietly asked what was going on. She hustled in and huddled with the hospital director. Apparently, the water company had come out and cut the pipes open.

What had happened? This very astute hospital administrator had been watching the water bill quite closely. She thought that the hospital was being charged an exorbitant amount for water, so she put a meter on the water flow to see how much water the hospital was actually using.

Because corruption is rampant in Uganda—they call it "feeding at the trough"—she suspected that the water company was dramatically over-charging the hospital. And sure enough, when she did the math, she could see it. She had the audacity to tell the water company that the hospital would not pay more than the proper price for the water that it actually used. In retribution, the water company came out and sawed the pipes open. More drama and negotiations ensued, but the water company was exposed.

The Ugandan hospital administrator had the financial literacy and math skills to monitor corrupt practices. Jacqueline Novogratz had the financial skills to do the books in the Rwanda micro-finance program and discovered that a director was embezzling money. When you are training about financial literacy—teaching how to create Excel spreadsheets, read budgets and do QuickBooks—say in very clear words that that these skills are crucial to fight corruption. In this way, you make the bridge between capacity building and empowerment.

Likewise, Economic Literacy Is Crucial

Economic capacity building and empowerment are key pieces in solving poverty. If this capacity building about money and economics were taken further, citizens would be more educated in macroeconomics; they would guard their nations against going into debt. There are pioneers paving that path: the African School of Economics (ASE) in Benin, founded by Leonard Wantchekon, professor of politics and international affairs at Princeton, is one such school:

ASE aims to meet the urgent need for an academic institution capable of generating the necessary human capital in Africa. ... Through its Ph.D. programs, ASE hopes to provide the missing African voice in many Africa-related academic debates. Through the Master in Business Administration (MBA), Master in Public Administration (MPA), Executive MBA and MPA (EMBA and EMPA), Master in Mathematics, Economics and Statistics (MMES), and Master in Development Studies (MDS) programs, ASE aims to provide the technical capacity that will enable more Africans to be hired into top management positions in development agencies and multinational corporations operating on the continent. This should foster sustainable hiring practices that will retain talent and experience in Africa.[2]

Why is this so important? If a country lives within its budget, like Botswana did, it never goes into debt and never has to take a loan from the IMF. The debts of many African nations were relieved in 2001 in response to a worldwide movement called Jubilee 2000. (We will discuss this more deeply in the advocacy chapter.) But the *Economist* magazine reported in March 2018 that in many African nations, debt is again growing. Debt cripples countries and leads them into a downward spiral.[3] Having economists and leaders who are economically literate is crucial to guiding wise economic policy.

John Kuada, professor of international management at Denmark's Aalborg Universitet, agrees that it is crucial for Africa to build its economic capacity. Scholars such as Dr. Kuada, originally from Ghana and the author of many articles, chapters, and books, are helping with this capacity building. His chapter "Culture and Leadership in Africa: A Conceptual Model and Research Agenda" suggests there may be knowledge gaps in existing African leadership studies regarding links between cultures and leadership practices in Africa, and that these links influence economic growth on the continent. His "Entrepreneurship as a Solution to Youth Unemployment in Ghana" is another example of how African scholars are contributing to the thinking and practices in international development.[4]

How Do You Help Problem Solve and Achieve Goals?

Problem solving may be an additional skill that local staff would like to learn to do more systematically. Problem solving is much like how a social worker does a needs and strengths assessment, where you break the solution into steps and strategies.

Teach people how to analyze a problem and break it into its component parts. This is a skill that you use in international development as well as in typical social work settings and in psychotherapy.

Teach people how to get from step A to step B. Discuss with them that most goals look overwhelming until you break them down into bite-size bits. Encourage people to identify a goal and then map the staircase or steps to attaining that goal. Discuss taking one step at a time, starting first with the easiest and moving on to the more challenging.

An example of teaching problem solving from my many years as a psychotherapist and social worker: when a client would present a problem, together we would dissect the problem. I would ask the client to describe the "who what when where" of the problem.

An example of problem solving comes from the altiplano of Peru and Bolivia. It is high—10,000 feet elevation—and dry, so it is hard to grow vegetables. NGOabroad's partner director in Peru had a brilliant solution to this problem: build greenhouses to grow vegetables.

Another example of brilliant problem solving: NGOabroad's partner organization in Rwanda, which is doing extraordinary reconciliation work, said to me: "We don't need help with the reconciliation work, but we need help with money to sustain our work." We had a long talk about how grant-writing is lots of work and only provides money for a short time. "Is there a way you can have a service or a product that will generate the income to sustain the organization?" They said, "Actually we have been thinking along those lines. We want to change half our headquarters into a guesthouse. Can you send us an architect who can help with the design and how we can landscape and make a very appealing courtyard and garden?" This model they envisioned has worked well in Kigali, the capital of Rwanda: Kigali's most popular hostel funds and sustains the Genocide Museum. I sent them an Australian architect who has done many projects for NGOabroad, and my Rwandan colleagues are well on their way to having a sustainable income for their organization.

What Is the Importance of Critical Thinking?

In addition, discuss the importance of critical thinking. A fundamental part of critical thinking is evaluating the accuracy of information—which is especially challenging in the digital age.

Rote learning is the usual method of teaching in many parts of the world. With your colleagues and the community and groups which you work in, simply and gently ask how they came to certain conclusions. Gently probe. Probably no other teacher or mentor has asked them to examine their logic. Questioning is often not taught or utilized in schools in many countries. (North American and European tutors are puzzled by why students never raise their hands to ask questions in our Ugandan secondary school.) Questioning may even be discouraged in repressive regimes, as authoritarian autocrats do not want to be criticized. This is another aspect of critical thinking that you can model and encourage.

In *The Blue Sweater*, one of the Rwandans ruefully noted after the genocide, "If we have learned anything, it is the horror that can happen when people don't think for themselves, but instead follow authority blindly. We have to teach our children judgment in our schools and businesses if we are to thrive truly as a country."[5]

How do you teach critical thinking?

In rote learning, the emphasis is on a lesson learned or memorized. In critical thinking, there is more emphasis on a problem to be solved. For example, when I was in Sierra Leone playing with primary age children at home after dinner, they could gleefully shout the answers to arithmetic problems that I posed: $1 + 1 = ?$ ... 2! ... $2 + 2 = ?$ ... 4! ... $4 + 4 = ?$ ... 8! ... But then I interjected, "There was a farmer who had two goats and a chicken. How many goats did the farmer have?" (I had not even created the part of the story problem where the farmer meets another farmer with one goat and five chickens.) The kids were bamboozled by my question. They clearly had never had story problems. They could not answer, "You said that the farmer had TWO goats."

Critical thinking has been a part of education in North America

In many countries, you are not encouraged to ask the teacher or authority figures questions, so foreigners can be out of step when they have a long list of questions.

since it was espoused by John Dewey. It is a part of our tradition, but less so in other countries. As educator Benjamin Bloom explains, "What is needed is some evidence that the students can do something with their knowledge, that is, that they can apply the information to new situations and problems."[6]

The Ontario Ministry of Education explains:

Critical thinking is the process of thinking about ideas or situations in order to understand them fully, identify their implications, make a judgement, and/or guide decision making. Critical thinking includes skills such as questioning, predicting, analysing, synthesizing, examining opinions, identifying values and issues, detecting bias, and distinguishing between alternatives. Students who are taught these skills become critical thinkers who can move beyond superficial conclusions to a deeper understanding of the issues they are examining. They are able to engage in an inquiry process in which they explore complex and multifaceted issues, and questions for which there may be no clear-cut answers.[7]

One of the ways that you help people build capacity in critical thinking is to walk through the steps in their logic and thinking. Have them explain how they would solve a particular problem. Another way is to ask people's opinions about what is going on around them and push them further to ask how they would improve things. All over the world, it is easy to complain or criticize and hard work to craft a solution. There is a clear connection between those who can think critically and creatively and leadership development.

How Do You Encourage Creative Thinking?

Equally important is encouraging creative thinking. It is good to remember that there are different kinds of creative thinking, and many in the developing world excel at it. People, by necessity, are ingenious at making things work. For example, the umbrella repairman who operated out of a cigar box in India; or the shade-tree mechanics who fixed the bus in Guatemala. They create solutions, often, with few tools or resources.

In India, my colleagues showed me the simple rice threshing machine they had invented so people would not have to thresh the

My colleagues in India invented a device to haul in these huge fishing nets.

rice in the road, and the ingenious winch that would help pull in the fishing nets so that they would not have to gather ten people to tug and struggle to haul in the nets. These inventions reflect the combination of creativity and problem solving.

When you work in other countries, it helps to have models from that region or continent. One of the most extraordinary stories regarding ingenuity is that of William Kamkwamba in Malawi, in *The Boy Who Harnessed the Wind*. There was a drought in Malawi in 2002, so William's father, a farmer, could not pay William's school fees. So William, though he could not yet read in English (as his first language was Chewa), would sit at the library. He was drawn to the diagrams in the book *Using Energy*. Out of scrap parts that he scavenged from the junkyard, he built a windmill that powered electricity for his family's home. The townspeople thought it was crazy until they saw that the windmill charged their cell phones! Most importantly, the windmill pumped up water for his family's parched fields.[8]

Creativity is essential in dreaming up solutions to the problems people face and to creating an enterprise to generate income.

"You see, we were brought up in a wrong way where business interests were not inculcated in us. People want to be workers and wait for their salary. They are not trying to create jobs. ... We were brought up to be workers not thinkers," explains Ugandan chemistry professor and entrepreneur, George Mpango.[9]

Often in financially stressed communities, simply dreaming up a business enterprise is very difficult. This is where building creative thinking skills can have real value. In many African countries, both the women and men are encouraged to sew to generate income. The problem with this is that then the market is glutted with tailors, and few make much money. Being encouraged to dream and create is important, but it is not emphasized in the educational systems in many countries. Yet creativity and critical thinking are essential for creating livelihoods and ultimately forging the economic prosperity of their country.

It is condescending and colonial to imply that those in the developing world are not creative. Here is where the difficulty is, I believe: at universities in the West, we are taught abstract thinking. We are praised for using big polysyllabic words and writing long essays. Where people work with their hands—whether it is the developing world or blue-collar America—you don't talk about ideas, you just do it. You talk and create in more concrete realities.

This is perhaps why asking people to dream up enterprises results in blank stares in a classroom but produces results if you walk around the community together to see what is selling. This is why the Maasai women with the Tanzanian social work director were doing so well: they were working with concrete realities, not abstract Western realities. The enterprises that they had dreamed up reflected the concrete reality in which they lived.

But it also may be that the people are doing a phenomenal job of dreaming up an enterprise—it is just dramatically different than the corporate job that you would have back home. Trevor Noah, comedian and host of *The Daily Show*, tells how growing up poor in South Africa, he managed to get by when there were no jobs: he very ingeniously made money by DJing parties and pirating CDs.[10] With his friend Bongani, who was a real hustler who knew how to leverage every opportunity, they began to do payday lending and had a pawn shop.[11]

You can extend capacity building even further. Institutions such as the African School of Economics are building economic competence, skills and literacy; the University of Global Health Equity is building capacity in public health and health services; organizations such as the African Capacity Building Foundation work to build strategic partnerships, extend grants, offer technical support and provide access to relevant knowledge related to capacity building in Africa. All over the African continent, African leaders and innovators are building the foundation for the skills and strengths—the capacity—of Africa to develop and blossom.

While much of the emphasis in this chapter has been on Africa, in the next book in the series about solutions, there is more focus on innovations emerging from Asia.

Thus far, we have been talking mainly about capacity building for individuals. But in international social work and international development, you may also build the capacity of organizations, which is what organizational development is all about, or communities, which is the purview of community development.

Like individual capacity building, community capacity building builds on local strengths and promotes community participation and leadership, as well as ownership of both the problems and the solutions.[12] The basis for sustainable, bottom-up community development lies in building community capacity.[13]

This book aims to help build your capacity, your strength, skills, competence and confidence. As I said in the introduction, I see building skills as much like how you build a house. You first start with the foundation. The chapters on needs and strengths assessment and capacity building are designed to provide your foundation. Once you have these skills built, you can move on to the next steps: working with the community in participatory development and community organizing, so let's examine those.

6

Partner to the Poor and Participatory Development

> The ends and means of development call for … people being actively involved—given the opportunity—in shaping their own destiny.—Amartya Sen[1]

"Absolutely not! We will absolutely not accept foreign midwives to come work here," exclaimed the Indonesian midwifery director indignantly on my field visit there. "They shove the local midwives out of the way and say 'Here, let me show you how to deliver a baby.'"

Similarly, the Tanzanian social work director—one of the most effective directors I have ever met—was also leery of foreigners. She was wary of me when I went to meet her and see her work. Riding together around some of the very remote, rural areas of the "up-country" of Tanzania near Mt. Kilimanjaro, though, she warmed a bit and explained: "These American students came here and said that they wanted to help me. Ha! They hijacked the whole organization! They went home and made a website and called themselves the board and the bosses. They never consulted me or helped me out in the rural areas here with the work that I do. To be honest, I don't trust foreigners as much now. It has left a sour taste in my mouth, but we are moving on and moving forward."

In contrast, there are many aspiring international development and international social workers who do not want to be so colonial and condescending.

"I don't want to be the 'Great White Savior,'" students will tell me when I talk about African directors' requests for their help in our international development, social work, public health, education, nursing, entrepreneurship, and democracy building programs. For example, the director in Kibera, the slums at the edge of Nairobi, Kenya, has wondered why so few people are stepping up to help.

I think (though this is an opinion not researched or evidence-based) the decline in interest in serving in Africa relates to Curtis Keim's *Mistaking Africa: Curiosities and Inventions of the American Mind* being widely discussed at universities in the United States. Keim debunks the myths and stereotypes which we have about Africa and lambasts the paternalistic practices that development in Africa has often entailed. I mention Keim because he is impacting not only African studies but international development in general: Keim challenges the paternalism inherent in our stereotypes, actions and interactions.

It was first Binyavanga Wainaima, a Kenyan writer and former director of the Chinua Achebe Center for African Literature and Languages at Bard College, who castigated the West for its stereotypes of the continent of fifty-four nations in his essay in Granta in 2005, "How to Write About Africa."

The goal posts are shifting. The new goal is to abolish paternalism.

I contend that it is not helping in Africa or any other part of the world which needs to be jettisoned, especially if that help is invited and requested; it is the paternalism which needs to be eliminated. Paternalism is the policy or practice on the part of people in positions of authority of restricting the freedom and responsibilities of those subordinate to them in the subordinates' supposed best interest. Keim is not the first person to condemn paternalism—an attitude of superiority, that you are or I am better than someone else. Kamla Bhasin and Robert Chambers—you will learn more about them later in this chapter—also practice an empowerment that comes from a deep sense of equality. Most of my colleagues in Africa simply call this working together as equals "partnership."

Because this attitudinal shift away from paternalism is so central to international development today, not just your skills but your attitude will impact how or if you thrive or fail in international development and even if you will be hired or accepted to work in Africa, Asia, or Latin America. This chapter examines what Paul Farmer called "solidarity" and will introduce you to the most important people who practice and espouse this egalitarian empowerment. We will also explore how Liberation Theology in Latin America and the groundswell of Gandhian thinkers and activists in South Asia laid the foundation for participatory development.

Partner to the Poor Is the New Paradigm

There is a new ethos inspiring and shaping international development. This is happening both from the top down in academia, as some of the most important development thinkers and practitioners articulate this new vision of partnership, and it is happening from the bottom up as people in Africa, Asia and Latin America insist that their input, voices and proposed solutions be heard.

Paul Farmer, former chair of the Department of Global Health and Social Medicine at Harvard Medical School and a physician and medical anthropologist, lectured all over the world about his indefatigable fight against tuberculosis, maternal mortality, AIDS and malaria in Haiti, Rwanda, Russia and Peru. His work inspired a generation to go into public health or international development.[2] As Farmer said in his lectures, he stretched what was thought possible; he made the problems of the poor compelling. [Note: After a lifetime of extraordinary service, Paul Farmer died in 2022 in Rwanda.]

An important part of Paul Farmer's contribution was his work as a medical anthropologist to help us understand the power relations, structural violence and social inequities that create what Farmer called "the pathologies of power." Farmer's lectures were rallying cries, exhorting people to act[3]; to end unnecessary suffering in the world. He emphasized that we have the means necessary to stop much of the suffering in the world. Farmer did not express a worry about being a Great White Savior, because he operated with such a sense of equality. The idea that some lives matter less—especially those of the poor—is what Farmer dedicated his life to reversing. Though Paul Farmer worked with a very tight team which eventually became the organization Partners in Health—Ophelia Dahl, Jim Yong Kim, Todd McCormack, Tom White, and later Father Jack Roussin in Peru—it was he who wrote and spoke so widely about partnering with and for the poor. Paul Farmer called his credo "pragmatic solidarity."[4]

Liberation Theology Influenced Paul Farmer

In the biography of Paul Farmer, *Mountains Beyond Mountains: The Quest of Dr. Paul Farmer, a Man Who Would Cure the World*, Tracy Kidder describes how Farmer was exposed to Liberation Theology. In 1980 when Archbishop Óscar Romero was murdered by a right-wing death squad in El Salvador, Farmer attended a vigil at the Duke University chapel. This inspired his reading about the branch of Catholicism called Liberation Theology, which Romero had been preaching and which led to his assassination. Latin American bishops spoke about the oppression of the poor, calling it "institutionalized sin." The Liberation Theologians believed that the church had a duty to provide "a preferential option for the poor." Farmer thought, "Wow! This isn't the Catholicism that I remember."[5]

In his book *Pathologies of Power: Health, Human Rights, and the New War on the Poor*, Farmer elucidated that what he meant by "preferential option for the poor" is "to fight to protect the rights of the vulnerable, over and above the rights of the powerful."[6] "Liberation theology," he wrote, "has always been about the struggle for social and economic rights."[7]

Paul Farmer infused a new attitude about poverty and

Archbishop Óscar Romero was a partner to the poor in El Salvador and an important figure in Liberation Theology.

privilege into international development. He was critical of those who are inclined to analyze instead of act: "ivory-tower engagement" and "seminar-room warriors."[8] "It is possible to forget the voices of the suffering as we sit in an air-conditioned office or lecture hall, we must not stop hearing the often silent voices of the poor. This type of community based listening and interacting will convince the hurting people that international organizations are not based on cost-effectiveness alone, and are willing to stand on the side of the poor."[9] Farmer went to Haiti for the first time in 1983. From his first experiences there, his work was steeped with this attitude of partnership and solidarity influenced by Liberation Theology.

Liberation Theology

Like the history of international development, community development and participatory development, Liberation Theology did not proceed in a linear way. It evolved more like spokes of a wheel or a fan, if one were to diagram it. Like Paul Farmer's Partners in Health initiative and many organizations, Liberation Theology started as an experiment and then took off. As with most movements, its ideas and actions motivate others and spread; it is a contagion. Liberation Theology was a movement or a trend arising principally as a moral reaction to the poverty and social injustice in Central and South America where the Catholic Church had and has a strong presence.

Dom Helder Camara and Leonardo and Clodovis Boff in Brazil, and Gustavo Gutiérrez in Peru, were and are some of the most prominent (though not the only) voices in Liberation Theology. The Boffs explain that Liberation Theology is a commitment to the cause and struggle of the millions of disenfranchised and marginalized people, a commitment to end Latin America's historical-social iniquity.[10] Liberation Theology's influence rippled around the world. Priests such as Desmond Tutu in South Africa, the Anglican archbishop who won the Nobel Peace Prize in 1984 for helping dismantle apartheid and pioneering the Truth and Reconciliation Commission, used Liberation Theology to help articulate the way people of faith must struggle for freedom.[11]

Why Is Liberation Theology So Important to International Development?

Liberation Theologians called upon the Church to abandon its longstanding alliances with the rich and the powerful and instead ally and align with the poor and oppressed—"a preferential option for the poor." Liberation Theology clergy were teaching Scripture in an entirely new way. Liberation Theology encouraged the poor to read the Scriptures in a way that affirms their own dignity and self-worth and their right to struggle for more decent living conditions and lives.[12] Catholic priests lived among the poor in "base communities," leading to unprecedented grassroots activism.[13]

It was a very new idea to live among the poor in these base communities, whether in the favelas of Brazil, slums of Lima, or the rural villages of Central America. Doing so, the clergy better learned the needs and the struggles of the local people. By living among the poor rather than at the rectory at the church, the priests were no longer such outsiders, but became more valued and trusted insiders. "You are one of us." This is the essence of solidarity. This is being a partner to the poor.

This attitude and practice of partnership and solidarity is what informs participatory development and thus profoundly impacts international development today. Later we will discuss how practitioners of participatory development encourage this immersion in the community, not being separated and living in mansions in walled compounds. The success of most development programs hinges on the deep connections to the communities that are cultivated in this way.

Leonardo and Clodovis Boffs' criticism of aid shapes best practices in international development and international social work today—capacity building, empowerment, working as equal partners in solidarity. "Aid—the 'Band-Aid' approach to social ills—increases the dependence of the poor, tying them to help from others, to decisions made by others: again not enabling them to become their own liberators."[14]

The Catholic Church is certainly not the only religion which does community development in other countries. The Mennonites, Seventh Day Adventists, Mormons, Methodists, Episcopalians and many evangelical churches all do missionary work or have international NGOs.

The Jewish faith emphasizes justice. "Tikkun olam" has become synonymous with social action and the pursuit of social justice. The magazine Tikkun proudly claims, "We are a prophetic voice for peace, love, environmental sanity, social transformation, and unabashedly utopian aspirations for the world."[15]

Other religions also act to support community development. In Sri Lanka, Sri Lankan community organizers leveraged the assistance of Buddhist monks in their community development. In the Muslim religion and throughout the Middle East and North Africa, it is often the local mosque which helps with the needs of the people and the poor.

For example: In Egypt, the organization El Gameya El Shareya gave food every Friday and money to help residents make it through the week. It gave money to orphan girls to help them furnish a house so they could be married. Most of the local poor acknowledge that none of them would have made it without the organization. For more than 100 years, El Gameya El Shareya has worked to compensate for the government's failure to supply the needs of Egypt's poorest citizens. At its peak, it had over 1,000 branches, operated 30 medical centers, and provided for 450,000 fatherless children, according to its Facebook page. This faith-based organization serves Egypt's poor.[16] In Islam, *zakat* is a religious obligation next in priority to prayer itself, to donate to charities to help the poor.

This credo of partner to the poor is intertwined with the new trend in participatory development.

Sri Lanka's Extraordinary Model of Participatory Development

Sri Lanka, once called Ceylon, is the teardrop-shaped island, about the size of Ireland, which sits like a tropical jewel in the Indian Ocean south of India. I have learned about Sri Lanka's exemplary model on my field visits there.

Ceylon declared independence from Great Britain on February 4, 1948. For twenty-four years Ceylon had dominion status, until 1972 when it became the Republic of Sri Lanka. Great Britain had set up all the tea plantations across the island.

Sri Lankan community development is interwoven with

reclaiming its religious and cultural heritage, especially after independence from Great Britain. In its population of over 20 million people, Buddhists make up 70.1 percent, Hindus 12.6 percent, Muslims 9.7 percent and Christians 7.6 percent. Most Sinhalese people are Buddhist; most Tamils are Hindu; and the Moors and Malays are mostly Muslim.[17]

In order to successfully implement a participatory development program in Sri Lanka's Buddhist communities, the Sri Lankan community organizers would first connect with the Buddhist monks in the area. This first step would gain credibility in the community. From there organizers would set up a family gathering where community builders would ask what the village needed most urgently. For example, do you need a road, irrigation, toilets, or schools? Then together with the village they would arrange a work camp to tackle that concern. The work camps were a way to get everyone involved, to learn their power and what they were capable of as individuals and as a community and gain confidence in what they could accomplish. At the afternoon break, as they rested during the heat of the day, they would discuss other needs and priorities. In the evenings there

In Sri Lanka, often the local Buddhist monk was the bridge to the community to form the foundation for the community and participatory development work.

would be cultural activities and fun—whether that was the kids putting on a skit or Buddhist chanting. The Sri Lankans believed that it was important that the Sri Lankan communities reclaim their culture and religion that had been repressed during the colonial era. They emphasized that the Buddhist tradition of service was central to the work they did.

Once the village had done a work camp project together, often with the monk guiding, they would set up a preschool program, thus drawing in the mothers. The curious and interested youth and men would then wonder what was going on and would check out these community developers. In this way, all the members of the community would be drawn in and services would be shaped to suit their needs.

At the core was the understanding that poverty is perpetuated by a sense of powerlessness. Thus, throughout the beginning work camp and the unfolding of the preschool and the mothers and youth programs, the goal was for the villagers to be involved, and little by little, task by task, grasp the power that they have to shape their own village and learn to make decisions which impact their daily life.

In this way the needs assessment was done, but not in a formal or Western way; likewise with capacity building. What began with a teacher taking his students to help in some villages has led to a methodology and movement for personal and community development. The skills and strengths are drawn forth as the people uplift their village. Through this model, 5,000 villages in Sri Lanka have been "awakened." (When I use the term "awakened" in this book, I use it as the Sri Lankans and as Gandhi and his protégés in India used it, not as it is used in the current parlance in the United States, meaning being politically correct and "woke.") This model of community and participatory development was indigenous, not something imposed by outsiders.

Gandhi Inspired an Entire Generation in South Asia

Sri Lanka's community mobilizers and Kamla Bhasin, one of India's most important participatory development thinkers and practitioners, stand on the shoulders of Mohandas K. Gandhi. (Often Gandhi is called Mahatma Gandhi. *Mahatma* means a person regarded with reverence or loving respect; a holy person or sage.) While Liberation Theology impacted Latin America, Gandhi influenced South Asia.

While Gandhi was most known for his non-violence work, which inspired Martin Luther King Jr., his contributions to development thinking are enormous. Listed below is a summary of his key principles and insights. He was truly a partner to the poor.

Gandhi was a partner to the poor who influenced much of South Asia.

1. In a sharp rebuke of India's traditional caste system, Gandhi was an advocate for the Dalits, the untouchables, the lowest caste in India. Gandhi called the poorest, most rejected and scorned people of India *harijan*— "children of God." Like Liberation Theology, Gandhi aimed to change the assumptions of a religion, in this case, Hinduism, to embrace the poor.[18]
2. He espoused the "uplift of all"; for a nation to flourish, every person must be lifted.
3. Gandhi passionately believed in the equality of all people and fervently opposed the separation of India into Muslim Pakistan and more Hindu India.[19]
4. Like the Liberation Theologians, Gandhi lived an austere life, saying, "Live simply, so that others can simply live." He was humble and did not claim to have all the answers. His autobiography was titled *My Experiments with Truth*.[20] In essence, his book implies, "I don't have The Answers; I have lots of questions that I have spent a lifetime trying to answer."
5. Gandhi advocated *Panchayat Raj*, a decentralized form of government where each village is responsible for its own affairs, as the foundation of India's political system. *Gram Swaraj* meant village self-rule and was at the heart of Gandhi's vision of economic development.[21] Village self-rule

promoted empowerment, developing community leaders
and the community's priorities rather than having the village
be ruled or run by outsiders or foreigners. The local people
were at the helm. This is fundamental to participatory
development.

6. Gandhi was prescient in anticipating the burgeoning slums
and how to prevent them. Gandhi believed, say my Indian
colleagues, that to prevent the flood of people from the poor
rural areas to the big cities looking for jobs, livelihoods must
be generated in the rural areas.

7. Gandhi rejected cultural imperialism and attempted to
throw off the shackles of the British colonizer, which had
seen British culture and way of doing things—from cricket
to crumpets to discipline in school to the civil service—as
superior. India and Sri Lanka were exploring and asserting
what was distinctly their own.

Why is this so crucial to understand? It is crucial because it
essentially was a rejection of Western cultural hegemony. In the
work you do in international development, you will likely find that
every nation on earth and every community benefits from capitalizing on such cultural pride and identity. Additionally, knowing
the contributions that other cultures and countries have made is
an antidote for cultural imperialism and paternalism. Google and
Facebook are not the only innovations in our world. This is why
the companion volume to this book highlights the ideas and development innovations that have been born in Asia, Africa and Latin
America.

Grassroots Organizations Grow Organically, Addressing Community Needs

At home and abroad, grassroots organizations usually grow in
an organic way: a small group of people coalesce around a particular
need or interest. Often there are a few movers and shakers who start
initiatives.

How did and do community organizations emerge? In both
domestic and international community development, one could say

that community development occurs because many organizations tackle the needs in that community: literacy, at-risk youth, family planning, clean water, economic empowerment, democracy building, environmental problems, women's rights, domestic violence, and sexual abuse, to name a few.

For example, here in my rather rural community, we have the dental van for people who cannot afford to go to the dentist; we have the very innovative program where people who cannot afford the exorbitant price of a home of their own can help each other build their houses—a modern incarnation of communities helping raise the roof beams together. The churches, as in many communities, provide meals for the homeless. One person who has ten acres envisions building small shelters for the homeless—a rural version of how to address homelessness.

In other countries, community efforts evolve in a similarly organic way. For example, people in communities in Kenya started bringing orphans to a Kenyan social worker. She first took in four kids; fifteen years later she has forty living at the home and over a hundred that they help in the community. Because so many kids are AIDS orphans or abandoned by alcoholic parents, she also developed programs within her fledgling organization to address the source of the orphans' problems. As her little children grow up, she builds in ways to help her kids emancipate, go on to college or secure gainful employment.

Likewise for a Rwandan social worker: people knew she would help them after the genocide. Women whose husbands had been killed in the genocide showed up on the Rwandan social worker's porch asking if she could help them to support their families, now that the breadwinner was gone. The Rwandan social worker started teaching hair cutting and sewing for fifty women at a time. She developed a child-care program so the women's children are taken care of while the mothers are in class or later working.

In Sri Lanka, how did another community organization evolve? A successful businessman was almost swept away in the tsunami in 2004, and his community was devastated by the powerful wall of water. His home became the medical center for people injured in the giant, crushing wave. His life suddenly changed from working in business to dedicating himself to community service. With the clinic anchoring how he helped his community, he took advantage of the

Tailoring, in which the Rwandan social worker began training women, is probably the most popular income-generating activity throughout Africa.

contributions pouring in from all over the world and built a computer lab, a dental clinic, a skills center for livelihoods and crafts, a social work outreach program, athletic fields for his beloved cricket and soccer, and a literacy program in the surrounding villages. You might say he jumped headfirst into community development and the organization's mission arose naturally from the sequence of events after that catastrophe.

In Lebanon, a group that operated a mobile medical van during a bloody civil war (1975 to 1990) later grew roots. Rather than doing emergency medical work, it set up clinics all over the country. This is yet another example of a small, organic, from-the-grassroots-up venture that solves real community needs.

In Ecuador, they had the brilliant idea to build a resort and restaurant around the hot springs, which brings in the money to do community development work in eight nearby villages.

Community development builds the capacity of the community.

Yossef Ben-Meir, who wrote a fascinating Ph.D. thesis on participatory development, defines community development "as a process of building the capacity of most or all the people of a community in order to manage development that addresses economic, social, political, and environmental objectives, and utilizes internal and external resources to improve human conditions."[22]

But now community development, which is the essence of what you will be doing in international development, has evolved further to participatory development. One of my colleagues, a Tanzanian director, was trained in participatory development in his studies at Harvard and considers this central to his success in the field in his work in Tanzania.[23]

Participatory Development = Needs Assessment + Program Development + Capacity Building

In previous chapters, we looked at how to do a needs assessment and how that leads naturally to program development, and how capacity building is an essential part of international development. The next step, if you are really skilled in international development, is to involve the local community in that needs assessment and designing the interventions. This is essentially what participatory development is.

In participatory development, local people are at the helm.

Participatory development is a development approach in which local communities and people control and own the process[24]: local communities plan, manage, and are the decision-makers in matters related to development.[25] Local people have a voice in matters which affect their daily lives. This is empowerment.

Participatory development is a rejection of paternalistic development models. When participatory development emerged, it was used by field activists who were frustrated by the failure of earlier models of development that advocated a top-down strategy for development.[26]

Participatory development moved from the periphery to center stage of development thinking in the 1990s. Participatory development is essentially a rejection of colonial ways of thinking, interacting and engineering change. It is an alternative to top-down development models that pressure developing countries and their communities by attaching conditions to aid that serve the interests of developed countries.[27]

Critics of existing international development practice such

as Kamla Bhasin, a respected social scientist, development trainer and outspoken feminist in India, contended that often the change agents or international development practitioners were paternalistic and doing everything themselves and without involving the community; doing things *for* people rather than helping people do for themselves.[28] [After a lifetime of rocking the boat, Kamla Bhasin died in 2021 in India.]

Robert Chambers is one of the most important thinkers and practitioners in international development. He is professor emeritus at the Institute for Development Studies at the University of Sussex in the UK and another of the pioneers in participatory development. He explains how participatory development is the antithesis of existing models of development: "The essence is change and reversals—of role, behavior, relationship and learning. Outsiders cannot dominate and lecture; they facilitate, sit down, listen and learn. Outsiders do not 'transfer technology'; they share methods which local people can use for their own appraisal, planning, action, monitoring and evaluation. Outsiders do not impose their own reality; they encourage and enable local people to express their own."[29]

For starters, assume local people are capable and can do for themselves. Chambers admonishes development practitioners to assume local people can do it unless they prove otherwise. In this way, you are helping the people build capacity—build their strengths and skills. Kamla Bhasin elaborated: a change agent works with the people, not for the people, and encourages and helps develop leadership skills of the local people.[30] Continued Bhasin: "Change agents must listen more than talk; learn more than teach and facilitate more than lead."

Participatory development practitioners are integrated into the local community. Bhasin believed that to be effective you must integrate and live with the people. This fundamental belief and practice, as examined earlier, is and was how in Liberation Theology, Catholic priests and nuns lived amidst the poor in base communities in Central and South America rather than living in lavish homes in walled compounds. They shared in the daily struggle of the poor and marginalized and lived in solidarity with and as partners to the poor.

So as discussed regarding pacing and leading in the chapter on capacity building, and in the chapter on attitude, Bhasin and the Liberation Theologians engaged in the daily tasks with the poor.

I recommend that you also join the local people in what they do every day: get up at dawn and fetch water (and see if you can carry it home on your head!). Then feed the family. Then before the sun is too high in the sky, head out to work in the fields. See if you get blisters and callouses. Paul Farmer was famous for how integrated he is in the community in Haiti—how many miles he walked— mountains beyond mountains—to do home visits that enabled him to understand the cause of certain peoples' medical problems. Like- wise, Paul Polak, who we will discuss in the next book in this series on solutions, would go to the fields with what he called "one acre farmers" to see how they did things and what the obstacles were, and spent long hours having a cup of tea to hear their struggles and dreams.

Bhasin cautioned about these potential mistakes:

1. Being paternalistic
2. Doing everything yourself
3. Emphasizing projects rather than long-term programs
4. Failing to adequately understand macro-issues and political forces
5. Failing to cooperate and coordinate with other change agents and stakeholders
6. Doling out material goods so it creates dependency
7. Doing things for people rather than helping people do for themselves.[31]

Putting These Ideas into Practice

Some thoughts on how you put partnering to the poor and par- ticipatory development into practice:

Grow More Comfortable in Group Contexts

Many people new to international development ask me for step- by-step instructions.

So, first step: become more comfortable and competent work- ing with groups such as sports teams or theatrical or musical groups. You may also learn how to be part of a team in a sorority or frater- nity, or in planning a fund-raising event or a conference with a team.

You may learn this group skill working at a summer camp or being a nanny or tutoring. If you are no longer a college student or maybe never were, you might learn how you fit in group dynamics in a parenting group, a union, or a hockey or soccer team.

You can learn a lot about yourself in these beginning group ventures. What are your strengths in a group context? When do you feel uncomfortable? Or as they say, what is your "growing edge"?

How Do You Gather the People?

Doing community organizing and community or participatory development assumes that you can gather the people so that you can connect to them. This can sometimes be hard to do. If you are living in the community, as the Liberation Theologians do, it may be somewhat easier.

For example, NGOabroad, at the request of our Cameroonian partners, had a nurse midwife come in to teach traditional birth attendants (TBA) in remote villages. This included how to monitor complications in childbirth to avert infant and maternal deaths and fistulas. It was a Cameroonian TV journalist colleague who said that she wanted the midwife to speak in her home village. The TV journalist was able to interview the midwife on TV so that thousands of Cameroonians learned what to watch for and what to do in case of a complicated birth. But when the TV journalist took the midwife to her home village, no one showed up for the talks.

Hmmm, what went wrong? First, the Cameroonian TV journalist had not "pumped and primed": she had not gotten the villagers excited about why this was so important. Because the Cameroonian journalist could not phone them or email them—as most rural villages are outside reception and the TV journalist now lived in Douala, nowhere near her home village—they did not really hear enough about it ahead of time. The villagers thought it more important to till their fields. In contrast, our Cameroonian social work director really prepares the villagers before anyone comes to do a talk—whether it is on purifying water, alternatives to violence (in our domestic violence program), public health, or entrepreneurship. She is always working out in those villages. So she tells them far, far ahead, "On May 24, at your midday break, come to the biggest house in the village ... you know, Vivian's house." They come. This is the advantage of an in-country partner, an implementing partner. They know everyone. They have tremendous credibility.

In the earlier account of how Sri Lanka uplifted the country, village by village, they would first align with the village's Buddhist monk. The monk knew everyone, and everyone respected the monk. The community development team that was sweeping the country would often begin by setting up a preschool program. In this way, the village would begin to see some activity happening and peek their heads around the corner to check out what was going on.

The Sri Lankans would energize and empower the village by tackling tangible, doable projects. They would have meetings at the midday break as people sought to escape the noon-day sun—relevant throughout most of the tropics. And they would have a cultural event, which was so important to Sri Lankans, who were reasserting their music and culture after independence from the British.

Music can gather the people. Once you have a captive audience, then on the heels of a cultural or musical performance, you can have a community meeting or discussion. For example, Serbians gathered a huge crowd with rock music in Belgrade's biggest square on the Orthodox New Year's Eve in 2000, then ended the show with reading the names of all who had died in Milošević's wars. The message was clear: Milošević must go. This group in Serbia was very effective at merging popular culture and community activism.

The question of gathering people vexes many Peace Corps workers, I am told. I remember someone telling me that Peace Corps workers would go door-to-door to invite people to the AIDS training. Or in southern Uganda, a former NGOabroad partner who ran a human rights program would put bus money on every chair in the audience. Was that a bribe to come? Not really: it was acknowledgment that most people would struggle to have the bus money to come to the training on human rights.

Many students whom I work with have phenomenal experience in putting on conferences or events at their college or university. They are creative in how they have gotten the word out. But sometimes the ways that you gather people in the West will not be pertinent in other countries. We work with a dynamite organization that is making alternative housing for people living in the slums. When doing an informal needs assessment about what kind of interns or volunteers they need, their operational director said, "We need help getting the word out that we are offering this housing option." They said they wanted people with a background in marketing or social media. Social media will work in urban locations in the developing world, but it is less likely to reach the rural villages that are outside reception. I said to the director, "Because your nation is so Christian, I would actually recommend that you talk to pastors so they mention it from the pulpit." In other words, I would take that Sri Lanka model of using the respected religious leader to spread the word and gain credibility. I also would make lots of posters to tack on walls and poles all over the slums—the same way that you put out the word about upcoming concerts. You must use your imagination, because gathering the people can be a challenge; but the challenge can be surmounted.

Listening Rather Than Having the Answers

It is crucial to learn how to ask questions that really draw people out. At a community gathering or meeting, talk to people at the break who were sitting on the periphery and not talking. This newly built connection will often make outsiders into insiders and make them more inclined to talk.

Have you ever noticed how good group leaders will say when you ask a question: "That's a good question"? I chuckle to myself when someone says it to me, but it works nonetheless in validating me or anyone else who asks a question.

Kamla Bhasin and Robert Chambers emphasized: It is really tempting sometimes to offer The Answer. It is often quicker to have The Answer rather than asking questions and helping others develop their own solutions, and often in international development the clock will be ticking on how much should be accomplished in six months or a year—the duration of the project due to the funding they obtained.

If you have The Answer and do everything, others learn nothing.

However, this is a fine balancing act: listening and eliciting and offering something yourself. For example, if I could repair the car myself, I would not take it to the mechanic. Thus, in international development, one of the ways I think that people such as Paul Farmer avoid this conundrum is to help when invited or requested, not impose help on others.

Facilitating Rather Than Commanding

At the heart of participatory development is the belief that the community and the people have many untapped strengths and skills; that people can figure out the answers. Your role is to be a facilitator—encouraging them to express their perspectives or priorities; helping wipe away what clouds their vision.

In a group context, notice other people's skills and strengths, and perhaps help make openings—tasks or roles—where those can shine. Help people over bumps and remove obstacles.

You can practice and polish this skill as facilitator in your home community or in college. The goal is to grow comfortable enough and skilled enough that you can transplant these skills to international contexts.

You Are Not the Expert—the People Are

I know that for myself, when I was doing my practicums in graduate school, I felt a tremendous weight: that I must know everything and I felt I could blow it and something catastrophic would happen, like someone would commit suicide. I think that this kind of insecurity and anxiety, in an international context, can produce some missteps, causing us to act as the authority or the expert, rather than with humility.

Several of the pioneers that examine privilege say one of the most egregious and offensive things is acting like a know-it-all; acting as an expert or authority can come across as arrogant, and thwart and sabotage your best efforts. Melinda Gates is an important model of how to resolve or rectify this: she deeply believes the experts are the people. Melinda, I think, is incredibly good at listening. Rather than thinking you have to have the answers, the most important first step is asking and deeply listening.

Local Community Involved from the Onset

Good participatory development and community development start with the discussion of needs and priorities. In days past, a country director might design programs in isolation in her or his office.

Good community programs do not start *ex nihilo*—out of nothing. They are birthed in the community itself.

Critical Consciousness

Kamla Bhasin believed that critical awareness building, like Paulo Freire's conscientization or critical consciousness, is the foundation of the work which you do together. Bhasin described this as "dialogue about the realities of the local situation to enable people to identify their own needs and problems and what kind of changes they want, how they would like to see them come about."[32] Paulo Freire cautions—or maybe it is more accurate to say blasts—what he calls the oppressor class for their lack of confidence in the people's ability to think, to want, and to know.[33]

In those first discussions about needs and priorities, Robert Chambers comments that you will have to go out of your way to not lead the discussion and call on people, because otherwise, some people will stay or grow silent. "Consciousness helps end the 'culture of silence' in which the socially dispossessed internalize the negative images of themselves created and propagated by the oppressor in situations of extreme poverty."[34] Sometimes, Chambers says, the solution is to have a local person or persons facilitate the discussion: "Conscientization means one both reflects and takes action on their social reality to break through prevailing mythologies and reach new levels of awareness—in particular, awareness of oppression, being an 'object' of others' will rather than a self-determining 'subject.'"[35]

Both Bhasin and Paolo Freire would say those first discussions and dialogues center around the question "What is wrong with this picture?" In *Pedagogy of the Oppressed*, Paulo Freire describes how he would show drawings or photos of interactions especially designed to elicit discussion; such images-to-elicit-discussion are well suited to people who cannot read. Critical consciousness is an exercise for people to describe their reality and their place in it, to gain perspective on how their problems relate to wider issues—with all the emotional impact and import of their reality and position.

To be honest in critical consciousness, you as an international social or development worker must be willing to reflect on your social reality, too. This is actually a crucial step, to shift how we relate in international interactions.

"Start where the client is."

Throughout my social work education, professors and practicum instructors seemed to talk in riddles. What they were saying seemed to make no sense, until you were out in the field and actually trying to apply what they were telling you.

The most important maxim that I remember from graduate school was the one that one of my favorite professors would say over and over again: "Start with where the client is."

It is likewise with community and participatory development. You may have some ideas about directions that you think will be helpful to head, but in the long run you will accomplish more if you start where the community is, where the people are. Start with their stated needs, priorities, concerns and complaints. Then, as outlined on the chapter on capacity building, you might add in your perspective or contribution. But let the local people lead the way. Often, the less that you have an agenda, the better you listen and truly engage with the people and the community.

An Attempt at Countering Cultural Imperialism and Paternalism: A Partnership Dialogue

The other day a Ugandan colleague Skyped me about a Master's of Public Health graduate who will be coming. In the part of the call described below, I was attempting to assuage the paternalism that I, myself, may perpetuate by (1) praising her smart idea of a needs assessment; (2) applauding the Ugandan government's Ebola prevention and response; (3) acknowledging the brilliance of a Ugandan—to balance my request to have our public health "expert" on the call.

"I'd like to do a survey of my community to see what topics in Public Health the people are most interested in so it will guide what the Public Health practitioner (MPH volunteer) presents," she said.

"Great idea!"

"I'd like to also show you what the Ugandan government promotes in Public Health."

"Could you send it?"

"And then," she said, "I'd like you, me and the MPH to get together on a Skype call to discuss all this."

"Great idea! I'd also like my Public Health teammate to be on the call. Would that be ok? Here, on this team, we treasure her as our 'walking encyclopedia.' She has proven time and time again to have helpful ideas. But be forewarned: do not be put off by how knowledgeable she is. She can be kind of a nerd. Do you have that word 'nerd' in Uganda?"

"No, what is a nerd?"

"Hmmm, let me give you a really good Ugandan example: the Queen of Katwe! (the name of the movie about her)—you know the chess champion in Kampala—what is her name?"

"Phiona Mutesi."

"The Queen of Katwe is absolutely brilliant! She was in this area, going to Northwest University. And every chess club in the Northwest invited Phiona to chess matches. When she came here, Phiona played eight people simultaneously! She was managing eight chess boards at once, and she still won every single one! The American chess players got absolutely drubbed! Your Queen of Katwe is so brilliant that she makes everyone else look stupid. That's a nerd."

At this, the Ugandan director was laughing.

Ask Instead of Assuming

As a woman, I appreciate men asking if I want or need help changing the tire, rather than assuming that I can't do it myself. Thus, one way to mitigate condescension or paternalism—the I-know-better-than-you—is simply to ask, "Can I help?" Or at the start of the day when locals are fetching water and wood, or in the group meetings, ask, "How can I help?" which puts them in charge.

Why Is Participatory Development Important?

Uphoff and his colleagues evaluated World Bank projects around the world and concluded that capacity building is more statistically significant than technical solutions or the amount of capital available for a development project.[36] Saying it another way: building the strengths and skills of the local people and community is what has the most enduring impact.

Further, in speaking about foreign aid, a World Bank research team found that when agencies sought participation as a goal, 62 percent of projects were successful—when not, only 10 percent.[37]

Summarizing, it is crucial to be "globally literate" if you aim to work in other parts of the world. Thus, this chapter emphasized the contributions of thinkers and practitioners from all corners of the earth, lest Westerners believe that we are the world's primary innovators and impose our ideas.

In the best practices of international development, the community participates in the needs and strengths assessment and in the design of the programs and their implementation. This is so important because international development is not just delivering services—in literacy or income generation or water and sanitation. It is empowering people and communities to have more voice in the decisions which impact their daily lives. In the Gandhian and South Asian tradition, they call this increasing empowerment "awakening." Being actively involved in participatory development helps villagers or local people awaken to their own power and capacity to create change. Thus empowered, they then realize how they can impact life in the community ... and in the nation. Participatory development is at the heart and soul of how you can create change, as can all the peoples of the world.

7

Community Organizing: Having a Voice

Because the real gut-punch of poverty is the powerlessness—not having a voice or a choice in the matters which impact your daily life—an important antidote is helping people learn how to gain and assert their power. This is the essence of community organizing.

Social work has a long tradition of community organizing and advocacy dating back to Jane Addams, because often to truly help people, you must help the entire community gain power.

As I say later in the chapter, it is crucial in community organizing to assess safety. In repressive or authoritarian regimes, speaking out or opposing the powers-that-be can be dangerous.

In international development, you may or may not do any community organizing which impacts political or economic structures. Often, though, you may do "sensitization" or awareness campaigns, such as the work we are doing in Uganda to decrease child marriage, teen pregnancies and thus fistulas (the tearing of internal organs resulting from obstructed births when a girl is too young to bear children); or the awareness-raising in Cameroon, where 48 out of 50 men said they beat their wives, to prevent domestic violence. Thus, how to work with an entire community is another important skill to learn in international social work and international development.

Community Organizing in Adjuntas, Puerto Rico

Adjuntas, Puerto Rico—nicknamed "Switzerland of Puerto Rico" due to the relatively chilly temperatures it endures—sits on

126

the slopes of El Gigante Dormido ("The Sleeping Giant") amidst the high peaks of the central mountain range. Tropical forests, including gigantic ferns and philodendrons and pockets of orchids and bromeliads, cover the hills. Veins of copper, silver and gold run through these mountains.

This tropical paradise was jarred when the Puerto Rican government approved a plan in the late 1970s to mine across more than 35,000 acres including the region of Adjuntas. Permits were granted for open-pit mining operations in 1980 and again in 1993. These open pit mines, much like the devastation that you see in Butte, Montana, would have spread pollution and toxic residues into the forests and rivers, endangering the ecological integrity of thousands of acres of mountain forests and the purity of the mountain headwaters.

The people of Adjuntas were not going to stand for it: they essentially said, "If you have come here to take our mountain; we have not come here to give it." Alexis Massol-González, a civil engineer by training, and Tinti Deyá Díaz launched the effort to first educate the people—a "sensitization campaign"—about what was at stake and the potential impact, and then rouse the local people to mobilize to prevent the destruction of their forests and water sources. They organized the community and launched a grassroots community campaign to prevent the mining. They won. In 1986, the government decided to reject the mining proposal and not give the mining permit.

Often, the opposition will bounce back and renew the fight. Sure enough, in 1993 the government again granted permits to mine in 36,000 acres of land in the municipalities of Adjuntas, Utuado, Lares and Jayuya. Tinti Deyá Díaz, Alexis Massol-González and the people of Adjuntas fortified their effort and gathered and galvanized an even broader coalition of citizens, drawing on environmental, scientific, student, cultural and religious sectors. They triumphed again. In response to the strong opposition by the people of Adjuntas, Puerto Rico's governor signed a law prohibiting open-pit mining in the region.

As in most community organizing, you do not stop just because you have succeeded in one campaign. You strategize and plan the next step: the local people wanted to protect the area from future development, to not have to keep fighting this fight over and over again to protect their mountains from being mined. Massol-González, Deyá Díaz and the people of Adjuntas proposed that the area be made into a preserve. Again, this was not granted initially but only after another broad campaign to win public support. Once again, they won. In 1996, the governor converted 303 hectares (748 acres) into a forest reserve which was duly named Bosque del Pueblo (People's Forest).

For the first time in Puerto Rico's history, a community was put in charge of managing a government reserve, which led to a new model of community-government cooperation. It was the first time a community-based group initiated the move to protect this region. Having garnered strong local community support throughout the previous campaigns, the local community stayed involved and proudly runs the reserve. The diverse alliance of people—scientists, specialists, artists, young people, adults and even the Puerto Rican diaspora—that helped defeat the mining efforts and make it a reserve continue to provide the blood, sweat and tears of the forest's management.

The people of Adjuntas and Puerto Rico did not only prevent the desecration of their mountains, forests and rivers; they also learned how to organize to make this all happen. They learned how to be change makers and community activists. They learned how to gain power and change policies and practices which impact their daily lives. Next, they built an enduring organization to address their collective concerns. Adjuntas coalesced as a community to form the organization Casa Pueblo. Casa Pueblo and community folks plant and cultivate shade-grown coffee in Bosque del Pueblo (People's Forest) to bring income to the community. They have their own radio station so that they can tell their stories and views and not have them filtered by others. They have thought of many angles. For his decades of work and leadership, Alexis Massol-González won a well-deserved 2002 Goldman Environmental Prize.

But as I say, you can rarely or never rest on your laurels. In 2012, the community once again rallied to defeat the Vía Verde project, the government's plan to run a gas pipeline through sensitive areas of Puerto Rico's interior. Once again, they confronted the challenge head on and stopped the building of the gas pipeline. Learning from their past experience about making protected areas, in 2013 the citizens of Adjuntas successfully lobbied the Puerto Rican government for the establishment of the "Corredor Ecológico del Bosque Modelo," protecting virgin forests in central Puerto Rico.

Their saga, story and successes continue. After the widespread destruction of Hurricane Maria in September 2017—the strongest hurricane to hit Puerto Rico in 86 years with winds up to 155 mph—Adjuntas once again rallied. Casa Pueblo launched a solar program so that the community will not depend on the dilapidated old power grid that gets knocked out during hurricanes.[1]

"Ten months after Hurricane Maria, Adjuntas still loses power any time a heavy rain or wind pounds the rickety power lines feeding this town high in the central mountains of Puerto Rico. That leaves its 20,000 people once again in the dark, without light, fresh water or air conditioning—except for a handful of homes and businesses glowing in the night thanks to solar energy," reports the *Christian Science Monitor.*[2] "The people of Adjuntas call those places lit by solar power 'cucubanos,' which is an indigenous Puerto Rican firefly."

Alexis Massol-González, the founding director, explains, "Casa Pueblo is part of a small but growing community movement for bottom-up social and political transformation that seeks, among other projects, to break dependence on fossil fuels such as coal, oil and natural gas to supply the colonial territory of the United States. Adjuntas Pueblo Solar is our new project with sustainable renewable energy that can provide power when the power grid fails and is a self-sustainable economic development model." This is a trend that I see all over the world: people asserting, "We are brilliant and competent [Alexis is a civil engineer] so that we can create our own solutions, thanks."

You could say that what Alexis, Tinti, Casa Pueblo and the community of Adjuntos have accomplished is a hybrid of community organizing and community development. Often they are intertwined. When the community is under siege or threatened, then they shift into the community organizing mode.

I asked Alexis Massol-Gonzalez, "What is the secret to your success?" He responded, "Casa Pueblo is not just about stopping the mining; we also build culture." Their radio station and economic development projects build community and connection, which creates a strong coalition of support. As Massol sees it, they balance their fight to protect their beloved mountains with upbeat community building. People are attracted and gravitate to a positive vision—what you are for ... rather than what you are against. Additionally, rather than burning out and fizzling, their positive vision has energized them over decades.

Note: One person's comment about including Casa Pueblo in a book about international social work and international development was this: "but Puerto Rico has been a territory of the United States since 1898." Yeah, I know. But Casa Pueblo's successes in community organizing have been extraordinary; it is an important model from which to learn community organizing. Additionally, I work with—and this book is for—people from all over the world.

Community Organizing = Needs Assessment + Capacity Building + Participatory Development

If you grow adept with the skills acquired in doing a needs assessment, capacity building, and participatory development laid out in the earlier chapters, then you have some of the skills which you will need in community organizing. The additional dimension in community organizing is that it usually involves an adversary or opponent; it usually is a struggle—as it is often called by those in the trenches—between the powerful and the powerless or disenfranchised. Community organizing is usually David meets Goliath, or Bambi meets Godzilla.

The goal of community organizing—an extension of participatory development—is to organize, mobilize and educate people to build a community's power and create effective ways for the community's needs and concerns to be heard and addressed.

Like capacity building and participatory development, community organizing aims to increase the people's voice to address social concerns or problems that the local people themselves have identified as important. (See the relationship to needs assessment?) Like capacity building and participatory development, community organizing aims to energize local community members to become more active in their society.

In the struggle and months or years-long saga to address some concern or problem confronting a community, the community learns their strengths and talents, and they learn to work together. Capacity is built at a community level as people learn how to wield power. The people of Adjuntas could rightfully claim, "We built the People's Forest and it built us."

Community organizing dates back to Jane Addams.

Community organizing is an important and respected branch of social work begun by Jane Addams, who helped poor, exploited and disenfranchised immigrants on Chicago's West Side in the 1890s. Once you become skilled in community organizing you can help either in your own community and country or internationally. I should note that I have rarely seen paid jobs for community organizers at an international level; the work is more often a subset of other roles and responsibilities. You will certainly see advocacy jobs, though, where you are educating the public about some issue and rousing people to action. If you are a rabble-rouser, there is a whole world which needs your skills.

Community organizing focuses on addressing social systems that exploit the poor and powerless, aiming to bring meaningful changes to people's lives, and empowering vulnerable or oppressed people. The goal of community organizing is to unite citizens around a common concern.

Community organizing often attempts to seize power from the powerful and transfer power to the powerless. It is this rectification of dramatic power imbalances—which underlie mistreatment, exploitation and disenfranchisement—that is at the heart of community organizing.

Community Organizing Is Risky

It is this confrontation with the powerful by the powerless that makes community organizing very risky.

Si Kahn, one of the leading and most respected community organizers in the United States, comments, "The list of important poor people's leaders who have been fired, evicted, beaten, jailed, shot at, and killed is tragically long."[3]

The powerful or the privileged rarely give up power without a fight.

Those who ally or align with the underdog may face the same

abuse and danger as those who bear the brunt of prejudice and exploitation. For example, in the United States, white allies who came from Northern towns and cities to help in the civil rights movement did so at considerable risk. The Southern Poverty Law Center lists the Civil Rights Martyrs, both black and white. For example, in June 1964, James Chaney from Meridian, Mississippi, and Andrew Goodman and Michael "Mickey" Schwerner from New York City were killed in what became known as the Freedom Summer murders.

The three men had traveled to Longdale, Mississippi, to talk with the congregation at a church which had been burned. After they left the church meeting, the three were arrested following a traffic stop outside Philadelphia, Mississippi, and then taken to the local jail and held for several hours. As they left town in their car, they were followed by law enforcement. Their car was pulled over. All three men were abducted, driven to another location, and shot at close range.[4] Chaney, Goodman and Schwerner were just three of the many people killed in the civil rights movement, which you could say was a giant community organizing effort of the powerless to confront the powerful to gain rights and respect.

Community organizing is not for the faint-hearted. It can be downright dangerous. Social work can be dangerous even in your home country. Those who work in child protective services may encounter dangerous situations, and they often are careful to protect their identities from people whom they have angered.

Community organizing is equally or more dangerous in other countries.

Community organizing surrounding environmental issues and causes can be especially dangerous. Often environmental issues hit the poor the hardest: whether the issue is the gas leak at the Union Carbide pesticide plant in Bhopal, India; toxic waste and dumps; or polluted water or air. The more affluent are able to hire lawyers who successfully lobby for "Not in My Back Yard." In the tropics, villagers or "land defenders" who have tried to prevent the cutting of their forest to be made into palm oil plantations are mowed down by thugs who represent the corporations that do not want their profits interrupted. Thus, the situation where and when environmental issues directly impact the health of the poor may become the flashpoint to ignite community organizing.

Global Witness, an environmental watchdog, monitors the land defenders who have been killed. The year of 2017 was a particularly grisly, with 207 land defenders killed. That is approximately four land defenders or environmental activists killed per week, as reported by the *Huffington Post.*[5]

One of the most famous environmental community organizers was Ken Saro-Wiwa. "Ken Saro-Wiwa was executed by a former military regime in Nigeria for fighting for the rights of the Ogoni," reported the German journalism site *DW (Deutsche Welle).* "Twenty years after his judicial murder, people in the region are still not benefitting from oil revenues."[6]

Ken Saro-Wiwa co-founded MOSOP, short for the Movement for the Survival of the Ogoni People, in the 1990s. *Deutsche Welle* continued:

> The group argued that oil production had devastated the region's environment, while bringing no benefit to its 500,000 people. Saro-Wiwa said that Shell had turned what was once an area of unspoiled natural beauty into a grubby lifeless moonscape. Oil from dilapidated pipelines and pumping stations seeped into the soil and destroyed it. For local residents, Nigeria's oil reserves hadn't brought affluence, just poverty and disease.
>
> The Ogoni took up the peaceful fight against Shell and the military regime of Nigeria. In 1993, Shell abandoned Ogoniland and has not been back since. This triumph turned Ken Saro-Wiwa and his people into a real menace for General Sani Abacha's military dictatorship. He had Saro-Wiwa arrested in 1994, allegedly for being responsible for the death of four Ogoni tribal leaders. Saro-Wiwa was hanged on November 10, 1995. He became a symbol for environmental protection and the human rights. [7]

Another more recent example of how an organizer was seen as a threat and "eliminated": Giulio Regeni, a 28-year-old Italian, was doing his doctoral research in Egypt on the street vendors' union. He was hoping the street vendors' union could revive the Arab Spring. Regeni was abducted on January 25, 2016. His body was found February 3, 2016. He had been extensively tortured and brutally murdered. Apparently, Mohamed Abdullah, who had been Regeni's contact to introduce him to street vendors, was an informant for the National Security Agency. Egypt is essentially a police state under Abdel Fattah al-Sisi.[8]

Social workers and development workers can be naïve, but they must instead be savvy.

I tell these stories so that you will not be naïve and in your zealousness step into danger. Because there is a risk to both you as a community organizer and to the community which you work with, Si Kahn, the quintessential community organizer, admonishes, "What's wrong is to put people in situations where they take risks without fully knowing it. ... We need to be certain the people we work with truly recognize the risks they are taking, the things that could go wrong, the losses they might suffer, before they make the decision to act, individually or together."[9] This is where ethics and community organizing interface.

How do you assess safety? This is an important question.

It is crucial to always do your homework. Before you step in to organize in a community in another country, check several resources. Human Rights Watch, Amnesty International, the Committee to Protect Journalists and Global Witness provide critical background on current trends in various countries. These watchdogs will tell you how repressive a president or government is; how they silence critics or journalists; how desperately they hang on to power—measures which imply the level of danger in a country. It can be staggering to learn all you need to know to effectively work in other countries. International Crisis Group's "Reports and Briefings" do a phenomenal job of helping you get up to speed with both background and current information.

As director of NGOabroad, I get requests from people who tell me, "I want to make a difference." And I get "cowboys" who want to go to Syria and take out Bashar al-Assad. My comment is: "If five million people fled a country, then it is not likely a safe place to go." I make such a big deal about safety because so many aspiring international development workers seem oblivious to safety. The other day I talked to a woman who wanted to go to Afghanistan. I said, "And you have only been to Latvia and Lithuania? You have to build the 'travel smarts' to go to more challenging places." I get social workers who want to help with sex trafficking. We do have a great placement in Nepal, but I warn people not to go to the brothels of Mumbai. Siddharth Kara vividly wrote how trafficked women would be beaten if they tried to escape the brothels, so this would be a dangerous place for you as well.[10]

A general rule of thumb: it can be very dangerous to stand between anyone and their profits—whether it is Shell Oil, a sex trafficker in Mumbai, a drug trafficker, or a mining or logging company.

As a good community organizer, figure out how to bring pressure that does not endanger you or anyone else.

When I was meeting with an NGOabroad colleague in Mongolia, I marveled at how the organization there had not run into any trouble for the democracy building, human rights and anti-corruption work it was doing. The Mongolian director smiled and sagely explained, "We don't do any naming or shaming."

Disclaimer: An Important Word of Caution

As we discuss the potential risks and dangers of some international work, I want to emphasize that the organizations examined in this book are highlighted because they are exemplary in some aspect of international development. They are not listed because I recommend that you work or volunteer with them or in particular countries.

I stress this for your safety. A book once published is static information that cannot capture the sociopolitical realities in an ever-changing world. A country that is safe under one president or prime minister can become quite dangerous under new leadership.

What is safe for you may not be for someone else. International development work or international volunteering must be carefully considered and individually tailored rather than plucked from this book.

Some of the organizations showcased in this book are in countries with challenging or dangerous sociopolitical situations. We recommend that you not go to, volunteer or work in organizations or countries just because they are mentioned in this book. This is a skills book, not a guide book.

Community Organizing Can Morph into a Social Movement

At the heart of community organizing, you are working with people who feel powerless or disenfranchised ... who feel they are not being listened to or heard. If community organizing is done extremely well or strikes a deep vein of public sentiment, it may

develop into a nationwide movement. For example, Gandhi's Salt
March led to the independence movement that ousted the British
colonizers.

Community activism taken a step further can morph into a
social movement. Augusta Dwyer, in *Broke but Unbroken: Grassroots
Social Movements and Their Radical Solutions to Poverty*, examines
how different social movements evolved.[11]

For example, indigenous people in Ecuador fought for over three
decades against oil drilling in the Ecuadorian Amazon. Much like
Shell in Ogoniland in Nigeria, Chevron dumped more than 16 billion gallons of toxic wastewater into the rainforest, leaving local people suffering a wave of cancers, miscarriages, and birth defects. This
became an important court battle.

The Confederation of Indigenous Nationalities of Ecuador,
which in Spanish is Confederación de Nacionalidades Indígenas del
Ecuador or, more commonly, CONAIE, is Ecuador's largest indigenous organization. Formed in 1986, CONAIE has pursued social
change on behalf of the region's significant native population using a
wide range of tactics, including direct action. CONAIE is best known
for its organization of popular uprisings ("levantamientos popu-
lares"), which have been known to include blockading of commercial
arteries and the seizure and occupation of government buildings.

The community organizing in the Ecuadorian Amazon has empowered the
indigenous tribes and morphed into a movement which is active in national
politics and IMF policies.

Its website states: "CONAIE's political agenda includes the strengthening of a positive indigenous identity, recuperation of land rights, environmental sustainability, opposition to neoliberalism and rejection of U.S. military involvement in South America."[12] CONAIE's work continues in challenging unrestricted oil exploration in their indigenous lands and in advocating against austerity policies in Ecuadorian government, which are explained in the next chapter.[13]

How Do You Actually Do Community Organizing?

Many of the same skills which you use in social work in your home community or internationally are skills essential for community organizing:

- trust building
- bonding—relationship building—or sometimes called "joining" in family therapy
- assessing the strengths of the community with whom you will work
- assessing the power structure and who key decision makers are
- energizing and motivating people
- building leaders and future community organizers

It is wise to get to know the community in which you will work before you even step foot into the area. Through the U.S. Census Bureau (if you are working in the United States) you can gain valuable information about the size and socioeconomics of the area. If you are working elsewhere, you can get valuable information from UNDP—the United Nations Development Programme. The local newspaper and your embassy can give you some idea of who some of the key decision makers and people with influence in the community are. Local leaders may or may not have a social media presence.

Before you even start talking to community members, wander around the town. Just as in doing a needs assessment, this is an important first step. Have a cup of coffee at the café or get a licuado—a smoothie made of tropical fruit in Central America—or fufu or dried fish on the beach in West Africa. Shoot the breeze with shop owners or street vendors. Get a sense of the place and where people hang out. And while you are sizing up the place, the local community will be watching your every move and trying to make sense of what this stranger is doing. Like chipmunks in a forest, their trill will send an alarm that someone new is in their territory.

The steps that you make in your entry can be crucial: The identity of your first contacts in the community sets up some alignments and suggests some alliances; which parts of the community you try to communicate with and which, if any, you try to avoid; where you live; how you dress; how you talk; and how you explain to the community what you are trying to do all lay important groundwork.[14]

You meet and speak not only with the poor and the powerless, but also the powerful, the elite in the power structure, those who hold the reins or marionette strings which determine how the community behaves. Note the deference patterns and observe who is the alpha dog. You want to establish a good working relationship with the powerful in order to cooperate on matters of mutual concern. You want to find your common ground and what you can agree on. Si Kahn advises—reflecting many years of polishing his community organizing skills—"Power structure people respond favorably when asked for advice, rather than when given it."[15]

In many ways this is what "liaising" is. To liaise is to establish a working relationship, typically to cooperate on a matter of mutual concern. You will see liaising as a qualification for many international development and international social work jobs, and it is discussed in the chapter on capacity building.

Si Kahn further recommends this (also like liaising): "A visit every few weeks to government and agency people that the organizer has made contact with can be helpful. If the organizer has accomplished things that she knows will meet with power structure approval, she should let them know—it will often mean increased neutrality on the part of the power structure."[16]

Note: I draw upon Si Kahn's thinking and his years of experience as a community organizer in the South and Appalachia because I like how practical he is. Saul Alinsky, based in Chicago, who wrote *Rules for Radicals* and *Reveille for Radicals*, was also a well-known community organizer.

The Questions Are the Key

Much as in psychotherapy, the questions the organizer asks the community are sometimes more important than the answers. One thing that you learn in psychotherapy is that a question makes people go within to answer. A good question makes people think deeply about possibilities, power structures and their predicament. Much like Paolo Freire's consciousness-raising, potent questions make people ponder, "What is wrong with this picture?" Questions do not have to be inflammatory or accusatory or point fingers. But good questions help people connect to the power within; they stir people from the inside outward; they lay the foundation for the motivation which will mobilize people. As people discuss community concerns and complaints, watch which have the most emotional valence. Which issues are they really willing to fight for?

Just Like in a Needs Assessment, Good Questions Identify the Priorities of the Community

And much like in a needs assessment, you want to listen and determine the concerns or problems which people in the community have. In an international context, concerns might be like these: they pay taxes, but never see any services delivered in return.... The government skims all the money off the top, so teachers never get paid so never come to school to teach.... Everyone in the room knows someone who has died of AIDS, but it is almost impossible to afford medication.... Everyone in the room has had malaria but no one can afford a bed net.... Politicians buy votes.... There is no decent road.... The water makes people sick.... The police hassle street vendors, saying they must get a business license, when really they are looking for bribes.... Half of the young people have no job.... Some youth are getting into drugs.

The community may come up with quite a long laundry list. The challenge is setting priorities together. Which issue will help the most people? Which issue do the people feel most strongly about? Which is most urgent and important to them? Let's say that out of the above list, they say they want to address the hassling that the police do. They say it is demeaning.

Being Sick and Tired of Demeaning or Abusive Behavior Fuels the Community's Action

If you recall, the Arab Spring in Tunisia was sparked by 26-year-old Mohamed Bouazizi, who was getting ready to sell fruits and vegetables in the rural town of Sidi Bouzid, Tunisia. Bouazizi was the breadwinner for his widowed mother and six siblings, but he didn't have a permit to sell the produce. When the police asked Bouazizi to hand over his wooden cart, he refused, and a policewoman allegedly slapped him. Angry after being publicly humiliated, Bouazizi marched in front of a government building and set himself on fire.[17]

Community Organizing and Events That Spark Revolutions Hinge on People Finally Saying "Basta!"—Enough!

Or "I'm sick and tired of being sick and tired."

"The dignity that comes from self-esteem is one of the most important tools the organizer can give to poor people. Belief in one's dignity as a woman or man is one of the strongest motivating factors; from it comes the refusal to be used or abused, the assertion that 'I have been pushed around too long, and I ain't going to be pushed around no more,'" writes Si Kahn.[18]

It was being sick and tired of being abused and demeaned that sparked #Black Lives Matter protests all over the United States in 2020 after the killing of George Floyd and Breonna Taylor … and many, many others. Protests against police brutality spread to Nigeria.

Though this book is not about social change in the United States, we can learn about community organizing from Alicia Garza, one of the founders of Black Lives Matter. Garza has distilled what she has learned from a decade of organizing into her first audio book, *The Purpose of Power: How to Build Movements for the 21st Century.* The 39-year-old organizer stresses that building a movement is not about the number of Twitter followers you have but about building alliances. She emphasizes: You don't tweet your way to political power; you have to put in the work. Garza explains that she cut her teeth in community organizing in fighting for affordable housing

People are ripe for community organizing when they are fed up and thus willing to take a stand about something which impacts their daily life or community.

in San Francisco's black communities. She learned that winning is about more than being right; it's about inviting people to be part of a change they may not have known they needed.

Garza founded Black Futures Lab in 2018, which has done an extraordinary needs assessment which Garza calls "the largest survey of Black people in America in 15 years." From this survey, or needs assessment, asking people's priorities, they have developed the Black Agenda, a policy platform reflecting "the most common concerns within Black communities across the political spectrum." This is how community organizing and advocacy merge together. This is how people can gain power and their concerns are addressed.[19]

In Community Organizing, You Work with the Community to Decide Goals, Strategy and Tactics

Goal: Where you want to end up
Strategy: How you plan to get there
Tactics: What you do—specific steps you take

Defining Our Terms: What Is a Strategy?

Strategy is deciding how you will rock the powers-that-be which impact your cause or area of concern.

Whether you diagram it on the proverbial butcher paper or map it out in the dirt, you ask the community: Who are the pertinent decision-makers whose behavior you want to change?

Simultaneously, you want to map out your group power and how you can concentrate it and capitalize on it; how you can leverage what you have; how you can be "the fly up the elephant's nose."

Defining Our Terms: What Is a Tactic?

Tactics are the activities which can mobilize power and are directed at a certain target or decision maker. When you consider a tactic, consider how it will give you leverage over a key target or decision maker.

Here is an example of what I thought was a brilliant tactic in Cameroon, where 48 out of 50 men said they beat their wives: They talked to the local chief about changing men's thinking and behavior. They enlisted an ally. They connected with a key leader in the community and invited the leader's participation.

Pick Strategies and Tactics That Are Winnable

With the community, pick an issue and a strategy that are winnable or achievable. Don't shoot for the moon. Start small and build the strengths and skills of the community members. Whether you are writing on butcher paper at the front of a room, or better, like Robert Chambers, you list all concerns or issues and the potential strategies and tactics with a stick in the dirt, you brainstorm as many strategies and tactics as you can. Then you weigh each possible approach to tackling the grievance or issue, considering your collective skills and capabilities, how much you can count on potential allies and how they could help. Through this thorough evaluation of various strategies, you determine which strategy has the most realistic chance of winning—of achieving the goal. It is only then that as a group you decide to move into action.[20]

You design your strategy by "starting at the finish line." Envision what victory or winning this campaign or cause would look like, then, working backwards, do your best to figure out the steps that will lead to that victory or finish line. Strategy is your overarching plan.

A huge part of strategy is pinpointing who the decision-makers are and identifying people in the power structure who hold the keys to achieving your goal. How can you impact their thinking, their perspective and ultimately their behavior? Then you break your strategy into tactics: what are the tools you will use to impact the decision makers? Often the community chooses to start with mild tactics: petitions, writing letters, making phone calls. But if the community does not feel there has been any response to mild tactics, it is likely to ratchet up the pressure to media exposés and newspaper articles to publicize the problem. There is a wide gamut of tactics that can be used: strikes, boycotts, picket lines, sit-ins, public hearings, confrontations, press conferences, paid advertising, meeting with public officials, direct actions, mass demonstrations, marches, petitions, letters, lobbying, leaflets, prayer services, silent vigils, civil disobedience, rallies and legal action.[21]

As in picking your strategy, you want to think about your tactics very carefully. Be cunning rather than impulsive. Tactics can change the ways in which your members see themselves and the ways in which they are willing to participate in the cause. Tactics affect how the public and your opposition see you too: Your tactics reveal your strength, your ability to sustain long campaigns, the depth of experience of your members and leaders. The opposition will clearly be watching and weighing your every move.[22]

Community organizing is a building block of democracy building and of how people gain power at a societal level. This societal or political dimension of community organizing, I believe, will become an increasingly important part of international social work and international development.

The rise of People Power made possible by social media and cell phones makes it fairly easy to gather protesters, but have the protesters built the skills necessary to take over and govern? It is one thing to protest austerity measures, corruption, or ruling by the elite. But if you topple the government, are you prepared to take the reins and run the country? Did you "start at the finish line" and give careful thought to what you want to achieve? Do you have not only a sense of what you are against but also a positive vision of what you want to build?

This is where community organizing skills morph into democracy building skills: looking at strategies, tactics, and long-term goals and nurturing leaders.

Building Coalitions and Bridges Is Essential

Van Jones, CNN sparring partner with Newt Gingrich, is very clear that it is important to listen to and work with people who do not share your own views—to build coalitions and build bridges across the divide. In his book *Beyond the Messy Truth: How We Came Apart, How We Come Together*, Jones recounts that his most important journalism mentor at the University of Tennessee at Martin was Dr. E. Jerald Ogg, someone who had dramatically different political beliefs than Jones. Ogg taught Jones, "We have different politics of the head but the same politics of the heart."

Jones recounts that when Newt Gingrich masterminded the "Republican revolution" of 1994, when Republicans gained 54 seats in the House of Representatives, Jones wanted to understand how Gingrich had engineered a political upset of such spectacular proportions. Jones read everything that Gingrich ever wrote and came to deeply respect what a strategist Gingrich is. It was ironic that they were chosen to be sparring partners on CNN.

But having learned from Ogg that you can work well with people with different points of view, Jones respected and respects Gingrich; they are close friends. It was Gingrich who told Jones one of his most important life lessons that became the cornerstone of his community organizing: "Your 'ninety percent enemy' can still be your 'ten percent friend'—on every point where you agree. Newt and I still passionately disagree on 90% or more of the issues. But in those places where our views align, we look for ways to work together. When it comes to fixing the justice system or the opioid epidemic, we owe it to ordinary people to try."[23]

So, while most people may think of community organizing as adversarial—the powerless against the powerful—Van Jones has found ways to build coalitions and build bridges. In 2015, Jones, Matt Hanen and Jessica Jackson organized the Bipartisan Criminal

Justice Summit. Republicans who cared passionately about this issue spoke at the summit—Newt Gingrich; Rick Perry, then governor of Texas; Nathan Deal, governor of Georgia—as did prominent Democrats: Attorney General Eric Holder and Senator Cory Booker of New Jersey.[24] Rick Perry had transformed Texas's criminal justice system—the state closed three prisons and devoted those monies to alternatives like drug courts, treatment programs and jobs—resulting in the incarceration rate dropping by 14 percent and crime rates dropping by 29 percent.[25]

Van Jones's style of organizing, his across-the-divide coalition building, is different than Si Kahn's but equally important. Building a strong coalition was central to the success of the community organizing to prevent the mining and build the People's Forest in Adjuntas, Puerto Rico.

Build Leaders and Community Organizers Who Will Carry the Torch

Social media has changed some of how community organizing is done. Facebook and Twitter were important tools in gathering people at Tahrir Square in Cairo and other flashpoints that created the Arab Spring. But revolutions do not necessarily build the new leaders and the democracy skills that will build a new society. Community organizing is not only bashing at the fortresses of power; it aims to build leaders as well.

As in capacity building, one of the functions of a community organizer is to recognize and cultivate leaders within the community and encourage people to step forward to sustain the cause of the campaign when the outside organizer leaves. It is much like parenting: part of your job is producing and building the skills of the next generation.[26] Si Kahn further explains, "People become leaders because they are tired of being pushed around. ... People become leaders when they see leadership as a real possibility for them. They go along thinking, 'I could never be like that.' One day they realize, 'I could be like that.' This realization—this 'awakening'—is the first step."[27]

It is important not only that the goals of the community organizing are reached—whether that is being treated better by officials, making sure there is not a toxic waste dump next to you, or whatever—but also that people who were disempowered now think of themselves differently. They feel worthy. They have found that they can master certain skills and impact how decisions are made. This is the intersection of capacity building and empowerment. People access the power within themselves to confront the powers that be, thus overturning the power structure which demeaned, discouraged, disenfranchised or exploited them.

The Real Goal Is People Realizing Their Power

Martin Seligman, in his pioneering work in psychology, found that learned helplessness is a phenomenon observed in both humans and other animals when they have been conditioned to expect pain, suffering, or discomfort without a way to escape it. Eventually, after enough conditioning, the animal will stop trying to avoid the pain at all—even when there is actually an opportunity to escape it. When humans or other animals start to understand (or believe) that they have no control over what happens to them, they begin to think, feel, and act as if they are helpless.[28]

If people cannot impact outcomes or the decisions which impact their daily lives, many quit trying and give up. This is the legacy of power structures that have been stacked against the poor: there is an insidious assumption that the poor cannot act on their own behalf. Thus, they may lose faith in themselves, their own abilities and their own power.

This is pertinent to what we are saying about community organizing and empowerment. As Alicia Garza explained in her book *The Purpose of Power: How We Come Together When We Fall Apart*: "Building a movement requires shifting people from spectators to strategists, from procrastinators to protagonists."[29] One of the most important outcomes of participatory development and community organizing is that previously discouraged or disenfranchised people discover their power. They learn that they can impact matters which affect their daily lives. Thus, participatory development and community organizing are antidotes to powerlessness and learned helplessness.

Martin Seligman has since spearheaded an entire branch of

psychology called positive psychology: how people gain mastery and control over their own lives. See his fascinating article coauthored with Ann Marie Roepke, "Doors Opening: A Mechanism for Growth After Adversity," which is very pertinent to our discussion about having the door slammed in your face and how adversity can build leaders.[30] Paul Stoltz in *Adversity Quotient: Turning Obstacles into Opportunities* emphasizes the importance of learning how to turn lemons into lemonade, to capitalize on challenges.[31] Gail Sheehy's book *Pathfinders* also notes that many community leaders were forged in the fire of adversity.[32] Angela Duckworth's research has more recently contributed insight about the importance of grit—persevering despite the odds.[33] So in capacity building, participatory development and community organizing, encourage and rally people to not give up despite the challenges. Remind them of Nelson Mandela's words: "When people are determined they can overcome anything."

Remind them of the lesson in Puerto Rico: we built the People's Forest, and the project and the struggle built us. Realizing your own personal and collective power is an important antidote to powerlessness and despair.

But be aware that the issues that people in other countries or cultures prioritize to organize around may be very different from the issues an outsider feels are important. Thus, if you have learned the lessons of participatory development and community organizing, you listen very closely to the local people's priorities; you don't impose yours. For example, Malala Yousafzai in the Swat Valley of Pakistan risked her life—and was shot—for pushing for girls to be educated. Throughout Africa and Asia, rather than being forced to marry at age 13, 14 or 15 and start bearing children, young women are saying, "I will choose when I marry." The next step is to defy the (male) village elders and tradition and assert, "And I will choose who I marry." Many of my colleagues in Africa and Asia see these two issues tied together: young women would prefer to get an education and fulfill their dreams than be forced to live a life of domestic servitude—exhausting days spent walking miles to fetch water and firewood, tilling the fields, washing the clothes by hand, making the meals, raising the kids … and never getting to fulfill their own dreams and potential. These issues are the priorities of local women, not something cooked up by foreign feminists or academic institutions.

Thus, the nucleus of a movement or an organization is born as people assert their concerns and priorities. People may first find their voices when they are outraged. This is how change-makers are born too.

For example, Mothers against Drunk Driving grew up around the kitchen table and morphed into an organization and advocacy movement that has changed attitudes and laws. Women who may have once felt timid found that a ferocious mother bear awakens when the safety or well-being of their children is threatened. Women find their voices and realize their power. In Argentina, the mothers of those who had "disappeared" under the military dictatorship would protest every Thursday in the central plaza to demand to know where their sons or daughters were. The organization Mothers of the Plaza de Mayo (Asociación Madres de Plaza de Mayo) was relentless and pressed for answers from the government in this way from 1977 to 2006.

At its root, community organizing is quite radical—because you are encouraging the disenfranchised or the powerless to get their concerns addressed, which potentially upsets the existing power structures. If community organizing is a true success, those who were disempowered are now empowered. And hey world, you'd better watch out!

8

Advocacy: Impacting Policies Which Create Poverty

> True compassion is more than flinging a coin to a beggar; it comes to see that an edifice which produces beggars needs restructuring.—Martin Luther King, Jr.[1]

In addition to jobs using the direct service skills in international development and international social work discussed in earlier chapters, there will be jobs in advocacy: advocating for and educating the public about policies which impact poverty and the quality of life in Africa, Asia and Latin America. For example, Oxfam is one of the most important international organizations that both works out in the field and works to impact public opinion and policy.

Advocacy is community organizing taken a step further. Advocacy is the intersection of economics, politics and activism.

Advocacy, whether by an individual, a citizens' pressure group, or an organization aims to influence decisions within political, economic, and social institutions by educating government officials and the public about the impacts of public policy, laws and budgets.

This chapter is devoted to what Martin Luther King Jr. calls "the edifice that produces beggars." In this chapter, we will examine austerity measures or "structural adjustments" and their impact on poverty all over the world. To be prepared to work in Asia, Africa, and Latin America or even in the MENA (Middle East and North Africa) region, it is helpful to understand how these policies impact ordinary people's everyday lives.

While communities will sometimes organize around a local issue, it is often the "austerity measures" of the International

149

Monetary Fund (IMF) which produce huge protests because it is ordinary people who feel the crush. But as we shall see throughout this chapter, a person's or institution's position on structural adjustment policies is often determined by their economic and political ideology.

Beyond simply educating about these policies, I will occasionally act as an advocate to recommend policies that would be less likely to increase poverty or reduce the quality of life of everyday people: pro-poor policies. We still have a long way to go to developing pro-poor policies that will help lift people out of poverty.

In 2020, the COVID-19 pandemic drove world events. It is clearer to see other factors in a more normal year, like 2019.

There was a wave—a tidal wave—of protests in October and November 2019. They may seem random, but there are some common threads which link them. My goal is to help you connect the dots and see the patterns. Friends and colleagues who read this chapter a year ago asked if I was fomenting revolution. Me, fomenting revolution? No, but revolutions were happening all over the world!

That year, 2019, was a "watershed moment"—a turning point from which I think there may be no turning back. After a year of protests in Sudan, Omar al-Bashir was removed from office in April 2019 after a 30-year dictatorship which was marked by civil war, oppression, genocide in Darfur, and human rights abuses. In October and November of 2019, ordinary citizens—both young and old, often across many sectarian divides—were demanding and pushing for change.

What is often behind the protests? All over the world you can find this pattern: a country does not live within its budget, so it must borrow money from the International Monetary Fund to keep the country afloat and pay its bills. The IMF loans the country money but requires very harsh belt-tightening measures—austerity measures or structural adjustment programs. These austerity measures are so harsh that protests break out decrying the belt-tightening.

How does this relate to poverty? The indebted country often struggles to pay back the loan. The most heavily indebted poor countries (HIPC) eventually paid out far more than they got from the IMF. Often the IMF asks a country to privatize health and education—to stop having the government provide those services. This is why all over the African continent, families struggle to pay school fees at the government schools (after government schools were privatized); why the families, themselves, must bring essential medical equipment if they go to the hospital. Structural adjustment programs are the economic policies that impoverish a nation.

Headlines of Some of the Protests of 2019

Lebanon: In what has been dubbed the WhatsApp revolution, Lebanon took to the streets.

Hundreds and thousands of Lebanese marched in October 2019 to express their economic and political grievances. These protests paralyzed the country's transportation and banking system.[2] Lebanese citizens suffered from tax hikes and dire economic conditions in the heavily indebted country. Lebanon's public debt stands at around $86 billion—more than 150 percent of gross domestic product, according to the finance ministry.[3]

Colombia: Protesters were angry over rumored austerity measures in the offing—which President Duque denied. The unrest began relatively peacefully but evolved into violent clashes. At least three people were killed.[4]

Ecuador: Tens of thousands of people, led by indigenous leaders, were expected to again bring Ecuador to a standstill. Civil unrest grew since President Lenín Moreno ended a decades-old fuel subsidy program as part of a so-called reform plan imposed by the International Monetary Fund after Ecuador took a $4.2 billion loan from the IMF earlier that year.[5]

Chile: Massive civil unrest and protests were ignited by a 4-cent raise in the Santiago Metro's subway fare. But the price of a commute over a year already amounted to over 10 percent of total income for more than half of Chileans. Young and old alike turned out for the protests over the increased cost of living; the privatization of the education system so students incurred huge student loan debts; low-paying jobs so it was difficult or impossible to pay back those student loans; cuts to older people's pensions; a poor public health system; and the stark inequality prevalent in the country. Chilean protesters called for a minimum wage and reform of the pension system in addition to reform of the neoliberal economic model that was incorporated under dictator Augusto Pinochet. The outrage in Chile was similar to that in Lebanon: essentially saying, "My taxes line the pockets of the rich while I can barely get by"—exacerbating the effect of the inequalities. (Former prime minister of Lebanon Saad Hariri and President Sebastian Pinera of Chile are both billionaires.)[6]

Argentina: Argentina's center-left swept to victory, ousting conservative President Mauricio Macri, as voters thumped the incumbent for failing to deliver on a promise to create more jobs and raise the country's standard of living. Macri, who was elected in 2015, had promised "zero poverty" and a resurgent economy. Instead, he left office with ballooning inflation, a plunging peso, a poverty rate that had risen from 29 percent to 35 percent and an outstanding $57 billion loan from the International Monetary Fund. His austerity policies further antagonized voters.

"We're tired of everything that has been happening," said one Argentinian. "When you have a friend who lost a job, a neighbor who can't make ends meet, it hits you."[7]

An acquaintance of mine who just presented training in nonviolent communication in Argentina said that what she heard the most in all the discussions was fear. "People are really scared. They don't

Protests occurred in autumn 2019 in Lebanon, Iraq, Chile, Colombia, and Ecuador. Many of them denounced the austerity measures or economic belt tightening imposed by the IMF.

know what is going to come next for Argentina or all of South America amidst all the unrest in Bolivia, Ecuador and Chile."

Greece: The worldwide Great Recession of 2008 hit Greece hard. Greece's economy tanked and it was headed for bankruptcy. The European Union, the European Central Bank and the International Monetary Fund loaned Greece a total of €289 bn ($330 bn) in three structural adjustment programs, in 2010, 2012 and 2015. They bailed Greece out.[8]

The economic reforms the creditors demanded in return brought Greece to its knees, with a quarter of its gross domestic product (GDP) evaporating over eight years and unemployment soaring to more than 27 percent.[9]

What was the human cost of the austerity measures in Greece? More pertinent to other chapters of this book, how do austerity measures create poverty? Oxfam reports:

- ⅓ of the population was on the threshold of poverty in 2012.
- 17.5 percent—over a million people—were living in households with no income.
- There was no basic social assistance system to provide a safety net of last resort.
- The suicide rate increased 26.5 percent, from 377 in 2010 to 477 in 2011.
- The public health system became less accessible, especially for poor and marginalized groups.
- ⅓ of Greeks had no health insurance.
- The crime rate increased.
- Far-right parties Golden Dawn and ANEL (National Patriotic Alliance in Greek: Ανεξάρτητοι Έλληνε) got 7 percent of the vote in the 2012 election due to the grave economic situation and a decrease in confidence in traditional parties.
- There was a growing crisis of xenophobic violence toward immigrants and political refugees.[10]

What brings people to the streets are "bread and butter issues"; things that affect daily life.

Tina Rosenberg in *Children of Cain: Violence and the Violent in Latin America* noted that Chileans did not protest when people were disappearing and being tortured under Augusto Pinochet. Between

1973 and 1990, 27,255 people were tortured and 2,279 were executed. But Chileans took to the streets when the price of TVs went up due to trade liberalization.[11]

I do understand the danger of opposing Pinochet or protesting when people are disappearing and being tortured. However, in neighboring Argentina, the Mothers of the Plaza de Mayo held vigils every Thursday for the disappeared—the "desaparecidos."

Tina Rosenberg elaborates years later about the evolution of her thinking on this:

> Most people don't care about human rights. They care about having electricity that works, teachers in every school and affordable home loans. They will support an opposition with a vision of the future that promises to make their lives better.
> Focusing on these mundane, important things is not only more effective; it's safer. ... The Burmese knew it was too risky to organize for political goals—but decided they could organize to get the Yangon city government to collect garbage. Gandhi wisely began his campaign of mass civil disobedience by focusing on Britain's prohibition on collecting or selling salt.... Movements grow with small victory after small victory. [12]

One of the purposes of this book is to give you context—some of the back story in history, politics and economics so that you can make more sense of what is going on in the world. The goal? To empower you; to make you a more effective change maker.

Structural adjustment programs, or austerity measures, impact "bread and butter" issues. People feel them acutely and respond accordingly. For example, in November 2019, Iranians took to the streets when the price of petrol went up. In 2018 in Tunisia, protests began in response to a new law that raised taxes on gasoline, phone cards, housing, internet usage, hotel rooms and foods such as fruits and vegetables. Protests in Haiti over high rice prices brought down the prime minister in April 2008. Elderly Greek citizens took to the streets in 2017 and 2018 when cuts to their pensions were proposed as part of austerity measures.

My mentors insisted that I study structural adjustments.

In the 1990s, I sought out mentors to guide me in understanding what was going on in the world in preparation for working internationally. Earlier, in college, I had taken a year of African history and literature and a year of Latin American history. (I recommend you all do the same.) But I needed to take it a step further. I asked a professor at the University of Washington to guide my further studies about

Africa, and I asked a professor at the University of Puget Sound to guide me about Latin America. Interestingly, both of them—they did not know each other—said: "If you want to understand Africa or Latin America, you must study structural adjustment programs and their impact." So I did.

In an effort to bridge ideological divides, I will say that there are two points of view on structural adjustments, as there are differing views on economics. On the one hand, you have the free-market advocates who believe that a country and an economy run better if you leave the market free and unfettered by government intervention. Ronald Reagan and Margaret Thatcher were strong proponents of this neoliberal or supply-side approach. On the other hand, you have people who say free markets do not "lift all boats" and that this neoliberal approach benefits corporations and harms people and the environment. The writers and thinkers who inform much of this chapter would say that structural adjustments have crippled countries.

How Did IMF Structural Adjustment Loans and Programs Emerge?

It is impossible to make sense of the poverty and desperation in Asia, Africa and Central and South America without a solid grasp of seemingly arcane economic policies. There is an invisible political-economic web that the Global South is trapped in. This is not a game of cat and mouse; it is a game of the spider and the fly.

The game of the spider and the fly is the set of rules, roles and interaction patterns that ensure that Northern dominance is maintained through structural adjustment loans (SAL) and structural adjustment programs (SAP). These are the ways the International Monetary Fund (IMF) writes the rules. Structural adjustment loans and programs have existed since the 1970s; they really gained momentum under the Reagan administration.

How did structural adjustments evolve? In the 1970s, the oil producing countries of the world, OPEC, collaborated to raise the price of oil. The price of gas at the gas pump skyrocketed. Richard Nixon went on TV and told America we could save oil by lowering the speed limit to 55 mph. People sat in long lines at the gas stations; this is now a way of life in many parts of the world.

As the price of oil soared, oil profits multiplied. Where did those profits go? Some stayed in Saudi Arabia and Kuwait, with sheiks buying Mercedes. But a tremendous amount was put in foreign bank accounts, says Howard Wachtel, author of *The Money Mandarins: Making of a Supranational Economic Order.*[13] Banks can never just let money sit. The way that banks make a profit and survive is to take money that someone has deposited and loan it out at a higher rate of interest.

By the 1970s, there were billions of dollars in oil profits, "petro dollars," that needed to be ploughed back into the economy, rather than gathering dust in a bank vault. Just as credit card companies send you and me solicitation letters, the banks were looking for places to loan to and make handsome profits.

It was largely during Robert McNamara's presidency of the World Bank that loans to Africa, Asia and Latin America mushroomed.

Some basic background regarding the IMF and World Bank:

In 1944, the World Bank and International Monetary Fund (IMF) were established at the Bretton Woods Conference, where 44 countries convened to agree on a series of new rules for the post–World War II international monetary system. The World Bank's loans helped European countries rebuild after World War II, while the IMF was initially designed to reconstruct the international payment system. The IMF now consists of 189 countries which work to foster global monetary cooperation, secure financial stability and facilitate international trade. The IMF depends on the World Bank for its financial resources.

In the 1970s, United States policy makers thought that the solution to the world's problems was for the Global South to join the industrial world. These policy wonks still regarded the "newly industrialized nations" as "graduating" or evolving in a desirable direction. A country won praise from the United States government if they spent big money on exports from us. Ironically, this would just sink them further into debt.

Structural adjustment programs and loans evolved at a time when it was unpopular for the United States to maintain its might forcibly. The U.S. public was taking to the streets, protesting the war in Vietnam. Corporate interests in other countries would and could no longer be protected with direct military intervention. This has everything to do with the covert way the structural adjustment measures were instituted.

What the United States experienced in Vietnam was a great humbling. Guerrilla war was victorious against American air strikes and fire power. Similarly, in Africa, people's movements were overturning the colonial powers. Most of Africa gained independence in the 1960s, starting with the Mau-Mau rebellion in 1952 in Kenya, where the Kikuyu people rebelled against the British. Jomo Kenyatta, one of the alleged leaders of the Mau-Mau, was jailed for nine years, until 1961. But upon his release, he successfully led the Kenyan people to independence. Other African nations followed.

This kind of insurrection is what made Western powers shake in their shoes; what we call "the demonstration effect" or what United States Secretary of State John Foster Dulles called the domino effect. The American government wanted to defeat any nation or rebel leader that showed a different path or a proclivity to communism. The American government muffled Cuba's success so that others would not turn to Communism. The American CIA was instrumental in defeating insurrections around the world, not wanting liberation movements to gain momentum and grow into a worldwide trend.

How could the West maintain dominance and its way of life if all the colonies achieved independence? How could the United States and Europe continue economic hegemony unless the former colonies were subservient?

U.S. "gun-boat diplomacy" wasn't working as a way to maintain power and position. The United States learned that in Vietnam. So the U.S. changed strategies but not goals. The U.S. government shifted to more covert methods, using the CIA rather than troops. The United States clandestinely overthrew governments that were not sympathetic to our interests. The U.S. government pursued covert action on many fronts.

Robert McNamara, president of Ford Motor Company, secretary of defense during the Vietnam War, and then president of the World Bank, articulated the new strategy: "Foreign aid is the best weapon that we have to ensure that our own men in uniform need not go into combat."[14]

Under McNamara's leadership, the World Bank increased its lending to African, Latin American and Asian nations. $2.7 billion was loaned in the early 1970s. This jumped to $8.7 billion by 1978. By 1981, America was loaning $12 billion annually to Latin America,

Asia and Africa. McNamara said that it was to help the poor and to subvert communism.[15]

"By promising development, cum limited social reform, containment liberalism hoped to take the wind out of the sails not only of communist movements but nationalists ... who were demanding fundamental changes in North-South relations," contends Walden Bello, Philippine sociologist and founder of Focus on the Global South.[16]

"Structural adjustment rolled back building Southern unity," asserts Kevin Danaher, co-founder of Global Exchange. "The 1970's ... set a global stage that seemed increasingly inhospitable to US interests. ... The debt crisis changed all that, opening doors of opportunity to reassert US hegemony and confront an assertive South. ... After 1982, the World Bank and the IMF became major instruments of an active attempt to restructure North-South relations, as well as guarantee the interests of commercial banks."[17]

Banking ambassadors were sent all over the world. Young graduates from the finest MBA programs, sporting three-piece suits, paisley ties and long sideburns which were the fashion of the '70s, spread like locusts, landing at almost every airport in the Global South: Rio, Santiago, Manila, Accra...

Not Allowed a Voice or a Vote but Must Pay the Price

The people of the Global South were not allowed input—a voice or a vote about structural adjustments—but had to pay the price. "Taxation without representation is tyranny."

Africa, Asia and Latin America were not asking the United States for these loans, initially. But U.S. bankers did a ferocious sales job. The bankers did not have to convince too many people. Structural adjustments were made behind closed doors. Usually the president, the financial minister, and a U.S. banker would hammer out the details. The people of Brazil, Chile, Ghana and the Philippines were not consulted, but it was the people who would have to pay.

A Guatemalan said it succinctly, "Look—your bank, I don't like it so much. It scratches where it doesn't itch."[18]

The bankers were primarily interested in finding big projects

"Look—your bank, I don't like it so much. It scratches where it doesn't itch"—insightful words from a local Guatemalan (courtesy David Zimmerly).

that would eat up big chunks of the petro dollars. So, for example, a dam was built on the Volta River in Ghana. Was it built for the Ghanaian people? Probably not: few Ghanaians can afford electricity, or even have access to it. More likely, it was for Kaiser Aluminum, which was enthralled with Ghana's rich bauxite deposits.[19] Kwame Nkrumah, the founding father of Ghana, fervently wanted Ghana to become an industrialized nation.[20] Spending lavishly to build industrial infrastructure, Ghana sank $600 million into debt by 1966.[21]

The money which the U.S. loaned went to roads and airports, ports and tall buildings, to building industrial infrastructure. Who did such projects employ? They employed contractors who came in from North America or Europe. They rarely employed or benefited the people in the recipient country. The office buildings of Nairobi, Lagos and Bangkok are often for corporate offices of expatriates, not for the people of Kenya, Nigeria or Thailand.

All over the world, these 1970s bank ambassadors loaned at 15 percent interest. They were loaning to countries who couldn't afford to pay the principal, let alone the interest. In Biblical terms, this is called usury. As a consequence, Latin America, Asia and Africa are in debt to American and European banks, and Southeast Asia is in debt to Japan, deeply in debt.

Don't get the wrong idea. Despite the anxiety when nations threaten to default on their loans or declare bankruptcy, the Global North is not suffering by loaning this money. The money flow is going in the reverse direction now. Africa, Latin America and Asia are sending more money to the Global North than Europe and America have sent south. As a debt collecting mechanism, this arrangement would make any credit agency's mouth water.

Susan George, prolific author on the subject of debt and founder of the Transnational Institute, estimates that in the period 1985–1989, the banks received $386 billion in payments from Africa, Latin America, and Asia while supplying it with only $43.5 billion in new funds. Debtors in the Global South have been paying their creditors an average of $30 billion more each year than they receive in lending. Getting her figures from the Organization for Economic Cooperation and Development, George reports that each month since 1982, debtor countries in the South remitted creditors in the North an average $6.5 billion (that's $6,500,000,000) in interest payments alone. This is as much as the entire Global South spends each month on health and education.[22]

The North magnanimously thinks of itself as providing "aid." The Global South resents us. Why? They see this as the worst plunder since Cortez. They don't think of it as aid. They think it is primarily intended to benefit the banks and corporations which receive most of the money. They think of it as paying in blood to sustain the neo-colonial way of life.

This arrangement of loaning big bucks to the Global South seemed quite all right until 1982. Then Mexico defaulted on its loan. Mexico said that it couldn't pay. "Yikes!" the United States gasped collectively. "If you do that, what's to keep Bolivia from defaulting … or Brazil??"

New arrangements were needed, and deals were cut. Bear in mind that Ronald Reagan was in office and "Reaganomics" ruled. The economic thinking of the day was that the free market, left unfettered, would solve economic problems. James Baker, Reagan's secretary of the treasury, recommended a plan. Paraphrased, it was:

"We will forgive your debt. That is, we will loan you some more money so that we can keep this whole ball rolling, if you'll agree to these conditions. We want you to structure your economy"—(hence the terms "structural adjustment program" and "structural adjustment loans")—"to maximize how the free market can operate, and so bring you out of this slump." The Reaganomic thinking was that governments pay too high a price and interfere too much. To supposedly get the economy back on its feet and booming, the United States government, which dominates the International Monetary Fund (IMF), insisted on these conditions:

Increase prices.

Decrease wages.

Discourage or outlaw unions.

Privatize the costs of health, transportation, and education. (That is, these services will no longer be provided by the government; citizens must pay out of their own pocket for these services.)

Devalue your currency, so that your exports are at a more competitive price. (This means inflation will go up and the price of imports will increase.)

Remove tariffs and trade barriers (read: open your country to goods from the U.S.)

Shift the economy to emphasize exports so that you can make some money on the international market.

Invite foreign investment and development.

Make government lean.

Save money by trimming the bureaucracy.

Sell state enterprises to the private sector to make government more efficient.

The Impact Was Devastating

Did these measures pull these economies out of a slump? Did it make them stronger, more vibrant economies? Debtor countries were 61 percent more in debt in 1991 than 1982. Just as when you and I are dealing with a 15 percent interest rate, it's almost impossible to get on top of your debt. To compound the burden of that debt, when interest rates are increased by the U.S. Federal Reserve, it increases the debt in the Global South by three to four times.[23]

The Transnational Institute where Susan George works

calculated that Sub-Saharan Africa's debt increased by 113 percent in the period 1982 to 1991. Over a barrel, by 1985 twelve of the top fifteen indebted countries submitted to structural adjustment programs. Of the forty-seven countries in Sub-Saharan Africa, thirty were undergoing structural adjustment programs.[24]

Structural Adjustment Programs Place a Country's Leader Between a Rock and a Hard Place

It is critical to understand how structural adjustment programs place a country's leader in an impossible situation. If you submit to the structural adjustment loan to avert the bankruptcy of your nation, then your electorate hates you. People are outraged as prices go up and wages go down. People riot in the streets as the government cuts subsidies to the bus system or for basic food supplies. A marginal existence plunges over the edge to despair and desperation. Crime rises. People who had honest jobs are now unemployed. People are hungry and homeless. The leader who signed on to the SAP is scorned by the public and expelled from office with the people spitting contemptuously and angrily. (See Cheryl Payor's book *The Debt Trap: The IMF and the Third World*, which recounts how Argentina and Brazil swung between these two poles.)[25]

Conversely, you can't win either. If you don't sign on to the structural adjustment program, then the World Bank and IMF make you a pariah to all creditors and nations with whom you would like to trade. You are cut off from imports. Like Indonesia, Malaysia, Korea, the Philippines, and Thailand in the autumn of 1997 during the Asia crisis, your country desperately needs the loan, so you will agree to anything.

If your country entered the industrial fold, where you were producing exports and raking in money, you may have placed your nation in the precarious position of exporting basic foodstuffs rather than being self-sufficient. As a pariah, no one will buy your exports—so you don't have money to import food, and people are put out of work. Unemployment rises. People take to the streets in protest.

In this teetering state, your nation wobbles and careens economically, politically, and socially. It is likely that you will be voted out of office or deposed by a military coup that is more sympathetic with U.S. interests. Repressive measures are instituted to silence the dissent. Tanks and troops are brought into the square filled with protestors. The people scatter; some dropped, downed by the guns. Dissidents begin to disappear.

These are the ways that structural adjustment programs affect the politics of the Global South. How they affect the daily lives of the people is just as devastating. The following figures are from the 1990s when many books were written about the debt and structural adjustment programs:

> Poverty: 1–2 billion people in the world live in absolute poverty.
> Hunger: Half the children in Sub-Saharan Africa are starving or malnourished.
> Jobs: More than 1 billion are underemployed or unemployed.
> Gap: The income gap between rich and poor doubled in the 1980s.
> In the Global South, the richest ⅕ is 150 times richer than the poorest ⅕.
> Education: In the 1980s in Africa, funding for education decreased by 25 percent.
> Health: In the 1980s in Africa, money spent on health decreased by 50 percent.[26]

A study for the Inter-American Development Bank, "Structural Adjustment and Determinants of Poverty in Latin America," concluded, "Harsh Structural Adjustments of the 1980's have significantly worsened poverty. Virtually every country confirms deterioration of living standards, and widening inequality in the last decade."[27]

Countries Sold Their Souls and Rainforests to Get Out of Debt

There are other parts to the structural adjustment story that people should know. Once in such a desperate predicament, countries consent to do anything to pay that debt. They sell their souls. They sell their children's food. They sell their forests and fisheries to raise export dollars. There is a direct correlation between countries with a high debt service ratio and deforestation, notes Susan George.[28]

Examples of the most indebted countries which are the most deforested? Haiti, the Philippines, Malaysia, Brazil. They all consented to the leveling of their forests to raise money to pay their debt. As Luiz Inacio "Lula" da Silva, former president of Brazil, said: "If the Brazilian Amazon is the lungs of the world; then the debt crisis is the pneumonia."[29]

The best indicator of the real hardships imposed by the debt is the debt service ratio. This reflects how much of a country's exports are devoted to payments on the debt.

In the Philippines the debt service ratio in the 1990s was 444 percent. That leaves no money for ecological protection or sustainability. There is no money for such luxuries. There is incredible pressure to log and convert the land to agricultural export crops.

Or take Cote d'Ivoire. The per capita GNP is $770. That means the gross national product, divided amongst the people, would leave $770 annually. That's not even the average annual income of most citizens. But if you took the debt that Ivory Coast owes, and divided it among the people, it would be $1,200.

Ivory Coast's debt so dramatically exceeds the wealth of the country that you can bet that Ivory Coast is selling its soul and its forests. Ivory Coast must earn hard cash by any means available. You could say they are prostituting themselves at an international level. Tropical forests once covered half of Ivory Coast. Now they cover only 5 percent.

Brazil is the top debtor and the top deforester. Brazil cut 2.3 percent of its forest every year in the 1990s. That's 50,000 square kilometers a year—equivalent to the destruction of the next ten deforested counties put together. If Brazil had left its forests intact, it could be producing ten times as much food as its gains from the newly leveled pastureland.

Costa Rica has a $4.7 billion debt. That's a heavy load for such a small country to carry. The debt divided among its people is $1,658 per person. Paying this debt takes 25 percent of Costa Rica's export earnings.

Forty-three percent of the world's forest cover was destroyed by the 1980s. Eighty to ninety percent of the forest cover has been lost in India, Ivory Coast, and the Philippines. Much of Brazil, Costa

Rica, India, Myanmar (Burma), the Philippines, Vietnam, Cameroon, Indonesia, and Thailand have been deforested. If logging is kept up at the current rate, these nations will be denuded of all forests in six to forty years.

Forests once covered one third of the planet.[30] Forests were extensive in Brazil, Zaire, Indonesia, Peru, Papua New Guinea, Venezuela, Colombia, Myanmar, Gabon, Mexico, India, Cameroon, and Malaysia.

Tropical forests once covered 80 percent of Haiti. Now it's only 5 percent. Haiti is almost completely clear-cut. Flying over Hispaniola, the border is obvious—Haiti is completely denuded, its red earth parched and eroding, no longer in the sheltering shade. In contrast, the Dominican Republic still has its tropical forests.

Malaysia, the Philippines, Cameroon, Ivory Coast. Let's take roll call. Structural adjustment programs stipulated that there be an emphasis on exports. That, coupled with encouraging foreign investors and business, is an invitation to logging companies to clear the trees.

What has this meant to people's lives?

The Philippines has steep hillsides. Deforestation has meant

Lush forests such as this one in Borneo once covered one third of the planet, but many were cut to pay off IMF debts.

landslides. It has meant that people who depended on the forest for their food are now hungry and that people flood the cities looking for a way to feed themselves and their families.

Parts of Africa were logged generations ago by the colonial powers. For example, in Kenya, trees were cut to make way for tea plantations for the British. Deforestation has led to desertification. The Sahel, which is the grassland south of the Sahara, has always been fragile. The Sahel could not support many people. For generations, the indigenous cultures of this region had rules and norms that regulated how these grasslands were grazed.

But as lands have been logged, seized by multinational corporations, or turned into desert, people have migrated in search of land which will sustain them. Africa is now a land of environmental refugees. Much like the Irish, who left during the potato famine, people are flooding across borders.

The economic pressures are much the same: a foreign power stipulating what you can eat and what you must export. In Ireland during the potato famine, England required that the Irish and Scottish would grow export crops: oats and barley. The oats and barley that the Irish grew were not to feed Irish families; they were for the colonial mother, for the profits of others. The Irish were supposed to get by on the potato. Rather than the rich variety of crops that the Irish had before, the potato was a monocrop. Monocrops are more prone to pests and disease, not having the genetic diversity to evolve strains that can combat disease. A fungal blight wiped out the potato crop. The crop that fed the Irish people failed. The Irish fled Ireland in search of sustenance and a better life.

Structural adjustments are just a new way of saying, "You'll play the game our way; you don't get any say-so in the matter. We'll extract your wealth and force you to do the work, and we'll take the profits."

The United States and the IMF are writing the rules as far as structural adjustment programs are concerned. In so doing, the U.S. and the IMF define life in the Global South: will there be any money left in the national budget for health care, or must it go to paying the debt? Is there money allocated to combat malaria, or has that been struck from the budget? Is the nation devoted to educating its people, or can it now not afford such luxuries, putting it on the shoulders of its citizens? Can citizens who live on a per capita income of $250 per year with a cost of living that is higher than in the U.S. possibly afford to send their children to school?

Structural adjustment programs (SAP) are a big part of perpetuating global inequality.

Commodity Prices Were Just as Crummy ... Just Get the Crumbs

My African professor also insisted that I study commodity prices, another arena which the Global North rules, indirectly determining if children in Africa will eat well or poorly. There is the same lack of input and democracy in decisions regarding commodity prices. The Global South is forced to sell cheap and buy dear. The price of agricultural exports on which much of Asia, Africa and Latin America depend is falling relative to the Global North's manufactured goods. This is one more sleight of hand that the Global North dictates and that has tremendous impact.

Joseph Collins and Frances Moore Lappé, in their book *The Twelve Myths About Hunger*, go so far as to say that more fairly determined commodity prices could eradicate the debts of African, Asian and Latin American nations. That is, if the price of raw materials had remained at what they were in 1973, or even 1979 (relative to our manufactured goods), most countries in the Global South—especially Latin America—would face no debt crisis today.[31]

But the Global North dictates commodity prices, so most African, Latin American and Asian farmers are caught in the squeeze as the fertilizer which the Global North supplies doubles in price, as do their taxes, but the price they can earn from their farm products falls.

This was what happened for farmers in Ethiopia in 1982. Farmers were required to sell their goods to the government at low, fixed prices. Without any increase in what farmers got for their crops, the government doubled the price for fertilizer and raised their taxes.[32]

It was a similar predicament for cotton growers in Sudan. Sudan had the greatest per capita debt of any nation. Determined to change that, the government offered incentives to boost production. Farmers and workers must have really kicked into gear, because in just two years, the volume of cotton exports tripled. But world prices fell over the same period, and total earnings improved only slightly.[33]

It was much the same story in Malawi. Malawi increased its sugar exports. But sugar prices plummeted, and so the foreign exchange earnings shrank by half.[34]

Like flies entangled in a spider web, leaders of the Global South are aware of the conundrum that has entrapped them. Julius Nyerere, the first former president of Tanzania, said: "Prices of primary commodities like cotton, coffee, cocoa, copper—which are export products of the Third World—go down in relation to prices of machinery, trucks, capital investments, and manufactured goods.... Third World countries sell cheap and buy dear."[35]

So, this is another way that the Global North holds the cards and writes the rules. We set the price. We charge high rates for our products and pay drastically below market value for products from the Global South, whether bananas or uranium. This has been the importance of the Fair Trade movement that emerged in the 1990s.

And how do we persuade, coerce, or cajole others into playing by our rules? We simply arrange the overthrow of any leaders who cross us. In 1974, President Haman Diori of Niger stood up to France.

In Asia, Africa and Latin America, farmers are forced to "sell cheap and buy dear."

He said that the price that France was paying for uranium was way below market value. He warned that if Prime Minister Messmer did not agree to a fairer price, he would denounce France at the United Nations. Several days before the new round of discussions were slated to occur, pro–French elements of the Niger army overthrew President Diori.[36]

Is this global world order democracy or a tyranny? Is there a tyrant at the top of the heap ruthlessly enforcing their rules? Or do the people who are impacted by the rules have a vote or voice in how the decisions are made?

Tyrannies are often just recycled feudal societies where the serfs must bring the food to a pudgy king while the peasants starve. Such an arrangement, being so grossly unfair, must be maintained by force. It's a precarious house of cards, as the peasants will only put up with this for so long.

Activism and Advocacy Trying to Change Structural Adjustments

The 1990s were a time of tremendous activism all over the world, trying to change SAP (structural adjustment programs), and of much advocacy—educating the public in the hopes they would press for policy changes. Organizations such as Institute for Policy Studies, Susan George's Transnational Institute, Global Exchange, Global Citizen, Make Poverty History, and 50 Years Is Enough were all working on this issue. Ultimately many of the thinkers and activists united to form the International Forum on Globalization.

Concern about austerity measures' crippling effects on people all over the world prompted an entire movement. The Jubilee 2000 organization originated during the African Council of Churches in Africa in the year 1990. Taking a page out of the Bible saying that every fifty years debts were forgiven, this whole movement advocated for debt relief—writing off the debts of the most Heavily Indebted Poor Countries. This movement coincided with the Great Jubilee, the celebration of the year 2000 in the Catholic Church.

Whereas much of the earlier advocacy work was done by pro-gressive groups on the left, by the year 2000, debt relief became a mainstream cause as more churches took it up—Anglicans/

Episcopalians, the Church of the Brethren, Catholics, and the Church of Christ. The National Council of Churches, the largest ecumenical body in the United States—which includes mainline Protestant, Eastern Orthodox, African American, evangelical, and historic peace churches—endorsed Jubilee 2000 and thus gave their immense weight to this movement.

Jubilee 2000 became an international coalition movement in over forty countries which called for cancellation of Third World debt. For example, the organization Freedom from Debt Coalition in the Philippines was very active—and still is. People were knocking on doors and giving community talks in many, many countries: Angola, Argentina, Australia, Austria, Bangladesh, Belgium, Benin, Bolivia, Brazil, Burkina Faso, Cameroon, Canada, Colombia, Cote d'Ivoire, Cuba, Czech Republic, Denmark, Ecuador, Finland, France, Germany, Ghana, Guatemala, Guyana, Haiti, Honduras, Hong Kong, India, Indonesia, Ireland, Israel, Italy, Jamaica, Japan, Kenya, Korea, Madagascar, Malawi, Mali, Malta, Mauritius, Mexico, Mozambique, Namibia, Netherlands, New Zealand, Nicaragua, Nigeria, Norway, Pakistan, Peru, Philippines, Poland, Portugal, El Salvador, Senegal, South Africa, Spain, Sri Lanka, Swaziland, Sweden, Tanzania, Togo, Uganda, United Kingdom, United States, Venezuela, Zambia and Zimbabwe.[37]

British economist Ann Pettifor founded and directed the global Jubilee 2000 campaign from the UK. Many would consider this worldwide advocacy campaign to have been very effective:

- It increased public understanding of the role of debt and of creditor institutions in the global financial system.
- It mobilized millions of people across the world—the Jubilee 2000 petition was signed by more than 21 million people.
- It was a groundbreaking use of the Internet for worldwide outreach, education and mobilization.
- It led to greater awareness in debtor nations of the nature and scale of the debt. This challenged the corruption behind much lending and borrowing, and increased accountability of governments to their people for foreign lending and borrowing.
- The resulting savings were subsequently used to reduce poverty, and to fund health and education programs in many countries, notes the Jubilee 2000 website.

On June 11, 2005, the G7 finance ministers (of Canada, France, Germany, Italy, Japan, the United Kingdom and the United States) at a meeting in Gleneagles, Scotland, agreed to cancel the debts of so-called Heavily Indebted Poor Countries owed to the IMF, World Bank and African Development Bank. Approximately $100 billion (in net present value terms) of debt was written off.

The 36 countries which had their debts cancelled under the scheme—the Multilateral Debt Relief Initiative—were Afghanistan, Benin, Bolivia, Burkina Faso, Burundi, Cameroon, Central African Republic, Chad, Comoros, Republic of Congo, Democratic Republic of the Congo, Cote d'Ivoire, Ethiopia, the Gambia, Ghana, Guinea, Guinea Bissau, Guyana, Haiti, Honduras, Liberia, Madagascar, Malawi, Mali, Mauritania, Mozambique, Nicaragua, Niger, Rwanda, Sao Tome and Principe, Senegal, Sierra Leone, Tanzania, Togo, Uganda, and Zambia.

The world's creditors (and in particular the World Bank and IMF) welcomed the fact that sovereign debtor balance sheets were being cleared of outstanding debt. Clean balance sheets made the above-named sovereign debtors attractive to both public and private creditors—and so they piled back in with new loans to sovereign borrowers. This time, China joined in the business—making loans in exchange for access to valuable African land, oil and other resources.

Because debt cancellation had made no difference to the structure of the international financial system in which creditors, investors and speculators are allowed free rein and are dominant; because there was no restraint on cross-border capital moving from creditors to borrowers—and back again; because the terms and conditions for borrowing did not include the ability to pay; and because creditors know that sovereign debtors (unlike commercial debtors) have no recourse to international bankruptcy law (there is no international law governing creditor/debtor relationships)—the debt merry-go-round swung back into action.

The result: African countries are again in debt.

On November 28, 2018, the German publication *Deutsche Welle* reported that eighteen African countries were in debt again.

"I think the fall in commodity prices or the fluctuations in commodity prices in the last two, three years has really affected the revenue inflows of a number of African countries. This has led to huge budget deficits, so governments have tried to plug the gaps. They've resorted to borrowing, especially from commercial sectors," said Tirivangani Mutazu, an analyst at the African Forum and Network on Debt and Development (AFRODAD). Additionally, countries incurred debts building roads, railways and ports.

"There are a number of countries already that are going to the IMF for bailouts so to speak. The IMF will of course demand they implement austerity measures," Mutazu said.[38]

Did Debt Relief Alleviate Poverty or Improve Lives?

That is a really important question—to look at impact.

And nowhere can I find data on whether debt relief of the IMF's HIPC Initiative reduced poverty in the previously debtor nations; nowhere. So I called Oxfam, because if anyone has a grasp of this research, it would be Oxfam. It is telling that they did not have a ready answer, but commendable that they were willing to look into it.

Oxfam sent me an article which corroborated this concern about former debtor nations again being in debt. "As of April 2019, according to the IMF, half of African Low Income Countries (LICs) are either in debt distress or at high risk of being so. ... With commodity prices very low, interest rates growing and exchange rates falling, less money on worse conditions is now arriving in Africa. ... Even countries at only moderate risk of debt distress are heavily cutting social spending ... on key sectors (health, education, and agriculture) by 12%."[39]

Sarajuddin Isar, Afghani Ph.D. candidate at the School of Oriental and African Studies in London, evaluated the progress of the HIPC countries using the Millennium Development Goals (MDG) as his means of measuring progress. Isar found this about the HIPC countries:

- Almost half still cannot meet MDG target for universal primary education.
- More than half still need to reach MDG targets pertaining to gender equality and the prevention of HIV/AIDS, TB and malaria spread.
- About half still need to reduce mortality rate of children

under five as well as ensure environmental sustainability MDG targets.

* Only a quarter are on track to eradicate extreme poverty and hunger or improve maternal health.[40]

So that is both good news and bad news, right? Half have made important progress; half have not achieved MDG targets. A bucket half empty or a bucket half full?

Later I found an article in the *Guardian* by Adrian Lovett, CEO of the ONE Campaign, who had more praise for what Jubilee 2000 accomplished: "Since 2005, new HIV infections have decreased by 33%; in sub–Saharan Africa almost one-third fewer children die before the age of five. And 35 million more children are now in school.... The extreme poverty figure has dropped from 43% of the world's people in 1990 to 21% in 2010."[41]

It is economist Richard Easterly who may have identified what the snag is: corruption.

Easterly did have an opinion on whether debt relief has helped. In his article in *Foreign Policy*, Easterly asserts, "Debt relief has become the feel-good economic policy of the new millennium, trumpeted by Irish rock star Bono, Pope John Paul II, and virtually everyone in between. But despite its overwhelming popularity among policymakers and the public, debt relief is a bad deal for the world's poor. By transferring scarce resources to corrupt governments with proven track records of misusing aid, debt forgiveness might only aggravate poverty among the world's most vulnerable populations."[42]

Easterly contends that poor nations suffer poverty not because of high debt burdens but because spendthrift governments constantly seek to redistribute the existing economic pie to privileged political élites rather than enlarge the pie through sound economic policies. Corruption—how the political elite, in Lebanon, Iraq, Chile and other nations, are pillaging state coffers—is a key driver of recent protests. People in many countries are taking to the streets, shouting, "We will not tolerate this any longer!"

For this reason, Easterly advocates that debt relief should only be given to governments that are not corrupt and where the money is not being grossly misspent. This is a new spin on behavioral economics—the kind of examination of impact and incentives that

Nobel Prize winners Banerjee and Duflo also advocate in determining which social programs actually work to help eradicate poverty.

Additionally, do central governments even know where their money is going? A recent IMF and World Bank study found that only two out of twenty-five debt relief recipients will have satisfactory accounting methods to track where government spending goes within a year. This is why capacity building needs to occur regarding accounting and economic skills.

To be honest, is there anywhere in the world that has high "economic literacy"—where people understand how economics impacts people's lives? If we talk about debt, let the United States not be too pious: we have a $22,000,000,000,000 debt! The United States has done a pathetically poor job of balancing its budget—of aligning income and expenses. We are not living within our means.[43]

If debt relief is not the magic bullet, what is?

I think it is important to hear Easterly's point: "Thirty-six poor countries received 10 or more adjustment loans in the 1980s and 1990s, and their average percentage growth of per capita income during those two decades was a grand total of zero."[44]

So, neoliberalism—allowing the free market full rein to solve social and economic problems—did not work. But to be honest, it seems neither did debt relief.

Notes Ann Pettifor, a British economist who launched Jubilee 2000 and who has expertise in the global financial system, sovereign debt restructuring, international finance and sustainable development,

> Quite right. Debt relief is just that: relief ... it is not cancellation, and it is not restructuring of the international system of creditor-dominance.... That is why Jubilee 2000's petition called for the creation of an independent international authority to mediate between private and public creditors and sovereign debtors (much as an independent authority mediates between states over territorial boundary issues)—to allow effectively for a nation state to become insolvent. Insolvency disciplines the borrower—but also the creditor. Without insolvency creditors carry on lending ... and politicians keep borrowing.[45]

In international development, both theorists and practitioners are getting less doctrinaire and more pragmatic. In other words, they try not to create solutions from ideology downward but rather from looking at what works locally and then scaling up. This new evidence-based approach is gaining traction, approaching things experimentally. This is where the emphasis is on impact and incentives. Easterly was thinking this way before or concurrent with Abhijit Banerjee and Esther Duflo, I believe.

The question remains: What does work? Some of the initiatives which have been working are more grassroots, social enterprises by and for the poor that have succeeded in spite of imposed SAP rules.

Additionally, would it work to reward governments that are not corrupt and self-serving? The Ibrahim Prize for Achievement in African Leadership aims to do just that. It provides an incentive—an award of $200,000 a year for life, exceeding the $1.3 million Nobel Peace Prize—to African leaders who have developed their countries, lifted their people out of poverty and paved the way for sustainable and equitable prosperity. Can we encourage and help create more people-centered governments that live within their budgets and create prosperity for their people?

Richard Easterly is an economist who has his share of critics. His detractors say that Easterly represents the Chicago School of Milton Friedman's neoliberal thinking, and he has decades of experience at the World Bank, which many view as the enemy.

But the field of economics has changed dramatically as new ideas have been infused. For example, after years of growing increasingly critical of the IMF and World Bank, Joseph Stiglitz "defected" from the World Bank and espoused more people-centered and pro-poor approaches.[46] James Wolfensohn invited Amartya Sen to speak to the World Bank in 1999, resulting in Sen's most succinct summary of his thinking in *Development as Freedom.* Jim Yong Kim, who was co-founder of Partners in Health with Paul Farmer (see the chapter "Partner to the Poor and Participatory Development")—one of the most important and visionary pro-poor health organizations in the world—was president of the World Bank from 2012 to 2019. Kim gave a speech entitled "Boosting Shared Prosperity."

Over the last several decades the World Bank has been listening and learning and has been revising and reforming. Just looking at the summaries of each World Bank president, you see how they are changing with the times, how Jubilee 2000 changed their thinking and policy, and their shift to trying to monitor corruption in the countries to which they loan:

Jim Yong Kim, July 2012–February 2019: Kim oversaw a bank-wide reorganization, a historic capital increase, the launch of the Human Capital Index, and a sizable investment in the fight against climate change.

Robert B. Zoellick, July 2007–June 2012: Modernized and recapitalized the bank, ramping up its crisis response and making it more accountable, flexible, fast-moving, transparent, and focused on good governance and anti-corruption.

Paul Wolfowitz, June 2005–June 2007: Good governance banker who pushed through controversial governance and anti-corruption strategies after extensive global consultations. He placed Africa at the heart of the bank's poverty reduction agenda.

James D. Wolfensohn, June 1995–May 2005: The "Renaissance Banker" who pushed through reforms that have made the bank more inclusive, with a renewed focus on poverty reduction.

Economics, like almost all academic disciplines, now has vanguard thinkers and practitioners with a global, enlightened and pro-poor perspective. Now there are economic think tanks such as the Institute for New Economic Thinking—economists who challenge conventional wisdom and advance ideas to better serve society. The old polarities of Republican and Democrat, Tory and Labor are beginning to dissolve and give way to old and new—those who want to preserve the old order or those who envision a new future that transcends old boundaries and polarities.

Even though neoliberalism has failed, as has debt relief, there are some valuable takeaways. Looking back at the intense passion of the 1990s and of the Jubilee 2000 movement, we see the dawn of caring how other people in the world lived and of examining the policies which impact poverty. It was compassion propelled by the Internet and new technologies. For the first time, the Global North and the Global South were able to talk to each other, instantly, and coordinate and organize. As newer technologies emerge, how we move together as a planet—humanity as a whole—will continue to change.

So perhaps I was naïve, along with my African and Latin American professors, to think that there was a panacea. Sad to say, there probably never is one magic bullet, no slam-dunk easy answer. Alas, no tooth fairy or Santa Claus either. Great hope was placed in micro-finance as a way to help many people out of poverty. Social entrepreneurship is seen by many as an answer. I think it is more helpful to approach dilemmas of global proportion in a more experimental, we-are-always-learning way, as Banerjee and Duflo advocate: evaluating what has impact—what worked and what didn't work and what needs to be tweaked. Once you have found interventions or approaches that work, you scale up. So rather than change happening from the top down, it is now happening from the bottom up.

It is commendable that there are continued efforts to find solutions to global poverty and a commitment to seeing that the lives of everyone on this earth are improved. I think there is no one solution, but many solutions, innovations and angles, and an exponential number of people and organizations dedicated to eradicating global poverty and improving the lives of billions.

You are not just the changer—the change agent. In equal parts, as you listen, learn and tweak, you are the changed.

III

Attitude

9

Attitude Is Everything

Your success or failure may depend on your attitude: "Check your privilege at the border." In international programs and projects, your success or failure may hinge on your attitude.

It is not just *what* you do but *how* you do it that can be crucial both at home and in other countries.

Lisa Adams, MD, has done TB (tuberculosis) care and prevention work all over the world for decades. She recounts how a TB project in Tanzania unraveled because she and her U.S. team inadvertently steamrolled over her Tanzanian colleagues. Adams, a medical professor and associate dean in global health at Dartmouth, in her TEDx talk titled "Global Health Partnership: Check Your Privilege at the Border," says this humbling experience was the most important lesson in her career in global health. She realized that good intentions in helping with TB are never enough; that she needed to slow down and understand her Tanzanian partners and their priorities; that she needed to understand that her own actions were overbearing and paternalistic in setting the agenda and strategies and basically spearheading the whole project. This potential failure proved to be the foundation for a new attitude in her work: equity in partnerships.[1]

A critical step in preparing to do international social work is not just learning essential skills and external realities but also examining assumptions and attitudes. This emphasis on attitudes is the most important new trend in international development today. What Dr. Adams found was that her Tanzanian colleagues were not cooperating with her project because they did not like her approach. Either we get it right or we may fail, as Dr. Adams initially did. To her credit, she listened, she learned, she rectified the situation and salvaged the project. This is the sharp cutting edge.

Privilege is being warm in winter, not shivering in Nepal.

This chapter explores privilege. I borrow perspectives and lessons learned from the white privilege awareness movement and soul searching that is going on across the United States in schools of social work and among seasoned social workers—though people from all walks of life are part of this movement. But privilege may not just be based on skin color. As an out-of-work white man in Indiana said, "I do not feel privileged at all."[2] In the first half of this chapter, we will explore how thinking and writing about privilege applies to international interactions. At the end of the chapter, we will look at tangible steps you can take. The intent of this chapter is to investigate the attitudes and assumptions behind power and privilege; because once you discover pernicious opinions or perspectives inside yourself, you are then in a better position to change them and, like Adams, improve your work all over the world.

There is much that we assume as the privileged and powerful.

Assume "Our Reality" Exists Elsewhere?

As with white privilege, aspiring international workers often do not know that we take many things for granted, things that shape our assumptions. Yesterday, I had a long conversation with a man who will soon receive his MSW. He had lived and traveled in India, Brazil, Peru and Guatemala, so he knew that not all the world was like back home. He wanted to either work or volunteer abroad. After much discussion, he could identify that he would like to do play therapy at a hospital with kids who have cancer.

"Hmmm, I don't know anywhere in poorer parts of Africa, Asia, Latin America that would have such a position," I commented. I continued:

It isn't that people or kids do not have cancer, it is that cancer is hard to detect. Most cancer detection while it's still in a treatable stage requires sophisticated and expensive equipment. In government hospitals, I have never seen an MRI (magnetic resonance imaging) scanner in the developing world. And cancer is expensive to treat. I have never seen radiation machines either, though they may be available in private hospitals or clinics. I have never heard of anyone getting chemo. I do know, though, that Kenya's famous environmentalist and Nobel laureate, Wangari Maathai, died of ovarian cancer. And doubtless, there are many people in the developing world—people living next to toxic sites or garbage pickers not to mention the people who cook indoors all over the world—who have increased rates of cancer. Several directors have asked for help sensitizing women about cervical cancer. But my point still stands that hospitals in the developing world rarely have pediatric cancer wards, they simply have a children's ward.

"Huh," I could hear him grasping and absorbing this.

I could tell from our long conversation that this social worker was very well meaning and well-intended; he was simply unaware how he had transposed his picture of the world on to other continents. I think that he pictured gleaming hospitals with all the equipment that we take for granted in Canada and the United States. It is these suppositions—that arise from our life of privilege—that are helpful to watch or examine once they have been discovered, and which he was very willing to do.

I know that I unwittingly made such suppositions. Decades before I had been many places in the world, I remember saying something to a man who had been in the Peace Corps somewhere in West Africa in the early 1970s. I said something about social services in Africa. He said, "*What* social services?" (Clearly, social services have blossomed all over the continent since the 1970s.) It was the first clue that my picture was dramatically inaccurate and that I had assumed that services or ways of life which we have here exist in other places. It was one of my first awakenings.

Note: Throughout this chapter, I refer to awakening or a light bulb going on, as I believe attitudinal and behavior change comes in this gentle, ah-ha, revelatory way. I use "awakening" as they do in Sri Lanka and India, acknowledging that change starts with the individual and ripples out into ever wider orbs of influence: to family, community then nation. I do not use the term "awakening" in reference to the modern American parlance of someone being "woke" or politically correct.

Note 2: Dr. Lisa Adams, perhaps because she has even more contact with medical resources, corrected me and said she knows of pediatric cancer wards and a cancer center in Tanzania, and that Rwanda also has a cancer center. Further, Dr. Adams said that most tertiary care hospitals in at least east Africa have MRI machines as well as CT scans. I humbly stand corrected, but also acknowledge that it was in Cameroon and Sierra Leone where people were reporting their brother dying of an ulcer which may have in fact been cancer. And also, if you remember Luke's story: many people do not have the money for the motorcycle taxi man or bus to get to those hospitals.

Privilege

I have extrapolated domestic discussions about racism to international interactions.

Much has been written about white privilege that can be applied to international interactions. Discussions going on in schools of social work about race and racism could be helpful in international social work. These discussions and writings about white privilege constitute a trend or a movement that can serve as a model to help shift attitudes about privilege.

The discussion about racism here at home is important to extrapolate to international dimensions because colonialism has left a legacy and vestiges of white as superior, as ruler; brown or black as servant or serf.

I suspect most people entering and graduating from schools of social work are goodhearted, well-intended people. But thinking of ourselves as goodhearted can allow us to put our blinders on. "I was taught to recognize racism only in individual acts of meanness … never in invisible systems conferring unsought racial dominance on my group," comments Peggy McIntosh, feminist, anti-racism activist, and senior research associate of the Wellesley Centers for Women.[3] If we think of ourselves as good people, we are exonerated; we may think that we are absolved of the responsibility to look at our unearned entitlement, unearned advantage, and unearned dominance coming from the so-called developed countries.

Of all that has been written about white privilege, it is Peggy McIntosh's thinking that I have found most helpful. In 1989, McIntosh wrote "White Privilege and Male Privilege: A Personal Account of Coming to See Correspondences through Work in Women's Studies."[4] I find McIntosh's juxtaposition between male privilege and white privilege sheds a great deal of light on the privilege, the power and the dominance that we have in international interactions; on our sense of entitlement; and on how oblivious we can be.

Oblivious to what is it like to not have a penny in your pocket? As Westerners, our privilege can lead to many erroneous assumptions and to totally missing others' realities.

The moment when the light bulb went on for me was when I read *The Blue Sweater: Bridging the Gap Between Rich and Poor in an Interconnected World* by Jacqueline Novogratz. She writes about her work distributing malaria bed nets in Tanzania. She had checked on this man who had previously been incapacitated by malaria and thus not able to work. He now had a bed net. But he had no bed to tuck the net under. He slept directly on the ground and tucked the malaria net around him.

A European NGOabroad volunteer in Ghana Skyped me. "I don't see what the big deal is about malaria. The Ghanaians could easily prevent it; there are malaria bed nets everywhere for sale." He was oblivious to the fact that most people cannot afford the $5 for a bed net. Like many people in Europe and North America, there may never have been a moment in his life, not a moment, when he did not have $5.

Another light bulb came on for me when I was talking to a Kenya

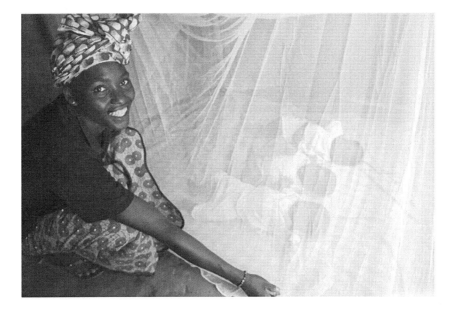

Mosquito nets save lives by preventing being bit by a malarial mosquito ... but many people cannot afford sleeping nets (courtesy Justin Douglass/World Vision).

school director: "Yes, skipping is our favorite sport here." "Skipping?!" "Yes, we find that it is great because it requires no equipment. We cannot afford soccer balls or basketball hoops."

I think that most people in the West assume that you play soccer with a proper soccer ball. In most parts of the developing world, kids play in their bare feet with a ball of rags which they have tied together on fairly hard, packed earth—dirt lot sports. I could see my obliviousness ... that I assumed people have shoes, balls and a manicured soccer field.

While people in the Western jet set have traveled to many countries, those who have far less money are lucky to be able to afford bus fare within their own country. The Cameroonian social worker we work with, based in the capital, Yaounde, had never been to the beautiful coastal town of Limbe. From Yaounde, it is a two-hour bus ride to Douala, then an hour shared taxi ride to the coast. Now admittedly, she does find a way to get home to her home village near Bamenda. But I suspect she either has other priorities like family or she does not have the money for bus fare and shared taxi to be traipsing around to places like Limbe.

The home-stay mom at NGOabroad's social work program in Dar es Salaam had never been to Zanzibar. To get to Zanzibar from Dar, you go down to the waterfront and catch the ferry boat. Looking back, I suspect that she cannot afford it either. Looking back, if I could do it again, I would have asked her if she wanted to come to Zanzibar with me.

In contrast, the world's wealthy people buzz all over the world.

It is now not uncommon for a student to go several places in a year. When I am returning an email or phone call to set up international career counseling or an international placement, people will pop me an email which says, "I am on 'alternative spring break' in the Dominican Republic but I want to go to Jordan in the summer." Or a student sent an email in December which said, "I will get back to you after I get home from Morocco." Or the teacher couple said, "We are just getting back from Costa Rica for spring break but we would like to go somewhere longer this summer."

This kind of dizzying jet-setting stands in sharp contrast to how others live. On the NGOabroad questionnaire I ask what countries someone has been to so I know what they have seen or experienced

"Sand lot" soccer in Brazil.

of other countries, what frame of reference they may have. (I also ask what experience people have of poverty and of other cultures— because you don't need to go to other countries to gain this valuable experience.) Many have a long list of countries to which they have been. Most people coming from the half of humanity that live on less than $8/day are lucky to have been on the bus to a neighboring country. There are many people in the United States or Canada who have travelled very little as well, who may not even have seen other parts of their own state or city.

This disparity in opportunity and privileges can lead to a lot of envy and potential ill will.

I think that most people coming from countries where people earn more than $32/day (one of Hans Rosling's "levels") cannot even guess what a person who earns less than $2/day will feel when they see your iPad, iPod and smartphone. How does that garment worker in Bangladesh who has worked 57-hour weeks and 100 hours overtime per month and earned $60/month feel when you or I land in her life with all our expensive electronic equipment? The cost of your smart phone is more than she earned all year. Over time, we can learn more about how we can change this enormous power and privilege disparity. The first step is not being so oblivious and being more aware of how others might feel.

As Peggy McIntosh says, "I have come to see white privilege as an invisible package of unearned assets that I can count on cashing in each day, but about which I was 'meant' to remain oblivious."[5]

What We Take for Granted

Often, we take our advantages and opportunities for granted.

Not everyone reading this book comes from privilege. But relative to the rest of the world, people of the West are privileged. Doors have opened for us so automatically that we expect them to always open. All too often a receptionist will tell a poor person in a cold voice that the doctor or the director is in but cannot see them, after the poor person has spent most of the day walking across town to knock on that door. For half of the world, they are more accustomed to doors and opportunities being slammed in their face.

One aspect of privilege is expecting to be attended to or waited on; not to be kept waiting. One Kenyan director exhorted me: "Please ask volunteers to be more patient!" Our self-important hurriedness can come across as arrogant. Project deadlines and planes to catch may seem irrelevant to people in-country. Dr. Adams's wanting to quickly forge forward with the TB project was what thwarted all progress. Adams humbly acknowledges that she has learned to slow down.

Obliviousness, an attitude of "It isn't my problem," is what Peggy McIntosh saw at the core of male privilege and at the core of white privilege. I believe it lies at the heart of what the privileged must awaken to and take ownership of, rather than denying; a shift from "It's not my problem—we don't care, we don't have to"—to taking responsibility to see that things change.

Privilege, inequities and the dismissive attitude that "it is not my problem" incenses or enrages people. Shelly Tochluk, who for years was a counselor and educator in California public schools and now is an education professor at Mount Saint Mary's University and author of *Witnessing Whiteness: The Need to Talk About Race and How to Do It*, elaborates, "We cannot recognize that economic and social benefits often come with our whiteness. We remain blind to the myriad ways that whiteness opens doors. ... Expectations of respect, attention, and courteous service from all people we encounter are experienced as normal. Then as we remain unconscious of the ways we receive unearned benefits, we act in ways that are thoroughly infuriating to people of color in our surroundings."[6] Take out the word "white" and insert "North American" or "privileged" and you see how this comment can easily be extrapolated to an international setting.

In the chapter on participatory development, we discussed not taking charge and dominating the conversation; these ideas are pertinent here. As the powerful and privileged, we are often unaware of our tendency to take over the direction of conversations. Often, we do not dedicate the time to listen, to learn and to gain the skills for success within another community. We are often unconscious of how people in Asia, Africa or Latin America read this lack of humility as enactments of privilege and racism. These were many of the behaviors of dominance or privilege that initially derailed Dr. Adams' project.

Increasing Awareness

How do we change the attitudes and actions that impact others? The first step is consciousness-raising—*conscientização*, as Paulo Freire called it: recognizing our role in the world around us, and changing things both little and large, or awakening, as my colleagues in Sri Lanka would call it.

Consciousness-raising happens over years and years. It takes time not because we are shirking or shrinking from the challenge, but because there is so much to learn. Those that I know who are actively engaged in groups and discussions about racism and white privilege all acknowledge that they will make mistakes; there will be gaffes. But the important thing to offer is an openness to learning when someone of color or from the less privileged parts of the world points something out to you. Be open rather than defensive, and thank them, because it is in these small moments that you learn so much.

Many in this movement that is examining privilege would say that we have been avoiding the very difficult dialogue that needs to take place. The anti-racism movement or the white privilege movement that is alive today provides an important model: people reading books together and discussing in groups how they can change is the kind of template we need to apply to shifting our attitudes and behaviors in international interactions.

The first step is learning lots and listening closely to other points of view. It is *sensitization*, as they would call it in East Africa. It is being open to learning ever more in discussions with people from other cultures, countries and ethnic groups. It is a question of continually learning, of listening especially to people who have been ignored or pushed aside or rushed past in our ever-so-busy, self-important ways. It is reflecting on how you have thought or perceived things—your attitudes and how you have interacted.

You become a more effective international worker as you learn from your mistakes.

Once you are aware of the deleterious impact of something you say or do, it is your responsibility to amend your behavior. For Dr. Adams, the unraveling of the TB project in Tanzania, and everything that she learned subsequently, transformed her and dramatically changed how she does global health. We are all humbly a work in progress, continually changing our thoughts, words and deeds.

There are many small ways that you can become more sensitive cross-culturally. Be mindful that most vendors, such as the shoe shine kid in Bolivia, may be supporting a whole family of eight. I am becoming more sensitive to not brushing past people in my oh-so-busy self-important gringo way. To not be so dismissive of other's needs is an important first step for me, and I suspect for many others.

A friend of mine is not only an incredible social worker but a model in this. When she is in other countries, she is very deliberate about how she buys her lunch at the market in Morocco, for example. She buys fruit from one vendor, nuts from another, juice from another. Her goal is to spread the wealth.

I have a colleague who is especially cognizant that in other countries people might be hungry. She has opined, "There is nothing so rude as to eat in front of hungry people." If she is on a long bus ride in some place like Cambodia or Botswana or Guatemala or Moldavia, if the bus stops for a bathroom and snack break, she will always buy food to share with everyone on the bus—something like a bag of peanuts that can be passed from one passenger to another. This small act of kindness reflects the beginning of awakening to the reality that most people who are poor are often hungry. This is a small but significant way that you can be more conscious and not so oblivious.

Who gorges and who is ravenously hungry epitomizes the inequity where the serfs toil and starve while the royalty or elite eat gluttonously at their feasts.

This whole issue of what we eat reflects the disparities. I had an NGOabroad intern email me from Uganda complaining about the breakfast served at the home stay. "We only get tea, toast and some fruit." That is like complaining that you were only served tortillas and beans in Mexico. I responded: "One of the reasons that we encourage a home stay is so that you can see how people live in other countries. Most Africans eat much more simply. They cannot afford a typical North American breakfast of eggs, hash browns, toast and bacon with orange juice and coffee." This is the kind of situation that I hope awakened her to the disparities.

When I help people get ready to go to their international

placements I get questions about food. Often, someone will say, "Is it ok that I am vegan?" "Sure, because it likely means more food for your host and their family. But just be aware in places where people have been or are hungry, they would never turn down some kind of food—that is a totally crazy idea to them!" Thus, I have never ever heard of someone with an eating disorder—either bulimia or anorexia—in the developing world. Rejecting food makes no sense to people who are so concerned about having food. It is also likely that while being a vegetarian is common because it is cheaper, your hosts will not be aware that adding a bit of meat broth or a scoop of butter to a meal would violate a vegan's dietary rules. It would be very odd and probably seen as rude to nit-pick about these details of what's for dinner. Be gracious and thankful, and eat.

Cultural imperialism or cultural humility?

Several of my colleagues in other countries have essentially expressed: "Do not assume or imply that your culture is superior. Don't push it on us."

For example, a colleague in Mongolia explicitly said: "We are a Buddhist nation. Please do not send interns or volunteers who want to proselytize." A prospective volunteer from the UK was considering volunteering in our Nepal program. After our lengthy, hour-long intake, she wrote an afterthought: "I am a new, born-again Christian. It is a very important part of my life. Will this be ok in Nepal?" Hmm, I hadn't fielded that question before but consulted with a Christian colleague in Nepal and responded: "There are a few churches in Kathmandu and Pokhara, more accurately just gatherings of people. Also important to note: Nepal actually has a law against proselytizing." But this question of Christianity cuts both ways. We are also partnered with faith-based organizations that want only Christian volunteers.

For this very reason, I spend lots of time preparing interns who go to our women's programs in various countries. I remind these interns: "It is important to not be dogmatic or too zealous, as then you won't be listening as well." I am especially aware of how fiery feminists interning in Jordan or Morocco placements may not have a solid understanding of the variety of Muslim worldviews, beliefs or perspectives. Arriving with your own deeply held beliefs and agenda is usually a mistake.

The same Mongolian director articulated it clearly to me: "We do not want people who have an agenda."

Stop trying to change us, and instead, change yourselves.

Part of privilege is an arrogant paternalism that implies, "I know what is best for you; I know how you need to change. I will decide the priorities and agenda." Part of the power of the anti-racism and white privilege movement is that it looks at how whites or the privileged or those in power can change in both attitude and behavior. Rather than trying to change others, people are working to change themselves.

Policy makers and politicians in the developing world often push back when the privileged and powerful nations tell other nations how to do things. For example, I remember Gabriel García Márquez, the Colombian author, saying, rather than trying to have the War on Drugs eradicate coca farms in Colombia, change the demand for cocaine in the United States. Rather than telling Brazil to quit cutting the Amazon rainforest to decrease global warming, why doesn't the United States or France (because it was Macron who beseeched Bolsonaro) quit driving so many cars which contribute to global warming?

Over time, I think that social work and international development can contribute to the structural changes which we need to make. Those who are trained in policy, advocacy and macro social work can help design the strategies and structural changes for how people in the richer nations can change to reduce poverty in other parts of the world.

As Peggy McIntosh emphasized, "Disapproving of the systems won't be enough to change them. ... To redesign social systems, we need first to acknowledge their colossal unseen dimensions. The silences and denials surrounding privilege are the key political tool here."[7]

What Can You Do?

1. Don't Be Awakened, Then Hit the Snooze Alarm and Go Back to Sleep

There are many causes that compete for our time and attention. When overwhelmed with the world's woes, we have the luxury to "switch the channel." Privilege affords us the ability to hear something and forget it, to be confronted with inequity and act for a time, but ultimately to take a break if we need to. The combination of privilege, resistance to hearing the pain of others, feigning offence, feeling paralyzed and staying angry are ways we allow the status quo to persist.[8]

2. Redressing Entitlement: Do You Expect to Be Waited On or Do You Pitch In and Help?

One of the most offensive forms of privilege and dominance is expecting to be waited on. This sense of entitlement—the belief that one inherently deserves privileges or special treatment—is what can derail all your overt and well-intended efforts in other countries.

Do you sit back and let the women arise at 5 a.m. to toil in the fields, then fetch the water so you may have your morning meal? Or do you note where the water source is, and fetch the water for the family the next morning? Do you help get the vegetables from the fields and peel and cut vegetables for dinner? Do you expect someone to hand wash and iron your clothes and not pay them? Do you pay them when they present you with unasked-for clean, folded laundry? Do you pay the kid who has been willing to be your guide and escort you back to your home stay or guesthouse when you are lost? Do you see people as whole human beings or as support staff for your life and activities?[9]

I find that most people, myself included, coming in to a new country have all sorts of questions and needs that may be quite important to us but that take up a great deal of time for our host or colleagues in-country. Being a bit needy is understandable, but how you convey and communicate your needs can be either culturally graceful or culturally gauche or imply that we expect to be served.

One woman coming into Sri Lanka wanted a very busy director to run around Colombo to see where she could get some electronic device so that she could be in touch with her family back home. It was asking too much. It had too many overtones of entitlement: that her needs superseded the work that he did to help his own people.

If I were able to do the above situation over again, I would have tried to solve her electronics quandary rather than her asking that of the busy Sri Lankan director. I sometimes recommend to people that they ask someone lower on the chain of command if the director is super-busy. Like everyone else in this process of learning how to reverse a sense of privilege, I am also learning.

I know that I asked many directors or people in other countries to tell me what kind of electrical outlets they have so I could bring adapters. Like the young woman above, I was asking people to help me—I thought that my need to have a laptop to work at and communicate from was oh-so-important—when they might have more pressing things to attend to. I have since discovered this handy chart that lists what kinds of adaptors are needed in various countries. It is great to be a little less needy! This is such helpful information that I will give you the link here: https://www.rei.com/learn/expert-advice/world-electricity-guide.html.

Rather than being waited on, the solution here is to make a daily practice of rolling up your sleeves and asking, "How can I help?"

Ironically, we had another volunteer in Sri Lanka who really wanted to help around the house; she didn't like being waited on. She was doing a home stay in the slums of Colombo. She found that her

Offer to help get the day's firewood (photograph by Quang Nguyen Vinh, Vietnam).

hosts would not let her help or lift a finger. But at least she offered and tried. Cultures vary so dramatically that it is helpful to know some of the cultural norms ahead. Books such as the *Culture Smart* series cover many countries, and *Worldwide Etiquette: A Beginner's Guide to Cultural Norms Around the World,* by Sarah Dunsworth, helps prepare travelers.[10]

Melinda Gates of the Bill and Melinda Gates Foundation recounts in her memoir, *The Moment of Lift: How Empowering Women Changes the World,* how important and illuminating it was for her and her daughter, Jenn, to help with daily chores in Tanzania. They went with their Tanzanian host to chop firewood, using dull machetes on gnarly wood stalks. They walked thirty minutes to fetch water and carried it back in buckets on their heads. Gates realized all this work meant a Tanzanian woman was in motion for seventeen hours a day. Gates humbly acknowledged the number of hours and intensity of the labor was a revelation to her. By participating in that labor she truly felt it in her body.[11]

3. Learning a Little, or Better, a Lot, of the Language Is a Sign of Respect for Another Culture

Though you may find some or a lot of English speakers in Asian countries (especially if they are from a part of the British Commonwealth and are from a former British colony), most have their own language—Lao in Laos, Vietnamese in Vietnam, Khmer in Cambodia, Sinhalese or Tamil in Sri Lanka, et cetera. I encourage people to get a grasp of basic language. For a nurse coming into Sri Lanka, I encouraged her to learn how to say, "How do you feel?" and "Where does it hurt?" in Sinhala. Google Translate makes this easy to learn. It is both pragmatic and culturally sensitive to learn as much of the language as you can. A simple greeting brings smiles, and conveys, "I understand that my language does not dominate the world."

Colleagues in Jordan emphasized to me: "Ann, do not send us anyone who cannot speak fluent Arabic! Otherwise, we have to put down the work that we are doing and go translate for them."

What I have seen recently is a giant surge—a tsunami, actually—in Westerners who are learning Arabic. I totally support that, but my colleagues in Lebanon and Jordan have made it clear that they

have organizations to run and Syrian, Iraqi, Yemeni and Palestin-
ian refugees to serve, and their purpose is not to help Westerners
learn Arabic. The Lebanese, Jordanians and Syrians have implied
that this deluge of Westerners-learning-Arabic feels like entitlement
to them—that Westerners expect people in the Arab world to help
them learn the language. The solution—and this is true of any language—is to work hard to learn Arabic at your university, practice
conversation skills back home or online, and/or take Arabic classes
while in-country.

4. Listen More Than You Speak

As Epictetus said, "We have two ears and one mouth so that we
can listen twice as much as we speak."

Listening is an act of humility; it powerfully conveys that what
someone else has to contribute is important. In contrast, acting and
speaking like the authority is usually viewed as superiority.

Melinda Gates is an important model. Despite her wealth,
Melinda Gates does not seem to act privileged. She is extraordinary
in her whole-hearted listening; in her capacity to "get it." She lis-
tens carefully all over the world to what people need and how they
would pursue a project. Melinda recounts the story of how she and
Bill Gates aimed to reduce HIV and AIDS in India. As outsiders,
they thought that they just needed to urge sex workers to cajole
their male customers to wear condoms. But the sex workers con-
vinced Melinda and Bill that the first issue was reducing violence.
The reality was that when the sex workers would ask a male cus-
tomer to wear a condom, he would beat them. The sex workers also
explained that they would be raped and beaten by the police. So the
sex workers devised a system where if a prostitute was being beaten,
she would alert twelve to fifteen other women and they would come
running and cause a public scene that would shame the offend-
ers into ceasing. Once the concern about violence was addressed,
the sex workers embraced reducing HIV transmission, which was
central to the AIDS strategy and success in India. It is because Bill
and Melinda Gates and their team are so willing to listen that they
could revise their strategy from "we know what is best for you" to
"let us listen to what the obstacles are for you and revise the plan
accordingly."[12]

5. Have the Courage to Reflect on
Your Attitudes and Actions

Because we all make mistakes and may have arrogant attitudes and ways of behaving which we are hardly aware of, it is important to watch yourself. Like Dr. Adams, you can transform a mistake into a breakthrough. Anti-racism and white privilege groups encourage people to make an honest inventory of ourselves. This self-assessment is important because it lays the foundation for behavioral change that can dramatically improve your effectiveness as a culturally sensitive international social or development worker.

For example, if I were to do a thorough self-inventory and improve my cultural sensitivity, I would have to admit that talking-like-an-authority is an area where I need to improve. So what I have begun to do is find models. Who are the people I know who empower others? Who has a refreshing humility? For me, I think Si Kahn is a good model and also a colleague in Morocco. I find that I need to pull back from this Western emphasis on making a point—on content—and, like Dr. Adams did, shift the emphasis from what I say to how I say it. Again realizing the importance of self-examination, I acknowledge that my very direct style probably does not wear well in cultures that are more oblique. And my way of blowing past introductions and niceties is likely seen as brusque and rude in cultures, such as in Africa, that start any encounter with asking about everyone in your family. These are the areas where I need to be mindful.

I think where I am also obnoxiously privileged and possibly condescending is suggesting to people that there is some easy answer which they have not considered. If you recall my conversation with Luke about finding a solution to his wife's malaria, when Luke said, "Yah Ann, I could put my wife and I on a motorcycle taxi and then we could go to the clinic," I had exclaimed, "There is your answer, Luke!" It implied that there was an easy answer that Luke had not thought of; that he had missed something obvious. Coming from this very American, can-do perspective, where things indeed are easier to solve, I thought I was God's gift in seeing some solutions. I do give both Luke and me credit for carrying that conversation further and Luke's laying out the obstacles like a deck of cards. I do give myself credit for listening, but I also think I do a fair amount of proselytizing or preaching or thinking I know something that the developing world does not. I think that I need to do lots more listening and have lots more humility and a lot fewer ready and packaged answers.

6. Be Open to Learning

Dr. Adams transformed her failure to success by her willingness to learn. People I know who are very involved in examining their own white privilege and racism acknowledge that they will make mistakes unwittingly. The important thing is learning from your mistakes. Welcome comments from people from other cultures and countries. Even better: invite feedback. Thank people for their feedback. Though it may be hard to hear at first, feedback is crucial to changing attitudes and actions.

7. Partnership of Equals

What employers are looking for, and more importantly what the local people and communities with whom you will be working are looking for, are those who can work as equal partners.

In summary, so you want to change the world? Great! We need people who are willing to tackle the challenges humanity faces. To change the world, you start with changing yourself.

Conclusion

The goal of this book is to address how most Westerners miss the mark: why they do not get hired, or why they fail to function effectively. My aim was to lay the initial foundation to help you work in international development, because there are few books that address the practical realities of what you *do*—that actually equip you. To summarize this book, three important arenas will make a huge difference in how effective you are in international development work.

1. Poverty

Problem: Most privileged people are clueless about how 80 percent of the world lives. Too Western; haven't gotten your hands dirty.

Solution: Learn about poverty; gain a grasp and understanding of the realities and challenges that the poor in this world deal with every day, what it is like to live on less than $2/day.

"Poverty is a state of relative powerlessness in which people are denied the ability to control crucial aspects of their lives."[1]

Poverty is not just about income and GDP. Equally important is having or not having power and respect, not having choices: "unfreedoms," as Amartya Sen calls them. The interventions and skills in international development are not just about improving quality of life but about empowering people. International development is not just about implementing programs in such areas as literacy, clean water or generating income. It is about nurturing the local people's strengths and confidence. Like a gardener or a parent, you plough, plant, weed, water and nurture to assist with a transformation: from people feeling powerless or actually being disenfranchised into people learning to have a voice; to articulate their needs, concerns and priorities; to untangle and solve personal or community problems and challenges; to exert their choice; to develop their power. As people realized in the community organizing example in Puerto Rico, "We build The People's Forest and it builds us."

2. Skills

Problem: People are graduating in international social work and international development, in global studies and international relations, without the skills needed in international development.

Solution: Build the tangible skills which are needed out in the field:

- Needs and strengths assessment, following through to program development
- Capacity building
- Having a "partner to the poor" approach and using participatory development
- Community organizing
- Advocacy—how to engage the public and impact policy.

3. Attitude

Problem: A patronizing or paternalistic attitude can negate all your well-intended work.

Solution: As important as *what* you do is *how* you do it. You must cultivate the right attitude as well.

* * *

What makes international development so exciting is that it requires a lifetime of learning. This book is meant to lay the foundation.

I saw a yawning gap, a real need for this book. I read voraciously about all things related to international development. Excepting the incredible books published by Practical Action and Oxfam in the UK—few of which make it across the ocean to North America—there are few if any books that tell you what to do and how to do it. My goal was and is to equip you for international development work.

Alas, a book is two-dimensional; it is difficult to write for all 7.8 billion people. Because of my roots in psychotherapy and direct service, I believe in a more personalized approach. The real value of the chapters on your perspective on poverty, on skills and attitude, comes as your breathe life into them, as you practice them.

Often, I talk to people who have taken the classes or completed the university courses—those provide great foundation—but haven't put in enough elbow grease yet. They are missing what Angela Duckworth calls "grit": not just the passion but the perseverance to truly learn a skill. As I say on my website, getting into international development is usually not a leap but a climb. Employers need people who have built the necessary skills, because the work can be very challenging. From what I have seen over many years, some job seekers are passive and expect that the job and the work will be handed to them; that they can pluck them off a shelf or buy them like a pair of shoes. I see many, many people who go in circles on the web, searching, searching, and searching. Often, my best advice is this: go get your hands dirty.

I had an interesting conversation with a man who did not grasp what I was saying when I told him, "The format of your résumé is great ... you have done a great job presenting what you have, but it is missing the essential content." He and his résumé were missing substance: skills and experience. He thought it was all about connecting on LinkedIn. I have written this book so it will make more sense if I say, "You are missing some of what is essential." This book's aim is to explain what is essential and where some people miss the mark.

The people about whom I can say "This person is going to get hired" are more active in their learning and extraordinary in how they connect to people. They are bridge builders and have an attitude of equality, like the Canadian nurse I showcased in the chapter on capacity building. The people who get hired are gems. The people in their community, in their neighborhood and in their workplace would all agree: "There's a gem." I have met high school students who are clearly gems. I mentioned earlier the high school student who was resettling Congolese and Syrian refugees in Pennsylvania and the high school student who worked with the homeless in the Tenderloin district of San Francisco. Both had a strong sense of service;

they would roll up their sleeves and say, "How can I help?" Both were building valuable skills and had the attitude which would get them hired. I am eager to see what they are going to do with their lives. I will say that an extraordinary ability to connect to people implies that you are an extrovert. I will also say that there is a way for everyone to contribute: one introvert wrote to me after she got a job in international development and thanked me for helping her find her niche ... not in the noisy limelight.

Thus, if you find yourself stumbling or feeling a bit adrift in a very big world—if you feel the learning curve is much too steep—if you would like coaching, training or consultations to hone and apply these skills and devise more individualized steps and strategies for how you enter international social work or international development, then see the NGOabroad website to consider setting up an appointment.

My mission is to help you become a potent change agent. When I did my "global needs assessment" at the outset of my shift into international development, I was overwhelmed by the many challenges humanity faces. Then I had this revelation—one of those moments when a light went on in my head—that has shaped what I want my contribution to be. I realized, "But ah-ha, there are so many people in the world who want to make a difference and who want to change the world for the better. If we can harness the talent and commitment of all those people to tackling the challenges, then we can make a difference." I deeply believe in both individual and collective people power.

I write this in 2020 and 2021 as the whole world is in lockdown, held hostage by COVID-19, the novel coronavirus SARS-CoV-2. The challenges are more immense and seemingly insurmountable compared to when I did that "global needs assessment" years ago. We can no longer dally or dither. This is a time which calls for action. Circumstance is forcing us to resolve problems which face humanity. I am proud of you for stepping up to the plate and offering to help in whatever way you can. May this book provide a foundation and equip you to mobilize that people power and transform this world.

Appendix: Discussion and Skills Development Guide for Classroom Use

Chapter 1: Why Social Work Is So Valued in International Development

1. Which of the social work skills listed in this chapter do you have a solid grasp of?
2. Which skills do you need to develop or improve so that you are more employable internationally?
3. How might you gain those skills? What is your plan of action?
4. Who might you talk to or approach to create the opportunity to get practice to develop or learn a skill?
5. Compare notes with your classmates or colleagues. If there is a common skill deficit, you might go to a workshop together … or ask a professor to address it … or ask your practicum supervisor if you can include practice in a certain skill in the work which you are doing.

Chapter 2: Know Poverty? How Does Half the World Live?

1. Is poverty something you have been exposed to or experienced?
2. How exposed to or experienced are you regarding poverty in your home or college community?
3. What do you know about how people live in other parts of the world?

4. How have you learned or lived this? What have been your moments of awakening?
5. "Poverty is a state of relative powerlessness in which people are denied the ability to control crucial aspects of their lives." Are there any aspects of your own life where you experience powerlessness to control crucial aspects of your life? Discuss this in small groups, then as a class.
6. What news sources, media or resources of any kind have been helpful in your learning about and more deeply understanding how half the world lives? Do some exploring and come to class to share your discoveries, realizations and "finds."
7. Watch Hans Rosling's TED talks. Come to class to discuss what was most illuminating: https://www.ted.com/talks/hans_rosling_new_insights_on_poverty.
8. Read Binyavanga Wainaina's essay "How to Write About Africa" and discuss in class:
   • What stereotypes do we/you hold? And what aspects about poverty are important to understand?
   • That is, how can you circumvent the stereotypes to understand how people live?

Chapter 3: Needs and Strengths Assessment to Program Development

1. Keep a journal of what questions or problems—what needs— you are facing in your practicum and how you would tackle those problems—your strategies. Thus, you get practice in identifying needs and crafting solutions on a frequent basis.
2. What would you say are the five to seven most pressing needs...
   • at your college or university?
   • in the town where you are going to college?
   • in the home community where you are from?
3. What is the consensus in your class on the needs of your community?
   • Does your list of needs agree or disagree with those of your colleagues? In what way?

- To what do you ascribe the disagreement or agreement about needs assessment?
4. How did you determine those needs?
   - Who is the community or what resources would you consult to determine community needs?
5. Now take it to the next step: How would you tackle those needs or problems? What groups would you gather? What interventions or actions would you undertake? What programs would you design?
6. Likewise, compare and contrast your solutions to those of your classmates or colleagues.
7. What have you learned about yourself ... about how you see problems and how you craft solutions? What are your filters, and what is your perspective?
8. Read *The Moment of Lift* by Melinda Gates.
   - How does Melinda Gates gather information and insights about needs in other countries? That is, how does she do a needs assessment?
   - What does she see as the primary needs in other countries?
   - Discuss her case example of how the Gates Foundation revised its AIDS strategy in India, after it had extensive discussions with the sex workers.

Chapter 4: Capacity Building: Creating Collaborators, Not Passive Recipients

1. Because capacity building has many strong resemblances to life coaching or mentoring, do a brief online review of life coaching or mentoring skills.
2. Do you have any experience as a mentor? What did you learn from this?
   - How can you further hone your skills as a mentor?
3. Exercise for class: What are the skills that you want to develop? That is, what strengths or capacities do you want to develop within yourself?
4. Pick someone in class with whom to pair—someone who you feel can help you develop that capacity—your mentor. Discuss with your mentor what your challenge is with this

skill—but also what your strengths are—what you have to build upon already. Practice a "session" where the mentor helps you develop a skill. At the end, critique how effective their "capacity building" was and how they might improve.

Chapter 5: Capacity Building: Other Steps to Empowerment

1. What do you know about financial literacy?
   What could you teach to others? Can you balance a budget? How do you keep track of income and expenses? Can you make a simple cash-flow chart? Do you know how to make and use an Excel spreadsheet? Are you competent with QuickBooks? Excel and QuickBooks are very useful, but they require a computer and programs. Pencil and paper can enable simple bookkeeping that is tremendously helpful.
2. How would you teach critical thinking to others?
3. What creative skills do you have? Musical, crafts, arts, fix-it? How would you teach creative thinking to others?

Chapter 6: Partner to the Poor and Participatory Development

1. What experiences have you had participating in a group? A choir, band, musical or theater production? … A sports team? … A school group or sorority or fraternity? … A religious or political group?
   What role do you often play? Do you prefer to be in the background but help get things done, or do you prefer to take a leadership role? Do you feel comfortable working in a group, or do you grow impatient with "group process"? What ways have you found to streamline "group process"?
2. First find a situation where you can *observe* community members stating their needs, rights or complaints—this may be at a city council hearing, a PTSA group, university students confronting or discussing something with the dean or the president, or a protest or gathering in your local community.

As you observe, reflect on how the group is presenting its concerns; and more importantly, how comfortable or uncomfortable you feel with the process.

3. Because participatory development really requires consummate group skills, if possible, find a place in your local community which offers trainings in running groups.

4. Ask your supervisor or practicum instructor if you can first observe then get practice in group work or leading a group activity.
    - Build your skill in including every member and allowing everyone to speak.
    - Watch whether you are often in command or are able to facilitate group members taking the reins.

5. If you have not heard Paul Farmer speak, watch him on YouTube.

6. What do you think about partnership among equals? How skilled are you in building solidarity, or using this approach?

7. If so moved, read more of Gandhi, the Liberation Theologians, Paul Farmer, Paolo Freire, Robert Chambers, Kamla Bhasin and Amartya Sen.

Chapter 7: Community Organizing: Having a Voice

1. In your own community—whether where you grew up or where you are going to school—what issues are people sick and tired of being sick and tired about? What issues are people rallying around?

2. How do you assess power structures in your own community? Who are the decision makers who adversely impact the poor or disenfranchised? How and why do you think the powerful are invested in keeping the status quo?

3. What strategies and tactics would you design to address the above concerns and power inequities?

4. What coalitions or "bridges" could be built to address the issues most important to you?

Chapter 8: Advocacy: Impacting Policies Which Create Poverty

1. How did structural adjustment programs evolve?
2. Why do people turn out in the streets to protest austerity or belt-tightening measures?
3. Who decides the terms of a structural adjustment loan? Why are the people who will be impacted by structural adjustments left out of the decision-making process?
4. What advocacy movement attempted to relieve the debts of Heavily Indebted Poor Countries?
5. Who were the key figures advocating for a change in policy?
6. Did canceling debts "make poverty history"?
7. What other policies or national or international measures might we consider to impact poverty in other countries? And to develop your skills in this, what would you do? Who would you write to? Or what decision-makers would you approach?

Chapter 9: Attitude Is Everything

1. Which points of this chapter struck you the most? Discuss in class.
2. Highly recommended: watch Dr. Lisa Adams's TEDx talk: https://www.youtube.com/watch?v=_NUEepj06pc.
3. Are there any resources or groups at your school of social work, at your college or in your community which examine racism or white privilege? Are there international students' groups at your college, or restaurants or organizations in your community, that could teach you about the realities in other cultures?
4. Do a searching self-inventory: what attitudes or behaviors do you have or display that you think will negatively impact your work in international social work? What gaffes do you regret?
5. What have been your moments of awakening? In what ways

have you, like Dr. Lisa Adams, turned a failure—erroneous assumptions, a misplaced attitude or action—into the foundation for a new way of seeing or doing things?

6. Who have been your most important teachers, mentors and models about privilege or the realities in other parts of the world? What friends, religious leaders or people have taught you the most?

7. What adversities have you personally overcome, and how have they shaped you? How has this galvanized your conviction to make a difference and contribute to the world?

Acknowledgments

Life is made rich by the people in it.

This book has been shaped by the people who had questions, who felt lost or clueless about how to jump into international development work and snag a job: e.g., the young man in Oklahoma who wanted to work in the MENA region; the "older" social work student in Missouri who did a mission trip in Haiti; the young woman from Sudan studying in the United States; the nurse from Alberta, Canada. Let me respect confidentiality, but this book has been inspired by and is for people such as these, the change-makers in the making.

This book is made rich by the people who have shaped my thinking. First and foremost, the countless and nameless people all over the globe who taught me about the world, how they live and what they need or want: the taxi driver in South Africa; the Maryknoll priest in Guatemala; the science teacher and the nurse in Kerala, India; one of the original staff at Capilano University in Vancouver, Canada who teased, "Yeah, I am going to come down and teach Americans manners!" I have many colleagues doing extraordinary work with whom I work all over the world, but it is conversations with certain people that really opened my eyes: Viswanathan, Beena George, Sandra Ross, Regina Nyamure, Florence Namusisi, Charles Maina Kariuki, Juan Carlos Monge, Felipe Patricio, Gloria Pinedo Bravo, and Erdengargal.

I wanted photos that show you, the reader, how half the world lives. I thank Charles Nambasi Waniala of Mbale, Uganda, for his photos of fetching water; Quang Nguyen Vinh and Thang Phan for their photos of Vietnam; and David Zimmerly for his photo of the Guatemalan woman. I am indebted to Dr. Md Zohirul Alam, who provided the photo from the Public Health Photo Contest by Subrata Dey of Bangladesh's coastal areas and the photo of Dr. Zafrullah Chowdhury training village outreach paraprofessionals from the Gonoshasthaya Kendra Archive. Additionally, I am grateful to nameless photographers on the Pixabay site who captured scenes from daily life.

Everyone should be blessed with a cheerleader and champion, the person who either encourages you through the hard times or carries you on their shoulders. Leslie McGee has been that person: she has read every page, revised my gaffes and glitches, and enriched my thinking. Likewise, Mary Ellen Walker, our "walking encyclopedia," has been invaluable for the multitude of international questions and concerns she sorts through with me daily.

While writing itself is a solitary sport, it takes a village to create a book. Many people in my inner circle read and commented: Davis Patterson, Jody Padgham and Joe Meeker in the first iteration of this book series. Maggie Lewis, Syd Jacobs, Barbara Dennard, Janet Staub, Nancy Afman, Maridee Bonadea, Alejandro Aguilera-Titus, and Christine McLaughlin all tugged my thinking. Others offered more technical help which made this book possible: Jay Borseth, Kim Johnson, Ofer Gneezy, Steve Schlossman, David Lubar, Bob Huppe, Dan Chasan, Si Kahn, Christopher Forrest, Lao Kiriazis, Kate Monthy, Susan T. Beer and Ann Strandoo.

I have told my local library that if we could choose where our tax dollars go, I would allocate my share to the many libraries which made this book possible. Becky Norman tracked down wheelbarrow loads of the more obscure books for me.

I thank the people on whose shoulders I stand: Robert Chambers, Deepa Narayan, Kamla Bhasin, Amartya Sen and Duncan Green—pioneers in international development. I carry the torch and follow the tradition which social work professors bequeathed to me: Jerry Kelly, Henry Maier and Lenora Mundt especially taught me *how* you do social work. This is why I think we need more *how*-to-do-it books in international social work and international development. I still remember my panic wondering *how* you conduct a counseling session. I had the pieces and some experience, but it was Lenora Mundt who kindly explained, "First ask them if you can take their coat...." I humbly acknowledge that, like me, most people need such simple instructions in their beginning steps.

Then there are the people in academic and professional circles who gave generously of their time … when, really, they did not have any to spare: Cathryne L. Schmitz at the University of North Carolina Greensboro; Manohar Pawar at Charles Sturt University, Australia; Brij Mohan at Louisiana State University; Lucy Jarosz at the University of Washington; Bill Richardson at University of Washington, Tacoma; John Lear at the University of Puget Sound; David Olson at University of Minnesota; Lori Bannai at Seattle University; Shelly Tochluk at Mount Saint Mary's University; Lisa V. Adams at Dartmouth; Olivia Scott Kamkwamba, Ann Pettifor, and Alexis Massol González.

This book started with stuttering and stammering, just a glimmer of what I wanted to say, what I felt people need to learn, and how to answer the many questions which come to me. It is a process to find your own voice. Thanks to McFarland and Co., which believed in the merit of this very practical book. It has been a pleasure to work with them, especially Susan Kilby.

I also want to acknowledge that this book captures what I know and think at this time. I am always listening and learning. If I am worth my salt, my thinking and understanding will evolve further.

My deepest gratitude goes to the many people who helped birth this book.

Chapter Notes

Introduction

1. Emily Fishbein, "'Stuck': Hope Fades for Refugees in Malaysia as US Closes Door," *Al Jazeera*, March 9, 2020.

2. "11 Facts About Global Poverty," DoSomething.org, https://www.dosomething.org/us/facts/11-facts-about-global-poverty.

3. "Mexico Violence: Why Were Two Butterfly Activists Found Dead?" *BBC*, February 14, 2020.

4. "Deadliest Year on Record for Land and Environmental Defenders, as Agribusiness Is Shown to Be the Industry Most Linked to Killings," Global Witness, https://www.globalwitness.org/en/press-releases/deadliest-year-record-land-and-environmental-defenders-agribusiness-shown-be-industry-most-linked-killings/.

5. Amartya Sen, *Development as Freedom*, 2nd ed. (Oxford and New York: Oxford University Press, 2001).

Chapter 2

1. Rosling, Rosling and Ronnlund, *Factfulness*, 27.

2. Net Impact, https://www.netimpact.org/blog/category/poverty.

3. Rosling, Rosling and Ronnlund, 6.

4. United Nations Department of Economic and Social Affairs, *The Inequality Predicament: UN Report on the World Social Situation 2005* (New York: United Nations, 2006).

5. Rosling, Rosling and Ronnlund, 52.

6. O'Brian, Hugh, "Hans Rosling: unveiling the beauty of statistics for a fact-based world view," *Perini Journal*, http://www.perinijournal.it/Items/en-US/Articoli/PJL-33/Hans-Rosling-unveiling-the-beauty-of-statistics-for-a-factbased-world-view.

7. Narayan, Lant and Kapoor, *Moving Out of Poverty*, 63–4.

8. Rosling, Rosling and Ronnlund, 27–30.

9. *Ibid.*, 60–3.

10. *Ibid.*, 111.

11. World Health Organization, "Malaria Fact Sheet 94," 2007.

12. Buechner, Maryanne, "How to Save 1.5 Million Lives a Year? Vaccinate the World's Children!" UNICEFUSA, February 14, 2017. https://www.unicefusa.org/stories/how-save-15-million-lives-year-vaccinate-worlds-children/31793.

13. Beall and Fox, "Urban Poverty and Development."

14. UNAIDS (Joint United Nations Programme on HIV/AIDS) Fact Sheet, 2017. https://www.unaids.org/en/resources/fact-sheet.

15. Chopp, *The Praxis of Suffering*, 74.

16. Sen, *Development as Freedom*, 20.

17. Oxford Poverty and Human Development Initiative, https://ophi.org.uk.

18. Stackhouse, 181.

19. Stackhouse, 150.

20. Green, *From Poverty to Power*, 8.

21. Green, 152.

22. Bonnet, Florence, Joann Vanek and Martha Chen. 2019. *Women and Men in the Informal Economy: A Statistical Brief*. Manchester, UK: WIEGO, 2019.

23. Green, 152.

24. Yang, *Calamity and Reform*, 34.

25. Narayan, Chambers, Shah and Petesch, *Voices of the Poor*, 46.

26. Wainaina, "How to Write About Africa."

27. *Ibid.*

28. Beall and Fox, 104.

29. Rosling, Rosling and Ronnlund, 34. Gapminder, Rosling's organization, encourages the use and spread of their information. They simply ask this citation: Free to use! CC (Creative Commons) by Gapminder.org.

30. Rosling, Rosling and Ronnlund, 35. Free to use! CC (Creative Commons) by Gapminder.org.

31. ILO (International Labor Organization), "Global Employment Trends 2007." https://www.ilo.org/wcmsp5/groups/public/---ed_emp/---emp_elm/---trends/documents/publication/wcms_114295.pdf.

Chapter 3

1. Carolina Sherwood Bigelow, "10 Little Known Facts About Poverty in Sierra Leone," The Borgen Project, July 15, 2018, https://borgenproject.org/tag/poverty-rate-in-sierra-leone/.

2. Aaron Stein, "10 Extremely Important Facts About Poverty in Rwanda," The Borgen Project, May 9, 2018, https://borgenproject.org/10-facts-about-poverty-in-rwanda/.

3. CDC, "2014–2016 Ebola Outbreak in West Africa," March 8, 2019, https://www.cdc.gov/vhf/ebola/history/2014-2016-outbreak/index.html.

4. Lisa O'Carroll, "Ebola 'leaves 12,000 orphans in Sierra Leone,'" *The Guardian*, March 4, 2015, https://www.theguardian.com/global-development/2015/mar/04/ebola-leaves-12000-orphans-sierra-leone.

5. Maier, *Three Theories of Child Development*, 1–292.

6. Bobby Wine, https://www.youtube.com/watch?v=00_KdOFIKtM and https://www.youtube.com/watch?v=HUF23GzojE8.

7. Elias Biryabarema, "Eight-Year-Old Rapper Strikes Chord in Uganda with Songs About Poverty,"

Reuters, February 5, 2020, https://www.reuters.com/article/us-uganda-music/eight-year-old-rapper-strikes-chord-in-uganda-with-songs-about-poverty-idUSKBN1ZZ1AN.

8. D. Reeler, "A Theory of Social Change and Implications for Practice, Planning, and Monitoring and Evaluation" (Cape Town: Community Development Resource Association, n.d.). http://www.managingforimpact.org/sites/default/files/resource/a_theory_of_social_change_and_implications.pdf.

Chapter 4

1. Eade, *Capacity-Building*, 14.

2. Eade and Williams, *Oxfam Handbook*, 9.

3. "FAO Capacity Development," FAO, http://www.fao.org/capacity-development/our-vision/en/.

4. Keim, *Mistaking Africa*, 37.

5. "Trevor Noah—Great Britain Not So Great," YouTube, August 4, 2015, https://www.youtube.com/watch?v=ADQCeC0tF0o.

6. Chambers, *Whose Reality Counts?* 7.

7. Bandler and Grinder, *Frogs into Princes*, 15; Bandler, *Richard Bandler's Guide*, 4.

8. Sara Miller Llana, "Chile Earthquake: President Bachelet Opens Up to Foreign Aid," *Christian Science Monitor*, March 1, 2010.

9. Tim Wyatt, "RAF Chinooks Recalled from Nepal Quake Effort Without Flying a Mission," *The Guardian*, May 15, 2015.

10. John Solomon and Spencer Hsu, "U.S. Didn't Accept Most Foreign Katrina Aid," *NBC News*, April 28, 2007.

11. Deborah Doane, "'The Indian Government Has Shut the Door on NGOs,'" *The Guardian*, September 7, 2016.

12. Pamela Abbotta, Roger Sapsforda, and Agnes Binagwaho, "Learning from Success: How Rwanda Achieved the Millennium Development Goals for Health," *World Development* 92 (April 2017): 103–116; Agnes Binagwaho et al., "Rwanda 20 Years On:

Investing in Life," *The Lancet*, April 3, 2014; Andrew Makaka, Sarah Breen, and Agnes Binagwaho, "Universal Health Coverage in Rwanda: A Report of Innovations to Increase Enrolment in Community-Based Health Insurance," *The Lancet*, October 21, 2012.

13. Kidder, *Mountains Beyond Mountains*, 16.

14. University of Global Health Equity, https://ughe.org/.

Chapter 5

1. Novogratz, *The Blue Sweater*, 61.

2. African School of Economics, https://africanschoolofeconomics. com/, https://africanschoolofeconomics. com/about-us/.

3. "Increasing Debt in Many African Countries Is a Cause for Worry," *The Economist*, March 8, 2018.

4. John Kuada, "Entrepreneurship as a Solution to Youth Unemployment in Ghana," in *Laboring and Learning*, ed. Tracey Skelton, Tatek Abebe, and Johanna Waters, *Geographies of Children and Young People*, vol. 10 (Singapore: Springer, 2017), 433–451.

5. Novogratz, 210.

6. Bloom, Engelhart, Furst, et al., *Taxonomy of Educational Objectives*, 38.

7. Ontario Ministry of Education, *The Ontario Curriculum Grades 9 to 12: Social Sciences and Humanities* (Queen's Printer for Ontario, 2013), 46, http:// www.edu.gov.on.ca/eng/curriculum/ secondary/ssciences9to122013.pdf, accessed January 29, 2019.

8. Kamkwamba, *The Boy Who Harnessed the Wind*, 1–293; Netflix, *The Boy Who Harnessed the Wind*, https://www. netflix.com/title/80200047.

9. Stackhouse, 97.

10. Noah, *Born a Crime*, 192.

11. *Ibid.*, 217.

12. Cavaye, *Capable Communities*, 112.

13. Lyn Simpson, Leanne Wood, and Leonie Daws, "Community Capacity Building: Starting with People not Projects," *Community Development Journal* 38, No. 4 (October 1, 2003): 277–286.

Chapter 6

1. Sen, 53.

2. Chris Beyer, "The Humanitarian Impulse," *The Lancet*, September 11, 2010.

3. *Ibid.*

4. Paul Farmer, "Pragmatic Solidarity," Center for Compassion and Global Health.

5. Kidder, 61–62.

6. Farmer, *Pathologies of Power*, 227.

7. *Ibid.*, 141.

8. *Ibid.*, 224.

9. *Ibid.*, 226.

10. Boff and Clodovis, *Introducing Liberation Theology*, 3.

11. Howson, *A Just Church*, 11.

12. Berryman, *Liberation Theology*, 5.

13. Mackin, "Liberation Theology/ Base Communities (South America)," 333-351.

14. Boff and Clodovis, 5.

15. "About Tikkun," Tikkun, https:// www.tikkun.org/about-tikkun.

16. Nicholas Linn and Emily Crane Linn, "Egypt's War on Charity: Egypt's Faith-Based Charities Have Become Victims of the Government Crackdown on Political Islam," *Foreign Policy*, January 29, 2015.

17. Department of Census and Statistics, Sri Lanka. http://www.statistics.gov. lk/pophousat/pdf/Population/p9p9%20 Religion.pdf.

18. Sagarika Ghose, "The Dalit in India," *Social Research: An International Quarterly* (Johns Hopkins University Press) 70, no. 1 (Spring 2003): 83–109.

19. Collins and Lapierre, *Freedom at Midnight*, 182.

20. Gandhi, *Autobiography*, title page.

21. Gandhi, *The Essential Gandhi*, 246–264.

22. Ben-Meir, "Participatory Development and Its Emergence," 59.

23. Powers and Allaman, "Participatory Action Research"; Mansuri and Rao, "Localizing Development," 2–13. https://openknowledge.worldbank. org/bitstream/handle/10986/11859/ 9780821382561.pdf?sequence=1&is Allowed=y.

24. Hampshire, Hills, and Iqbal, "Power Relations," 340–1.

25. Cary, 144.
26. K. Botchway, "Paradox of Empowerment: Reflections on a Case Study from Northern Ghana," *World Development* 29, no. 1 (2000): 136.
27. Ben-Meir, 181.
28. Bhasin, "Participatory Training," 29.
29. Chambers, *Whose Reality Counts*, 103.
30. Bhasin, 37.
31. Bhasin, 39.
32. Bhasin, 25.
33. Freire, *Education for Critical Consciousness*, 60.
34. Chambers, *Can We Know Better*, 135.
35. Goldbard, *New Creative Community*, 44.
36. Uphoff, Esman, and Krishna, *Reasons for Success*, 192.
37. Isham, Narayan, and Pritcheet, "Does Participation Improve Performance?," 87.

Chapter 7

1. Casa Pueblo website: http://casapueblo.org/.
2. Danica Coto, "After hurricane, Puerto Rico Switches on to Renewable Energy," *Christian Science Monitor*, July 26, 2018.
3. Kahn, *How People Get Power*, 47.
4. "Civil Rights Martyrs," Southern Poverty Law Center, https://www.splcenter.org/what-we-do/civil-rights-memorial/civil-rights-martyrs.
5. Arthur Neslen, "4 Environmental Activists Are Killed Every Week So We Can Have Snacks, Meat and Coffee," *The Huffington Post*, July 24, 2018.
6. Adrian Kriesch, "Why Nigerian Activist Ken Saro-Wiwa Was Executed," *DW (Deutsche Welle)*, November 9, 2015, https://www.dw.com/en/why-nigerian-activist-ken-saro-wiwa-was-executed/a-18837442.
7. *Ibid.*
8. Declan Walsh, "Why Was an Italian Graduate Student Tortured and Murdered in Egypt?," *New York Times*, August 15, 2017.
9. Kahn, *Creative Community Organizing*, 65.
10. Kara, *Sex Trafficking*, 200–221.
11. Augusta Dwyer, *Broke but Unbroken*, 1–176.
12. "Confederation of Indigenous Nationalities of Ecuador" CONAIE, https://conaie.org/proyecto-politico/.
13. Kimberley Brown, "Ecuador's Indigenous People Are Leading the Anti-Government Protests," *The Washington Post*, October 10, 2019, https://www.washingtonpost.com/world/the_americas/ecuadors-indigenous-people-are-leading-the-nations-anti-government-protests-they-have-a-record-of-ousting-presidents/2019/10/10/ab9d7f1e-eaa2-11e9-a329-7378fbfa1b63_story.html.
14. Kahn, *How People Get Power*, 2.
15. *Ibid.*, 24.
16. *Ibid.*, 26.
17. "The Arab Spring: A Year of Revolution," NPR, December 17, 2011. https://www.npr.org/2011/12/17/143897126/the-arab-spring-a-year-of-revolution.
18. Kahn, *How People Get Power*, 45.
19. Arwa Mahdawi, "Black Lives Matter's Alicia Garza: 'Leadership Today Doesn't Look Like Martin Luther King," *The Guardian*, October 17, 2020.
20. Kahn, *Creative Community Organizing*, 165.
21. Kahn, *Organizing: A Guide*, 187.
22. *Ibid.*, 188.
23. Jones, *Beyond the Messy Truth*, 128.
24. *Ibid.*, 146.
25. *Ibid.*, 148.
26. Kahn, *How People Get Power*, 23.
27. Kahn, *Organizing: A Guide*, 23.
28. Courtney E. Ackerman, "Learned Helplessness: Seligman's Theory of Depression (+ Cure)," Positive Psychology, https://positivepsychology.com/learned-helplessness-seligman-theory-depression-cure/.
29. Garza, *The Purpose of Power*, 144.
30. Ann Marie Roepke and Martin E. P. Seligman, "Doors Opening: A Mechanism for Growth After Adversity," *Journal of Positive Psychology* 10 (2015): 107–115.
31. Stoltz, *Adversity Quotient*, 5.
32. Sheehy, *Pathfinders*, 17.
33. Duckworth, *Grit*, 1–14.

Chapter 8

1. Martin Luther King, Jr., from the speech "The Three Evils," Atlanta, Georgia, August 31, 1967.

2. Kareem Chehayeb, and Abby Sewell, "Why Protesters in Lebanon Are Taking to the Streets," *Foreign Policy*, November 2, 2019.

3. "Lebanese Continue Protests, Demand Government to Fix Economy," *Al Jazeera*, October 20, 2019.

4. "Colombia Anti-Government Protesters Clash with Police," *DW (Deutsche Welle)*, November 22, 2019.

5. Amy Goodman, "Indigenous-Led Anti-Austerity Protests Shut Down Quito Forcing Ecuadorian Government to Move Capitol," *Democracy Now*, October 9, 2019.

6. Jimmy Langman, "From Model to Muddle: Chile's Sad Slide into Upheaval," *Foreign Policy*, November 23, 2019.

7. Scott Neuman, "Argentina's President Macri Defeated as Voters Cast Verdict on Ailing Economy," NPR, October 28, 2019. https://www.npr.org/2019/10/28/773980251/argentinas-president-defeated-as-voters-cast-verdict-on-ailing-economy.

8. "Greece Emerges from Euro-Zone Bailout After Years of Austerity," *The Guardian*, August 20, 2018.

9. *Ibid.*

10. Cavero.

11. Rosenberg, *Children of Cain*, 179.

12. Tina Rosenberg, "How to Topple a Dictator (Peacefully)," *New York Times*, February 13, 2015.

13. Wachtel, *The Money Mandarins*, 16.

14. Bello, Cunningham, and Rau, *Dark Victory*, 11.

15. *Ibid.*, 12.

16. *Ibid.*

17. Danaher, *Fifty Years Is Enough*, 25.

18. Broad, *Unequal Alliance*, xvii.

19. Nicholas Burnett, "Kaiser Shortcircuits Ghanian Development," *Multinational Monitor* 1, no. 1 (February 1980).

20. Hilke Fischer, "Ghana's Kwame Nkrumah: Visionary, Authoritarian Ruler and National Hero," *DW (Deutsche Welle)*, February 2, 2016.

21. Alden Whitman, "Nkrumah, 62, Dead; Ghana's Ex-Leader," *New York Times*, April 28, 1972.

22. George, *The Debt Boomerang*, xiv.

23. *Ibid.*, xv.

24. *Ibid.*, xvi.

25. Payor, *The Debt Trap*, 143–166.

26. Danaher, 22–23.

27. Brecher and Costello. *Global Village or Global Pillage*, 27.

28. George, 4.

29. *Ibid.*, 1.

30. McKibben, *Hope, Human and Wild*, 12.

31. Collins and Lappe, *The Twelve Myths About Hunger*, 91.

32. *Ibid.*, 20.

33. *Ibid.*, 91.

34. *Ibid.*

35. "A Note on the Tanzanian Economic Dilemma." *Bulletin of Tanzanian Affairs* 14 (January 1982).

36. Abraham, *The Missing Millions*, 20–21.

37. Thanks to Ann Pettifor for sending me the list of countries that participated in the Jubilee 2000 Coalition, because the Jubilee 2000 website no longer exists.

38. Daniel Petz, "Africa's New Debt Crisis," *DW (Deutshe Welle)*, November 28, 2018. Emphasis added.

39. Jaime Atienza, "Is Africa Facing Its Second Debt Crisis?" *Oxfam Intermon*, July 16, 2019.

40. Sarajuddin Isar, "Was the Highly Indebted Poor Country Initiative (HIPC) a Success?" *Consilience: The Journal of Sustainable Development* 9, no. 1 (2012): 107–122.

41. Adrian Lovett, "Make Poverty History? A Decade on from Gleneagles, It Is a Genuine Possibility," *The Guardian*, July 6, 2015.

42. Richard Easterly, "Think Again: Debt Relief," *Foreign Policy*, November 16, 2009.

43. Bill Chappell, "U.S. National Debt Hits Record $22 Trillion," *NPR*, February 13, 2019. https://www.npr.org/2019/02/13/694199256/u-s-national-debt-hits-22-trillion-a-new-record-thats-predicted-to-fall

44. Easterly, "Think Again: Debt Relief."

45. Private correspondence with Ann Pettifor.

46. Richard Stevenson, "Outspoken

Chief Economist Leaving World Bank," *New York Times*, November 25, 1999.

Chapter 9

1. Lisa V. Adams, TEDx talk at Dartmouth, published June 27, 2019, https://www.youtube.com/watch?v=_NUEepj06pc.
2. Jones, 19.
3. McIntosh, "White Privilege: Unpacking the Invisible Knapsack," 113..
4. Peggy McIntosh, "White Privilege and Male Privilege: A Personal Account of Coming to See Correspondences Through Work in Women's Studies" (Wellesley: Center for Research on Women, 1988), working paper 189. This piece was later transformed into: McIntosh's "White Privilege: Unpacking the Invisible Knapsack."
5. McIntosh, "White Privilege: Unpacking the Invisible Knapsack," 109.
6. Tochluk, *Witnessing Whiteness*, 20.
7. McIntosh, "White Privilege: Unpacking the Invisible Knapsack," 113.
8. Collins and Jun, *White Out*, 119.
9. Kivel, *Uprooting Racism*, 57–8.
10. Dunsworth, *Worldwide Etiquette*, 1–37.
11. Gates, *The Moment of Lift*, 120–1.
12. *Ibid.*, 240–253

Conclusion

1. Brower, Grady, Traore, and Gidda, "The Experiences of Oxfam International."

Bibliography

Abbotta, Pamela, Roger Sapsforda, and Agnes Binagwaho. "Learning from Success: How Rwanda Achieved the Millennium Development Goals for Health." *World Development* 92 (April 2017): 103–116.

Abraham, Kinte. *The Missing Millions: Why and How Africa Is Underdeveloped.* Trenton, NJ: Africa World Press, 1995.

Alinksy, Saul. *Reveille for Radicals.* New York: Vintage, 1989.

_____. *Rules for Radicals: A Practical Primer for Realistic Radicals.* New York: Vintage, 1989.

Bandler, Richard. *Richard Bandler's Guide to Trance-formation: How to Harness the Power of Hypnosis to Ignite Effortless and Lasting Change.* Boca Raton, FL: Health Communications Inc., 2008.

Bandler, Richard, and John Grinder. *Frogs into Princes: The Introduction to Neuro-linguistic Programming.* Boulder: Real People, 1979.

Beall, J., and S. Fox. "Urban Poverty and Development in the 21st Century: Towards an Inclusive and Sustainable World." *Oxfam Research Reports.* Oxford: Oxfam GB, 2006.

Bello, Walden, Shea Cunningham, and Bill Rau. *Dark Victory: The United States and Global Poverty.* Oakland: Food First, 1999.

Ben-Meir, Yossef. "Participatory Development and Its Emergence in the Fields of Community and International Development." Doctoral thesis, University of New Mexico, 2009.

Berryman, Phillip. *Liberation Theology: Essential Facts About the Revolutionary Movement in Latin America—and Beyond.* New York: Pantheon, 1987.

Bhasin, Kamla. "Participatory Training for Development: Report of the Freedom from Hunger Campaign/Action for Development Regional Change Agents Programme, April–May, 1976." Geneva: Food and Agriculture Organization of the United Nations, 1977.

Binagwaho, Agnes, et al. "Rwanda 20 Years On: Investing in Life." *The Lancet* 384 (2014): 371–375.

Bloom, Benjamin Samuel, Max D. Engelhart, Edward J. Furst, Walter H. Hill, and David R. Krathwohl. *Taxonomy of Educational Objectives. Handbook I: Cognitive Domain.* New York: David McKay, 1956.

Boff, Leonardo, and Clodovis Boff. *Introducing Liberation Theology.* Maryknoll, NY: Orbis, 1987.

Boo, Katherine. *Behind the Beautiful Forevers: Life, Death, and Hope in a Mumbai Undercity.* New York: Random House, 2014.

Brecher, Jeremy, and Tim Costello. *Global Village or Global Pillage: Economic Reconstruction from the Bottom Up.* Cambridge, MA: South End, 1998.

Broad, Robin. *Unequal Alliance: The World Bank, the International Monetary Fund and the Philippines.* Berkeley: University of California Press, 1988.

Brower M., H. Grady, V. Traore, and D.W. Gidda. "The Experiences of Oxfam International and Its Affiliates in Rights-Based Programming and Campaigning." In *The Experiences of Oxfam International and its Affiliates in Rights-based Programming and Campaigning*, ed. Paul Gready and Jonathan Ensor, pp. 63–78. The Hague: Oxfam Novib, n.d.

Brown, Judith Margaret. *Gandhi: Prisoner of Hope*. New Haven, CT: Yale University Press, 1991.

Cary, L. Introduction. In Cary, L. (ed.), *Community Development as a Process*. Columbia: University of Missouri Press, 1970.

Cavaye, Jim. *Capable Communities: A Guide to Community Development*. Rochester, NY: Cavaye Community Development, 2000.

Cavero, Gonzalo. "The True Cost of Austerity and Inequality—Greece Case Study." Oxford, UK: Oxfam Case Study, September 2013.

Chambers, Robert. *Can We Know Better: Reflections for Development*. Rugby, Warwickshire, UK: Practical Action, 2017.

_____. *Whose Reality Counts? Putting the First Last*. London: Intermediate Technology, 1999.

Chopp, Rebecca. *The Praxis of Suffering: An Interpretation of Liberation and Political Theologies*. Eugene, OR: Wipf and Stock, 2007.

Collins, Christopher, and Alexander Jun. *White Out: Understanding White Privilege and Dominance in the Modern Age*. New York: Peter Lang, 2017.

Collins, Joseph, and Frances Moore Lappe. *The Twelve Myths About Hunger*. Oakland, CA: Institute for Food and Development Policy, 1982.

Collins, Larry, and Dominique Lapierre. *Freedom at Midnight*. New Delhi: Vikas, 2009.

Danaher, Kevin. *Fifty Years Is Enough: The Case Against the World Bank and the International Monetary Fund*. Cambridge, MA: South End, 1994.

Doane, Deborah. "The Indian Government Has Shut the Door on NGOs." *The Guardian*, September 7, 2016.

Dowden, Richard. *Africa: Altered States, Ordinary Miracles*. London: Portobello, 2010.

Duckworth, Angela. *Grit: The Power of Passion and Perseverance*. New York: Scribner's, 2016.

Dunsworth, Sarah. *Worldwide Etiquette: A Beginner's Guide to Cultural Norms Around the World*. CreateSpace, August 23, 2016.

Dwyer, Augusta. *Broke but Unbroken: Grassroots Social Movements and Their Radical Solutions to Poverty*. Black Point, Nova Scotia: Fernwood, 2011.

Dwyer, Peter, and Leo Zeilig. *African Struggles Today: Social Movements Since Independence*. Chicago: Haymarket, 2012.

Eade, Deborah. *Capacity-Building: An Approach to People-Centred Development*. Oxford: Oxfam, 1997.

Eade, Deborah, and Suzanne Williams. *The Oxfam Handbook of Development and Relief*. Oxford: Oxfam Publications, 1995.

Easterly, Richard. *The Elusive Quest for Growth: Economists' Adventures and Misadventures in the Tropics*. Boston: MIT Press, 2002.

_____. "Think Again: Debt Relief." *Foreign Policy*, November 16, 2009.

_____. *The Tyranny of Experts: Economists, Dictators, and the Forgotten Rights of the Poor*. New York: Basic, 2015.

_____. *The White Man's Burden: Why the West's Efforts to Aid the Rest Have Done So Much Ill and So Little Good*. New York: Penguin, 2007.

Farmer, Paul. *Pathologies of Power: Health, Human Rights, and the New War on the Poor*. Berkeley: University of California Press, 2004.

Fischer, Hilke. "Ghana's Kwame Nkrumah: Visionary, Authoritarian Ruler and National Hero." *DW (Deutsche Welle)*, February 2, 2016.

Freire, Paolo. *Education for Critical Consciousness*. New York: Continuum International, 2005.

_____. *Pedagogy of the Oppressed*. New York: Herder and Herder, 1970.

Galeano, Eduardo. *Open Veins of Latin America: Five Centuries of the Pillage of a Continent*. New York: Monthly Review Press, 1971 and 1997.

Gandhi, Mohandas K. *Autobiography: The Story of My Experiments with Truth*. New York: Dover, 1983.

_____. *The Essential Gandhi: An Anthology of His Writings on His Life, Work, and Ideas*. New York: Ballantine, 1962.

Garza, Alicia. *The Purpose of Power: How We Come Together When We Fall Apart.* London: One World, 2020.

Gates, Melinda. *The Moment of Lift: How Empowering Women Changes the World.* New York: Flatiron, 2019.

George, Susan. *The Debt Boomerang: How Third World Debt Harms Us All.* London: Pluto, 1992.

Gibson, Barbara. *The Complete Guide to Understanding and Using NLP: Neuro-Linguistic Programming Explained Simply.* Ocala, FL: Atlantic, 2011.

Goldbard, Arlene. *New Creative Community: The Art of Cultural Development.* New York: New Village, 2006.

Grande, Reyna. *The Distance Between Us: A Memoir.* New York: Washington Square, 2013.

Green, Duncan. *From Poverty to Power: How Active Citizens and Effective States Can Change the World.* Oxford, UK: Oxfam International, 2008.

Guha, Ramachandra. *India After Gandhi: The History of the World's Largest Democracy.* New York: HarperCollins, 2007.

Gutierrez, Gustavo. *A Theology of Liberation: History, Politics, and Salvation.* Maryknoll, NY: Orbis, 1988.

Gutierrez, Gustavo, and Gerhard Ludwig Muller. *On the Side of the Poor: The Theology of Liberation.* Maryknoll, NY: Orbis, 2015.

Hampshire, K., E. Hills, and N. Iqbal. "Power Relations in Participatory Research and Community Development: A Case Study from Northern England." *Human Organization* 64, no. 4 (2005): 340–1.

Heinrich, Joseph. *The WEIRDest People in the World: How the West Became Psychologically Peculiar and Particularly Prosperous.* New York: Farrar, Straus and Giroux, 2020.

Holt, Rachel. *NLP: A Changing Perspective.* Scotts Valley, CA: CreateSpace, 2014.

Howson, Chris. *A Just Church: 21st Century Liberation Theology in Action.* New York: Continuum, 2011.

Isar, Sarajuddin. "Was the Highly Indebted Poor Country Initiative (HIPC) a Success?" *Consilience: The Journal of Sustainable Development* 9, no. 1 (2012).

Isham, Jonathan, Deepa Narayan, and Lant Pritcheet. "Does Participation Improve Performance? Establishing Causality with Subjective Data." *World Bank Economic Review* 9, no. 2 (1995). Reprinted in *Assessing Aid: What Works, What Doesn't and Why.* World Bank/Oxford University Press, 1998.

Jones, Van. *Beyond the Messy Truth: How We Came Apart, How We Come Together.* New York: Ballantine, 2017.

Kahn, Si. *Creative Community Organizing: A Guide for Rabble-Rousers, Activists, and Quiet Lovers of Justice.* Oakland, CA: Berrett-Koehler, 2010.

_____. *How People Get Power.* Washington, D.C.: NASW, 1994.

_____. *Organizing: A Guide for Grassroots Organizers.* New York: McGraw-Hill, 1982.

Kamkwamba, William. *The Boy Who Harnessed the Wind: Creating Currents of Electricity and Hope.* New York: William Morrow, 2010.

Kara, Siddharth. *Sex Trafficking: Inside the Business of Modern Slavery.* New York: Columbia University Press, 2009.

Keim, Curtis. *Mistaking Africa: Curiosities and Inventions of the American Mind.* Boulder: Westview, 2014.

Khoo Thwe, Pascal. *From the Land of Green Ghosts: A Burmese Odyssey.* New York: Harper Perennial, 2003.

Kidder, Tracy. *Mountains Beyond Mountains: The Quest of Dr. Paul Farmer, a Man Who Would Cure the World.* New York: Random House, 2003.

Kim, Jim Yong, Joyce V. Millen, Alec Irwin, and John Gershman. *Dying for Growth: Global Inequality and the Health of the Poor.* Monroe, ME: Common Courage, 2002.

Kivel, Paul. *Uprooting Racism: How White People Can Work for Racial Justice.* Gabriola Island, Canada: New Society, 2017.

Mackin, Robert Sean. "Liberation Theology/Base Communities (South America)." *Wiley Online Library,* January 4, 2013.

Maier, Henry W. *Three Theories of Child Development.* Lanham, MD: University Press of America, 1988.

Makaka, Andrew, Sarah Breen, and Agnes Binagwaho. "Universal Health Coverage in Rwanda: A Report of

Innovations to Increase Enrolment in Community-Based Health Insurance." *The Lancet* 380, spec issue 2 (2012): S7.

Mansuri, Ghazala, and Vijayendra Rao. "Localizing Development: Does Participation Work?" A World Bank Policy Research Report. Washington, D.C.: World Bank, 2013.

McIntosh, Peggy. "White Privilege: Unpacking the Invisible Knapsack." In *White Privilege: Essential Readings on the Other Side of Racism*, ed. Paula S. Rothenberg, 109–113. New York: Worth, 2005.

McKibben, Bill. *Hope, Human and Wild: True Stories of Living Lightly on the Earth*. Boston: Little, Brown, 1995.

Meredith, Martin. *The State of Africa: A History of the Continent since Independence*. London: Free Press, 2005.

Narayan, Deepa, Robert Chambers, Meera K. Shah, and Patti Petesch. *Voices of the Poor: Crying Out for Change*. Washington, D.C.: World Bank, no. 13848, March 2000.

Narayan, Deepa, Pritchett Lant, and Soumya Kapoor. *Moving Out of Poverty: Success from the Bottom Up*. Washington, D.C.: World Bank, 2009. http://documents.worldbank.org/curated/en/653631468043174245/Moving-out-of-poverty-success-from-the-bottom-up.

Noah, Trevor. *Born a Crime: Stories from a South African Childhood*. London: One World, 2016.

Novogratz, Jacqueline. *The Blue Sweater: Bridging the Gap Between Rich and Poor in an Interconnected World*. New York: Rodale, 2009.

Odede, Kennedy, and Jessica Posner. *Find Me Unafraid: Love, Loss, and Hope in an African Slum*. New York: Ecco, 2016.

Payor, Cheryl. *The Debt Trap: The IMF and the Third World*. New York: New York University Press, 1975.

Petz, Daniel. "Africa's New Debt Crisis." *Deutshe Welle (DW)*, November 28, 2018.

Pham, Andrew X. *The Eaves of Heaven: A Life in Three Wars*. New York: Crown, 2009.

Powers, Cara Berg, and Erin Allaman. "How Participatory Action Research Can Promote Social Change and Help Youth Development." Berkman Klein Center. December 17, 2012. https://cyber.harvard.edu/node/97242.

Roepke, Ann Marie, and Martin E. P. Seligman. "Doors Opening: A Mechanism for Growth After Adversity." *The Journal of Positive Psychology* 10 (2015): 107–115.

Romero, Oscar. *The Scandal of Redemption: When God Liberates the Poor, Saves Sinners, and Heals Nations*. Walden, NY: Plough, 2018.

Rosenberg, Tina. *Children of Cain: Violence and the Violent in Latin America*. New York: Penguin, 1992.

Rosling, Hans, Ola Rosling, and Anna Rosling Ronnlund. *Factfulness: Ten Reasons We Are Wrong About the World—and Why Things Are Better Than We Think*. New York: Flatiron, 2018.

Sen, Amartya. *Development as Freedom*. 2nd ed. Oxford and New York: Oxford University Press, 2001.

Sheehy, Gail. *Pathfinders*. New York: Bantam, 1982.

Snyder, Steven: *Leadership and the Art of Struggle: How Great Leaders Grow Through Challenge and Adversity*. San Francisco: Berrett-Kohler, 2013.

Sparks, Allister. *The Mind of South Africa: The Rise and Fall of Apartheid*. New York: Ballantine, 1991.

Stackhouse, John. *Out of Poverty: And into Something More Comfortable*. Toronto: Random House Canada, 2000.

Stevenson, Richard. "Outspoken Chief Economist Leaving World Bank." *New York Times*, November 25, 1999.

Stoltz, Paul G. *Adversity Quotient: Turning Obstacles into Opportunities*. New York: John Wiley, 1997.

Tochluk, Shelly. *Witnessing Whiteness: The Need to Talk About Race and How to Do It*. Lanham, MD: Rowman and Littlefield Education, 2010.

Uphoff, N., J. Esman, and A. Krishna. *Reasons for Success: Learning from Instructive Experiences in Rural Development*. West Hartford, CT: Kumarian, 1998.

Van Dyke, Nella, and Holly McCammon. *Strategic Alliances: Coalition Building and Social Movements*. Minneapolis: University of Minnesota Press, 2010.

Wachtel, Howard. *The Money*

Mandarins: Making of a Supranational Economic Order: Making of a Supranational Economic Order. New York: Routledge, 1990.

Wainaina, Binyavanga. "How to Write About Africa," *Granta* 92, 2005.

Yang, Dali L. *Calamity and Reform in China: State, Rural Society and Institutional Change since the Great Leap Famine.* Stanford: Stanford University Press, 1996.

Index

"[A] smartly written, swiftly moving, well-researched, clear-eyed treatment of one of the most remarkable figures of the first half of the twentieth century."

—Jonathan Kirshner, *Boston Review*

"Although British economist Keynes is mostly remembered for the theory that bears his name, in his first book, journalist Carter reveals that his ideas have far more to offer to today's world of rickety economies and creeping authoritarianism. . . . In this sweeping intellectual biography, Carter traces Keynes' career from his first forays into public policy during WWI, through the bumpy 1920s, and the Great Depression, to its end in the behind-the-scenes negotiations of WWII. He vividly describes Keynes' world, which encompassed both European realpolitik and the Bloomsbury Group, and illustrates how his academic, cultural, and political activities influenced his ideas. . . . Carter's timely study is highly recommended."

—*Booklist* (starred review)

"In this illuminating and well-researched book, Carter, senior reporter at *HuffPost*, not only explains Keynesian economics, but also provides a comprehensive portrait of British economist John Maynard Keynes. . . . Readers who want more biographical information about Keynes will be captivated by this depiction of his life and thinking."

—*Library Journal* (starred review)

"Making an impressive book debut, journalist Carter offers a sweeping, comprehensive biography of economist, political theorist, and statesman John Maynard Keynes (1883–1946), one of most influential figures of his time. . . . An absorbing, thoroughly researched life of a singular thinker."

—*Kirkus Reviews* (starred review)

"Journalist Carter debuts with a compassionate and richly detailed exploration of the life and legacy of economic theorist John Maynard Keynes. . . . Carter makes complex economic concepts accessible, and eloquently untangles Keynes's many personal and professional contradictions. This is an essential portrait of the economist and the man."

—*Publishers Weekly* (starred review)

"A brilliantly wrought, beautifully written life of John Maynard Keynes that wonderfully captures the many dimensions of one of the most captivating intellects of the twentieth century."

—Liaquat Ahamed, Pulitzer Prize–winning author of *Lords of Finance*

"Zachary D. Carter has given us an important, resonant, and memorable portrait of one of the chief architects of the world we've known, and know still. As Richard Nixon observed, we're all Keynesians now—even if we don't realize it. Carter's powerful book will surely fix that."

—Jon Meacham, Pulitzer Prize–winning author of *The Soul of America*

"*The Price of Peace* has the thrilling pace of the best journalism, the analytic heft of the best scholarship, and the gorgeous visual detail of the best movies. It takes in the whole world of Keynes, from the gossip of Cambridge to the ethics and aesthetics of Bloomsbury to the mathematics of probability to the skullduggery of Versailles, and to the improbable triumph of the man himself. It's that rare thing in writing: a genuinely cinematic history of ideas."

—Corey Robin, author of *The Enigma of Clarence Thomas* and *The Reactionary Mind*

"*The Price of Peace* is a towering achievement. Carter blends a nuanced and sophisticated financial history of the twentieth century with the intimate personal drama and political upheaval of an epic novel. . . . A masterful biography of a unique and complex social thinker."

—Stephanie Kelton, author of *The Deficit Myth*

"With an eye for the apt phrase and the telling detail, Carter has written a thoughtful and sweeping biography of Keynes and his ideas, extending through the twentieth century and into our own time. Carter gives life to the effortless brilliance, frank appetites, and ethical commitments that made Keynes and Keynesianism so immensely consequential in philosophy, art, money, politics, letters, and war. . . . A terrific book to read about a fascinating character."

—Eric Rauchway, author of *The Money Makers* and *Winter War*